To Ann,

With love and appreciation, who shared the vision, much of the hard work and was an encourager. More than that she had to surrender her husband for long periods. Worse still she almost lost the household computer!

By any measurement, Jesus is one of the towering figures of history. David Gates offers a wonderfully helpful introduction to his life and significance set in his real historical context and free from the myths that swirl around him. I am impressed at how much helpful information this book contains which is presented in a very easy manner. It assumes little, explains a lot and is a great starting point for those who want to know more about a man who changed everything.

Rev. Dr Derek Tidball
Former Principal London School of Theology, 1995–2007

To David & Valerie,
Christmas 2009
David

Jesus –

A^Serious Beginner's Guide

~~~

*Almost everything
you'll need to know*

David P Gates

ATHENA PRESS
LONDON

Jesus – A Serious Beginner's Guide
Almost everything you'll need to know
Copyright © David P Gates 2009

All Rights Reserved

No part of this book may be reproduced in any form
by photocopying or by any electronic or mechanical means,
including information storage or retrieval systems,
without permission in writing from both the copyright
owner and the publisher of this book.

ISBN 978 1 84748 602 8

First published 2009 by
ATHENA PRESS
Queen's House, 2 Holly Road
Twickenham TW1 4EG
United Kingdom

Every effort has been made to trace the copyright holders
of works quoted within this book and obtain permission.
The publisher apologises for any omission and is happy to
make necessary changes in subsequent print runs.

Scripture quotations in this publication, unless otherwise
stated, are from the New International Version® NIV®
Copyright© 1973, 1978, 1984 by International Bible Society®.
All rights reserved worldwide.

The quotation from Spiritualism, K N Ross is used with the
express permission of SPCK, London.

Printed for Athena Press

FOREWORD

David Gates has done a stupendous service for the serious enquirer into the life of Jesus. An expert Bible student with first-hand knowledge of the land in which Jesus was born, the author takes the reader on a journey that can only be described as captivating.

The style is inviting and cheerful; the background research is meticulous, yet unobtrusive; difficulties are met head-on, yet with an informed authority that is attractive in its modesty and reverence. Geared for 'beginners', this book will, however, also be an eye-opener for many who, like me, have been reading and preaching from the Bible over a lifetime.

The Rev. Richard Bewes OBE.
Formerly Rector of All Souls Church,
Langham Place, London W1

WHO IS THIS BOOK FOR?

If, at the beginning of a book, I come across the word 'Introduction' or worse still 'Preface' I am not completely happy. To be perfectly honest this is the part of any book that I, as a reader, am often tempted to skip. Please, if you feel the same, may I ask your patience and – to help, I've even changed the name. So, do read these paragraphs!

Is this book exactly what it says on the cover and the title page? Is it a book just for serious beginners? Yes, it is, but it is also something more.

Please, let me explain. The first eight chapters are for those who wish to simply understand about the earthly life of Jesus. This is, as you will realise a vast subject, so I have had to reduce the material to looking at the early life and childhood influences and then later at the period that led to his trial and execution. I have tried to keep it as straightforward as possible. However, as the story is not fiction there are certain historical facts and historic people that we come across as we read about this life story. Chapter 9 is for travellers to Jerusalem. The final chapter, number 10, looks into the continuing meaning of the life of Jesus.

To help the questions that you may have as you read the early chapters I have included a *Short Dictionary* section, plus what I have called a *Supporting Cast*, this is a list of articles, or 'profiles', about the friends and foes of Jesus. You can read about Caiaphas, Judas, Pontius Pilate, Mary Magdalene and others. Many readers may want to dip into these two sections that are found at the back of this volume. Let me tell you a little about the *Short Dictionary*. This will give you more details on various subjects. For example, Aramaic might intrigue you. This was one of the languages spoken in the Holy Land during the time of Jesus and, in fact, by Jesus himself. If you wish to know more, the *Short Dictionary* section is there to help you. Here you will find some answers but I hope that the answers you find will be a match for the questions you bring to the section. Again, I have tried to keep these simple but I hope that more advanced students will find them helpful. There are articles on crucifixion, the Sanhedrin and what an apostle was, plus many more.

The *Short Dictionary* and the *Supporting Cast* sections are, to the best of my ability, well researched and readers with a greater grasp of who Jesus is will find them informative. In fact, these were written almost independently and, as 'stand alone' articles are complete in themselves, more informed readers with a basic knowledge of the life of Jesus could well benefit. Just use them for research.

At the foot of each page there are often notes that give more detail and also draw attention to various sections at the back of the book. This should ensure that reading the narrative ought to be a smooth process. Technical phrases are minimal and more complex details 'unpacked' in the footnotes. The use of unexplained Latin tags is a 'no-no'!

As you flick through the pages you will find that I have tried to keep the text into manageable bite-sized chunks. This is to help readers with limited time, such as journeys on public transport, or who are likely to have frequent interruptions. It also helps those who wish to look back to check on facts that they came across earlier.

Quotations from Scripture are mostly printed in full, in order that it may be 'something to read on the train' to work or elsewhere where there is limited space and without having to work out how the writer is using the Bible to make good his points. They also tell you what the quotation actually says. All biblical quotations are printed in **bold** and *italic*. On the subject of Bible versions there are several very good translations, from the original languages of the Old and New Testaments available to readers and I, for the most part, have used the *New International Version*. This version is readily available from retail outlets.

Jesus's disciples wrote the four accounts of his life and death, but in spite of that, these accounts are very objective. If you read them for the first time you may be surprised at the honesty of them. They do not gloss over the faults and failings of the leading disciples of Jesus. Rather their accounts have the ring of the totally authentic!

IS THIS BOOK FOR YOU?

As I have said in the title above, this is intended as a guide to help you to decide whether *Jesus – A Serious Beginner's Guide* is for you. It may be that you have questions about the sections I have just written about. So, let me see if I can help you.

Anyone who picks up a book will ask him or herself whether the volume they are examining will be of any benefit or amusement to them. The question may not be in such black-and-white terms and questions such as price and attractiveness will present themselves at, or before the point of deciding to make it their own.

Finding our way around a programme, and that is what this is, can sometimes be a problem but let me make it easier for you. Let me say that my intention is to make this as readable as possible, so that, as mentioned earlier, serious enquiry can usually be undertaken without having a Bible within reach. And with my avoidance of technical language I hope that using an English dictionary can be forgotten as well.

Studying the Bible and the life of Jesus is a lifetime's work. There is always something more to discover. Degree-level training at a college gives time and depth with the opportunity of looking at the original languages of the Bible. It was a formative and fruitful time for me and for my fellow students. Yet, in spite of that, it is a humbling experience to discover, on occasions, that a less experienced reader of the Bible has grasped the meaning of a verse or a sentence better than you have – for all your academic training. This helps to keep the teacher from becoming 'too big for his breeches'.

Therefore, I present this book compiled by a slightly more advanced student to other students eager to learn about that totally unique human being – Jesus. May it be a guide and source of pleasure to you all!

David Gates, March 2009

ACKNOWLEDGEMENTS

As is the case with many things, as my task got bigger I began to realise that I would need help. One of my first helpers who greatly expanded my understanding of *Passover* and matters Jewish was Maurice Rollnick. He spent time with me and lent useful literature, Maurice is an active member of our local branch of the *Council of Christians and Jews*. I most gratefully give thanks to him and Pat, his wife, for their encouraging patience, hospitality and friendship.

There is another debt that I owe to Maurice, which neither of us would see at the time. Although, I think that Maurice may have suspected it. This was my increased appreciation of the Jewish roots of the Christian faith. It is true that I knew this before, in theory, but my appreciation has been deepened.

It is my sincere hope that some Jewish people will be able to enjoy this book and actually benefit from it as they seek to find out about their greatly neglected prophet *Yeshua*.

Secondly – but she would probably be rather embarrassed – a word of thanks must go to Vera Bramwell. It was she who, during some discussion, mentioned one aspect of the Passion, which was well worth pursuing. It was one that I had not thought much about. I thank her for her interest and prayer for this project.

Thirdly – my interest in things Jewish led to my discovery of the work of Rev. John Fieldsend, a Messianic Jew, and of the contribution that he is making to develop an increased awareness of the traditions that Jews and Christians share. I have been very glad of some practical advice from John and wish to put my gratitude on record.

Fourthly – I need to mention Dr John Warren, a chemist by profession, and also a friend with a very logical mind who gave guidance on some early chapters.

Fifthly – my grateful thanks must go to the Rev. Paul Dunthorne. He gave wise counsel on the final chapter. Thank you, Paul, for taking time from your busy ministry to do this task.

Lastly – but only as his offer of help came just before publishing – is Roger Newton. I most gratefully thank him for the quality time that he gave me and to this project. I feel that his wise and gracious suggestions have added to the readers' ability to grasp the meaning I was trying to convey.

Also I have to express appreciation for the loan of many very useful books from friends. These expanded my knowledge and supplemented my own library. Reading the work of others has really advanced my own development. At times it was like 'standing on giants' shoulders' as fresh ideas and inspiration came.

My most sincere and lasting thanks go to all concerned in this huge project.

David Gates, March 2009

CONTENTS

Chapter 1.   *Jesus in the Twenty-first Century*   21

Jesus, a Brief Profile
Jesus and the Enlightenment
Another Book about Jesus?
Where Do We Begin?
Jesus and Modern Times
Jesus – our Modern Historical Perspective
Jesus – our Modern Cultural Perspective
Jesus – an Early Glimpse
The Holy Family

Chapter 2.   *Jesus – the Early Years*   45

Jesus the Carpenter
A Prophet from Galilee
Disciples
Jesus – a First-century Picture
Jesus, the Gospels and this Book
Mark, Matthew, Luke, John
The Events that Led to Jesus's Arrest
The Cleansing of the Temple
The Triumphal Entry into Jerusalem
The Raising of Lazarus – a crisis point

Chapter 3.	***The Last Supper***	84

The First Passover
Jesus and Passover (*Pesach*)
'Seder', the Celebration Meal
In Jesus's Day
Jesus's Inner Group
The First 'Lord's Supper'
The Role of Judas
The Thinking of Caiaphas
Did Caiaphas Prepare Pilate for the Trial?
The Difference of a Day
The Fundamental Change
The Final Hours

Chapter 4.	***The Arrest and Trial***	117

The Arrest
The First Hearing
The Second Hearing
Peter's Lapse
The Third Hearing
The Oath of Testimony
Was the Trial before the Sanhedrin Legal?
The Fourth Hearing – before Pilate
The Fifth Hearing – before Herod Antipas
Back to Pilate, the Final Hearing

Chapter 5.	***The Taking Up of the Cross***	142

Where Did Jesus Die?
Jesus's Crucifixion
Joseph of Arimathea and Nicodemus
The Last Rites
The Centurion
The Repentant Robber
How Did Jesus See the Cross?
The Cross – a Moral Objection
What Happened the Next Day?
Did Jesus Really Die?

Chapter 6.	***Raised from the Dead***	173

Easter Day – the Road to Jerusalem
The First Easter Morning
Mary Magdalene's First Visit
The Other Visitors
Peter and John's Visit (***John 20:3–10***)
Numbers – a Crucial Issue for Some!
Why is Mark's Gospel Different?
Jesus and his Dealings with Mary
  Magdalene
The Stone that Sealed the Tomb
Did Jesus Really Rise?
The High Priests' Unbelievable Story

Chapter 7. *Later that First Easter Day* 202

The Travellers on the Road to Emmaus
The Stranger on the Road to Emmaus
At the Village of Emmaus

Chapter 8. *The Lesson on the Emmaus Road* 217

The Lesson from the Stranger
The *Messiah* and the Suffering Servant
A Simple Approach to Prophecy

Chapter 9. *The Perils of Being a Pilgrim* 242

What Do You Expect from your Trip?
The Pilgrims' Jerusalem: Essential Viewing!

1. The Church of the Holy Sepulchre
2. The Garden Tomb
   Impressions and Evaluations
3. Gordon's Calvary
4. Temple Mount
5. The Western (Wailing) Wall
6. Gethsemane and the Church of All Nations
7. Bethlehem (Beit Lahm)

Is this a Guidebook?
The Final Hurdle

Chapter 10.   ***The Jesus of Faith and Humankind***   266

The Ascension

What Happened at 'the Ascension'?

The Meaning of the Ascension

'The Man who is God'

Can We Really Call Jesus Son of God?

Before Creation

The Divine 'Bridge' and the Human
  Condition

Humanity – God's Plan

Humanity – the Marred Image

Restoring the Special Relationship

A Very Remarkable Offer

In Conclusion

The Supporting Cast   299

*The friends and foes of Jesus: Annas, Caiaphas,
Herod Antipas ('the Fox'), John, 'the Beloved'
Apostle, Judas Iscariot, Mary Magdalene, Mary
Mother of Jesus, Peter the Apostle, Pontius Pilate.*

A Short Dictionary   365

*Words, phrases, customs, ceremonies that occur or
are mentioned in this book.*

Bibliography   437

Chapter 1

JESUS IN THE TWENTY-FIRST CENTURY

Jesus is not *quite* back in fashion but the last few years have shown that there is more of an interest in him as a historical person. In 2004, the film *The Passion of the Christ* created much interest not merely in the western world but also in the Middle East and beyond.

Then more recently the pseudo-historical novel called *The Da Vinci Code* has been filmed. This gives an alternative life of Jesus and some have enjoyed it and quite possibly have believed some elements of the story. This far-fetched supposition of author Dan Brown and the filmmakers has not impressed academics because they call for some very strange conclusions that historians, sometimes called 'time detectives', are not buying. It would have been a useful beginning if Dan Brown had paid more attention to the Bible[1] than to the many traditions, many very strange and untested, that he has chosen to believe.

There have been a few books that have tried to disprove the fact that Jesus actually existed. In fact, recently I wrote a letter in answer to a correspondent

---

[1] There is an article about the **Bible** and how to use it in the *Short Dictionary* section towards the back of the book.

who had urged readers in our local newspaper to reject the historical Jesus. As his arguments were poorly thought out and his quotations often used 'selectively' this was not a tremendous challenge. In fact, we can forget this notion being a serious challenge to Christian belief. The vast majority of scholars, even the most sceptical, have no serious doubts about the existence of Jesus in first-century Judea.

JESUS, A BRIEF PROFILE

But what is really known about Jesus in the twenty-first century? Let me give a brief introduction to this subject.

A little more than 2,000 years ago a series of events took place that influenced the life of most of the inhabitants of this planet. To begin with it changed the way we, in the west and in most parts of the world, calculate time. Today we speak of time *BC*, meaning before Christ, or being *AD*,[2] which means we are, for example, in the 2,009th year since the birth of Jesus Christ. There are many other influences that the life of Jesus gave us. We shall look at some of them later. Let's get on with the life of Jesus.

In the province of the Roman Empire called Judea, now part of modern Israel, a boy was born. His birth came at

---

[2] *Anno Domini* is, as I am sure you will know, a Latin Phrase meaning 'in the year of our Lord', in other words, Jesus Christ. As we live in a society that wishes no offence to anyone it has become popular to say 'the 2009th year of the Common Era' (CE). This has meant that BC is now 'Before Christian Era' or (BCE).

a very inconvenient time for his mother. The Emperor Augustus thought that it would be a good idea to find out the total population of his Empire. This meant that everyone had to return to his hometown for a census. We read about this in the early verses of *Luke's Gospel Chapter 2*. This meant that, by Imperial command, the heavily pregnant Mary,[3] the mother of Jesus, had to give birth shortly after the arrival of her and her husband in Bethlehem. This was the hometown of Joseph, Mary's husband.

The birth itself was natural, although in the night sky there was a strange conjunction of the planets. This attracted the attention of astronomers several hundred miles to the east. They realised that someone mightily important had been born, no less than a king! Other things were happening locally.

Down the hill in the fields, close to Bethlehem, a group of shepherds were guarding their sheep. Suddenly they became scared stiff. A shining figure in white appeared. They must have been petrified with fright! Then they realised that it was an angel who told them: ' *"Do not be afraid. I bring you good news of great joy that will be for all the people. Today in the town of David a Saviour has been born to you; he is Christ* (Messiah) *the Lord" '* (*Luke 2:10–11*). These men, at the bottom of the social pile, were the first to learn of the birth of the long-expected *Messiah*. He was the one who had been

---

[3] Please see **Mary, Mother of Jesus** in section at the back called *Supporting Cast*.

predicted for centuries in the holy writings, what many people call the Old Testament. *Messiah* was an extra-special king who would bring in a new age. The Jewish writings indicated that he would be both human and also divine.

Although the birth of Jesus was spectacular it is his conception that is unique. Mary also had an angelic visit from God's special messenger Gabriel. She was fearful.

' *"Do not be afraid, Mary, you have found favour with God"* ' (*Luke 1:30*). Well, that wasn't totally reassuring. What did God want? She suspected that the LORD had a special job for her. And that could *well* be challenging!

Gabriel had come to tell her that she had been chosen to carry and give birth to God's *Messiah*. She pointed out to the angel that she was a virgin and, although betrothed, could not be expected to have a son until she married. She pointed out that she was a 'good girl' and lived by the highest standards of her day. Sex before marriage was a 'no-no'! I think that she thought that that might let her off the hook. Not so, God had other ideas!

In short God's plan was to 'short-circuit' the normal manner of reproduction and to use his own Holy Spirit to begin the pregnancy without physical contact. Male semen was not needed. Mary must have swallowed hard but she said to Gabriel: ' *"I am the Lord's servant"* ' (*Luke 1:38*). The angel also had a word with Joseph her husband to be.

Although Jesus was a unique child, in many ways his upbringing was, as far as we can tell, fairly conventional by the norms of a Jewish boy in the first century.

At about the age of thirty, Jesus became a travelling teacher and was often called 'rabbi'. As well as a teaching ministry he had gifts of healing, which were remarkable to say the least. No, 'remarkable' is not sufficiently strong a word to describe him – 'miraculous' fits far better. He was instantly successful as a teacher and worker of miracles and this aroused the jealousy of the religious establishment in Jerusalem. Jesus also showed them up for what they were: hypocrites, and they schemed against him. In this they had some help from one of Jesus's own close followers, a man called Judas Iscariot.

At the main festival of the Jewish year Jesus was arrested in Jerusalem by night. The legality of Jesus's trial has been widely discussed but the High Priesthood and the Jewish Council, known as the Sanhedrin, got a conviction on a charge of blasphemy! The penalty was death. Imposing the death penalty was something that the priests could not enforce themselves. The Romans made sure that nobody useful to them would die merely because they were unpopular with the Sanhedrin Court. A Roman execution meant a slow agonising death by crucifixion.

Pilate, the Roman Governor, did not really want to execute Jesus but he ordered that Jesus be put to death.

Jesus died on a Friday, outside Jerusalem at about three o'clock in the afternoon. Everyone thought that that was the end.

On the following Sunday, women relatives with some friends, visited the tomb to perform the last rites, the anointing of Jesus's body. Jesus had been placed in a burial chamber dug from a cliff side. The large stone at the entrance would have to be removed but that was the only obstacle these women expected. But things were not as they had expected. It seems that these ladies had not known that the Sanhedrin had got permission to place a Roman guard on the tomb. However, this detail of men had gone – something had deeply disturbed them!

The large stone was lying on the ground and the body of Jesus was nowhere to be seen. Some of the women went quickly into Jerusalem and told Peter and John, disciples of Jesus, who were hiding in the city. These two then rushed to the tomb! The shroud that had been over the body of Jesus had not been disturbed, the sashes around where the body had been were still in place. They had been tied around Jesus's corpse to keep his shroud in place. It was John who was the first to realise the amazing fact that the body had passed through the fabric without disturbance. John then remembered that Jesus had spoken, on several occasions, of *rising from the dead*. Later that day reports began to be received that Jesus had been seen alive.

At supper time, that same Sunday, the disciples of Jesus were together and had just heard a man called Cleopas recounting that he and a companion had met Jesus earlier that afternoon. Then, in spite of the door being locked – Jesus was in the room with them! He assured them that he was no ghost, showed them the scars of crucifixion and shared some food with them. Then, after that, over a period of about six weeks, Jesus met with his disciples. He taught them and encouraged them to continue the work he had begun.

Then, one Thursday, he met with them telling them that he had finished his earthly work for the time being. He had earlier made it plain that he would return to earth, at some time in the future, to complete the work of making his kingdom universal. Then they saw him being taken into the heavens. The disciples finally saw two angels who assured them that his return to earth would also be from the clouds. The physical body was no longer seen but on several later occasions people had visions of Jesus.

This, in brief, is the history of Jesus. In the following Chapters we will look more closely at these events.

JESUS AND THE ENLIGHTENMENT

Interest in Jesus has gone through some strange phases over the years. During the middle of the eighteenth century a German scholar, Samuel Reimarus, published a work that tried to get away from the view of the life of Jesus that had been unchallenged for centuries. He was looking for the historical person behind the Gospels. Well, in no sense did he open a floodgate. But there has been a steady stream of literature seeking, by using historical methods, to find what the real man who lived during the first century was actually like. One of the most controversial of the writers to follow Reimarus was David Friedrich Strauss whose *Life of Jesus* was published in England in 1846.

Samuel Reimarus and those who have tried to look for a historical Jesus, leaving aside the Gospels, have very little historical material to work with. There are a few documents that show the rise of Christian faith in Europe from the later years of the first century but only one helps us to pinpoint Jesus as a historical person and this is Tacitus's report on the persecution of the Emperor Nero following the great fire of Rome (AD 64). After the fire Nero looked around for someone to blame and found a group of people mostly drawn from the lower social classes *'hated for their abominations, who are commonly called Christians. Christus, from whom their name is derived, was executed at the hands of the procurator Pontius Pilate in the reign of Tiberius.'* This helps us to date the death of Jesus to the governorship of Pilate during the years AD 26–37.[4]

---

[4] Tacitus went on to say that this *'pernicious superstition thus checked for the moment, broke out not only in Judea, the first source of the evil, but even in Rome, where all things hideous and shameful from every part of the world find their centre and become popular'* Tacitus, Annales, XV, 44

Of course, one of the greatest proofs for the life of Jesus is the community that he founded. It began during his lifetime and in spite of huge opposition from the Jewish Authorities, then later the Roman Empire, prospered and eventually changed the society that had tried to destroy it. Yes, for all its many faults, that community known as the 'Church' endures.

ANOTHER BOOK ABOUT JESUS?

So, is it time for another book that takes a look at the life of Jesus? There are many available although not so many actually in print. They are mostly excellent. However the trouble is that most of these will tend to be technical. Such books are usually written by scholars for serious students – students who hope to use the material they read for higher education. This does not help the more casual enquirer who does not wish to wade through a load of academic jargon. This book is written for people who wish to know the facts and need to get to the nub of the matter easily!

Many of us have grown up with the notion that we live, or have lived until recent times, in a Christian country. Perhaps, to be more realistic still, we ought to say in a country with a Judeo-Christian tradition. Pessimistic people, in the United Kingdom speak of a *post-Christian* Britain but Britain has been in a similar position before. In the late seventeenth century, during a time of lawlessness, some people must have wondered about the Christian faith and whether it had any future. Then in the eighteenth century men of God such as the Wesley

Brothers, George Whitfield and the like delivered a mighty change. Britain became, once again, Christian. To be more accurate Britain became more Christian.

In modern times, western countries have had to accept what is called *multiculturalism*. Some, mainly older people, find this unsettling and it calls for understanding and acceptance on all sides. However, my purpose here is not to talk about *multiculturalism*, I want to write about some of the traditions that have shaped our modern society. They are not multicultural they have a Christian origin.

Education and caring for the sick came from the monastic movement. Some people from a socialist background have stated that with the coming of the Industrial Revolution employers realised the benefits of a better-educated workforce. There is probably some truth in this but centuries before this time monks and nuns were caring for the sick and providing at least a basic education. Improvements in the conditions of the work force, particularly children, were brought about by Christian influences and teaching such as: *'we must help the weak, remembering the words the Lord Jesus himself said: "It is more blessed* [praiseworthy] *to give than to receive" ' (Acts 20:35).*

Personally, I believe it is premature to write off America, Britain and other Western countries as 'post-Christian' and although Jesus is attracting more interest there needs to be a growth of understanding. So, what are we in the twenty-first century to make of Jesus?

WHERE DO WE BEGIN?

Let me ask a few questions! How many of our younger people, or more mature ones, realise that the name *Christ* is not the ancient equivalent of a surname? It is a title and means 'one who has been *anointed* or chosen'. In early times in the Holy Land, God's choice would be shown by the pouring, or anointing with oil upon the head of the one who had been chosen. The kings of Israel were often anointed, perhaps long before they were crowned. The shepherd boy David was chosen as the second king of Israel. Jesus is one of his descendants. The title Christ is from a Greek word. The title *Messiah* also means, 'anointed one', but is a Hebrew[5] word.

In our rather less than fully Christian English-speaking societies, how many people use the title 'Christ' in the right way? It is often used as a word to express surprise, anger and similar feelings. Such an exclamation is still considered blasphemous by some. This is not to say that it would not have happened in the past but then it would have produced more shock and in past centuries possibly some correction. Modern humans, many of whom would consider themselves as Christians, have lost the reverence that they used to have for the title.

This is very different for many Jews. During my preparation for writing, I visited some websites to gain

---

[5] More information on **Hebrew**, the language and the people, can be found in the *Short Dictionary*.

further information on the Jewish faith. Here I found a great reverence for the divine name. It was written 'G-d'. For both Jews and Christians the second of the Ten Commandments is binding upon those who would call themselves committed Jews or Christians: '*You shall not misuse the name of the LORD your God, for the LORD will not hold anyone guiltless who misuses his name*' (*Exodus 20:7*, also *Deuteronomy 5:11*).

In Christian faith, Jesus is held to be God alive in a human body (and we shall look at the arguments in support of that later in this book). How many realise that using the name of God or Christ improperly breaks one of the Ten Commandments,[6] which is a summary of the Law of God? As I said we have moved on as a society but many have not made any progress in terms of a spiritual understanding.

For readers who wish to look again at Jesus let me present this book. I do not for one moment imagine that this will help everyone. But I hope and pray that it will be a starting point for you. The best books on the subject of Jesus are still the Gospels. Do read them, and as one convinced disciple told one enquirer, who later, after he had met Jesus personally, became another disciple, ' "*come and see*" ' (*John 1:46*).

JESUS AND MODERN TIMES

During the twentieth century there were several who

---

[6] Take a Bible and see either or both the Old Testament books *Exodus 20:2–17, Deuteronomy 5:6–21*.

tried to explain the Christian faith as merely a set of rules on which we should pattern our behaviour. Again those who put forward these ideas wished to try to get away from the Jesus of the New Testament to find the historical person. These people wished to promote the moral teaching of Jesus. As to the other matters of what happened to Jesus this, apart from the crucifixion, was unclear. It was because of this uncertainty that some began to avoid speaking about 'Christianity' or the 'Christian faith' and coined the term 'the Christ event'. During my own time at college we looked with interest at the writing of Rudolph Bultmann who, during the 1940s, published an essay. He assumed that behind the stories in the New Testament we would find a rather different Jesus.[7] The theologian missionary Albert Schweitzer's also looked at this subject.

This does not seem a very fruitful line of enquiry and there have been some who have begun with this and then had to reject it. Frank Morison was one who was influenced by some of the same ideas that attracted Bultmann. He was to have a radical change of mind. We shall be looking with interest at his work in later chapters and will find him extremely helpful.

This Historical Jesus School argued that we should start with the Golden Rule which states: *'in everything, do to*

---

[7] One of the weaknesses in Bultmann's understanding was that he lacked knowledge of Hebrew and the Aramaic spoken in Jesus's time. This may have caused him to miss certain important facts hidden in the original writings of that time. Bultmann's essay was written in 1941 and is entitled *New Testament and Mythology*.

others what you would have them do to you, for this sums up the Law and the Prophets' (*Matthew 7:12*). This for them was the all-important thing.

Well, this is partly true as far as it goes and if we were to live by this teaching, life on earth would be so much better. However, many atheists and those of other faiths would say that this Golden Rule is worth living by. In fact, many of the precepts that Jesus taught are also taught by other world religions, some of them older than the Christian faith. If we ask how this can be I would say that God's rules for the life of humankind are so important that he has given them from the earliest times to all peoples.

After all, as humans we are made in the image of God.[8] This means that we are made to share with God a sense of what is moral. So, we ought not to be surprised that such a powerful teaching is so widespread. However, humanity's problem is not a failure to believe in goodness; no, its difficulty is in living a morally upright life!

There is another point to make about the Jesus of the New Testament. If we are to understand his teaching in its fullness and understand its relevance, it is important to see the context. What was it that led to a certain teaching being given? Sometimes it came in the form of a *parable* (a story with a moral lesson) and this is often a result of Jesus being challenged by the religious authorities of his day, to explain why he was doing

---

[8] We shall be looking at what this means later in Chapter 10.

something or was taking a particular stance. Yes, we do need the historical Jesus but our source can only be the Christian Scriptures. These are reliable and do help us to know what he did during his earthly life.

The problem, for us, with the New Testament is that it does not feed our modern obsession with having a full biographical picture of Jesus. This is certainly not because the Gospel writers were disinterested in such things, rather they were concerned with functioning day-to-day as Christian believers, very often in a hostile environment, such as Nero's persecution of the Church in the mid-60s of the first century. Many of them felt that pressure of time prevented them from finding the facts that they knew could be of interest to their first readers and others, such as us, coming after them. Thus, their accounts often deal with the vital points and not with interesting details.

JESUS – OUR MODERN HISTORICAL PERSPECTIVE

Let's face it we all, every one of us, has our own mental picture of Jesus. This is partly a historical thing and partly a matter of culture. We will begin with the historical view. As far as history is concerned we have the Gospels to give us the events of his life but this fails to tell us what he actually looked like.

With no help available what are we to do? Are we left with our imagination? The answer seems to be yes, unless we take seriously a length of cloth preserved in Italy.

The Shroud of Turin is a sheet of woven linen, 14.5 x 3.5 feet, which bears the image of a bearded man with bodily wounds that are fully consistent with the victim of a crucifixion. *The Shroud* also has bloodstains. The height of the man has been estimated to be about six feet. The material of which *The Shroud* is made has been identified as coming from the Middle East and seems to have been discovered, or rediscovered, in the year 1357. To preserve both the image and the material on which it appears, it is now only exposed to view every few years and if you are among the few able to see it you would have to look very carefully to see the image.

However, in 1898 *The Shroud* was first photographed and the Italian who processed the plate discovered that the negative image on the material was startling. The positive image that he had photographed was faint. He decided that the negative was the most important. He wondered whether he was looking at the face of Christ.

As you can imagine, sceptics insist it is not genuine. They claim that *The Shroud* is nothing more than a clever medieval 'hoax'. To dismiss it easily in this way is difficult because this is to believe that modern state of the art technology was available to the hoaxers. It cannot be a painting – it is too lifelike for that. Still the sceptics continue to claim that *The Shroud* was woven no later than the Middle Ages. Those who believe in it say, with some scientific evidence, that it has three-dimensional characteristics. Also, the blood and body fluids are definitely genuine.

The experts also say that, from much earlier, there is evidence of the image of Christ being seen on a sheet. It was called the *Cloth of Edessa*. Edessa was the capital of ancient Syria[9] and it seems to have been known of in the third century if not earlier. Could *The Shroud* be the *Cloth of Edessa* rediscovered?

Much of our modern mental picture of Jesus[10] as the man with the beard seems to come from our knowledge of *The Shroud of Turin*. Interestingly, there are some very ancient pictures of Jesus that show him as clean-shaven. These are quite rare.

In most cases I am very wary of artefacts claiming to have been touched by Jesus or his disciples. On the other hand it does seem an extraordinary item, which challenges even the sceptics. Perhaps this will be proved to be an extremely clever hoax. Nonetheless, the Shroud has influenced the way we think of Jesus and modern research appears to confirm that we are correct.

Computer users will be interested in looking at websites on this subject and I include the address of two in particular for your interest. The first is www.shroud.com. However, one of the most dynamic sites I have visited is www.shroudimage.com, where

---

[9] Edessa is now in Turkey and is known as Urfa (Sanli Urfa) and is located in south-eastern Turkey

[10] Many of the great painters of the past lived during times when the wearing of beards was customary. This cultural idea would also have contributed to assuming that Jesus was bearded.

readers can see a computer-enhanced portrait of the well-known image of the head on *The Shroud* given flesh, hair and eyes. The effect is stunning! With these tools you can then decide whether the image on *The Shroud* is an unexplained phenomena, a clever hoax or – as a British ITN newsreader once suggested it might be – 'evidence of the Resurrection'.

JESUS – OUR MODERN CULTURAL PERSPECTIVE

Let's now look at the cultural issues that affect the way we look at Jesus and his teaching. Jesus, although very much a Jew, made it quite plain that he was for everyone. He is therefore universal but this does not mean that humankind's image of what he is really like will be uniform. Each different person and each different tribe or nation will see him differently. This will depend on their circumstances and on the society from which they come. A remote African tribe will see his teaching often differently from an industrialised western society. For them Jesus's parable about a lost sheep will probably have different shades of meaning and produce a stronger reaction because it will be an all too familiar problem of life.

This can be a strong point and a weakness. Those of us who are Christians are not at liberty to take our particular version of the faith and to apply it to an entirely dissimilar culture. That remote African tribe will need to apply their Christian faith to their own society. There is a difference between many societies and this could well apply to our African tribe. English-speaking peoples, particularly Americans, see themselves as individuals. Other cultures feel themselves not just as members of a community but *as the* community! This is seen in Japanese culture, where to step out of line and to behave like a westerner may well meet with disapproval.

Let me be quite clear that the faith that Jesus taught has quite a number of regulations that are absolute. Unlawful killing, theft, giving false evidence in court and adultery are examples. Let's suppose that our African tribe before becoming Christian practised ritual killing. This would be one of the things that the tribe would hopefully immediately reject outright.

But Christian faith as well as having the moral absolutes that Jesus taught has, at times, developed a large cabinet of regulations. In the eighteenth century alcohol was for many a social problem. As a reaction many Christians abstained from drink. True, certain people in the Bible abstained from wine and strong drink but there is no blanket commandment on this issue; there is no, *'thou shalt not drink alcohol'*. For young men and women during those years there was a pressure to abstain. It was towards the 1960s that this began to change.

Let me return to the main point that I wish to make, that is that Jesus is universal but we all see him in various ways. Back in the 1970s there were two musicals that packed in the theatregoers. One was

Godspell, which portrayed Jesus as a charming and charismatic man who was out to help humankind. This was a partial truth because he was far, far more than just a do-gooder. Then there was *Jesus Christ Superstar*, which contained, and I quote from its literature, a *'twentieth-century attitude and sensibilities'*.

As far as my own Christian faith is concerned my own attitudes and values are shaped by the twenty-first-century society in which I live. Fortunately, I have realised that these may be far from perfect and need to be constantly measured against the teaching of Jesus Christ.

JESUS – AN EARLY GLIMPSE

Some of the first believers did have access to the childhood life of Jesus. We take the Gospel of Luke as an example. Luke was a Gentile and possibly a later convert, so his sources were those people who had personally known Jesus as he explains in the first chapter of his Gospel. Luke's concern was with the miraculous events, not the mundane. However, he does give us a glimpse into the boyhood of Jesus which helps us to understand the family relationships that later developed. This incident is likely to have come from Mary, Jesus's mother.

When Jesus was about twelve years old, Mary and Joseph travelled to Jerusalem to celebrate Passover. After the Feast they had left Jerusalem, then after travelling for a whole day they found that Jesus was not among their friends in the party, which would have been fairly large. One can imagine confusion and then fear setting in! It is likely that they decided to stay where they were in the hope that Jesus would catch up with the party. After a restless night they decided to return to Jerusalem. The most obvious place was to return to where they had stayed but he was not there. The next day, the now frantic couple decided to go to the Temple as Jesus had loved being there.

There he was, having a deep conversation and asking very searching questions of the teachers of the Law of Moses. Mary's rebuke is answered in a simple but very profound way.

'Why were you searching for me?' he asked. 'Didn't you know I had to be in my Father's house?' But they did not understand what he was saying to them. Then he went down to Nazareth with them and was obedient to them (Luke 2:49–51).

Here is a uniquely different boy who, although reasoning with his parents like a twelve-year-old, has a depth and grasp of things which sets him out as being different to others. He is able to converse with the wise men in the Temple and must have created quite an impact.[11] Mary and Joseph are confused and not sure of how to deal with the situation. However, we are told that Jesus was a dutiful son and obedient.

---

[11] There is a view that this happened immediately after Jesus's *bar mitzvah*. I am not quite convinced by this opinion.

THE HOLY FAMILY

Mary and Joseph had a family with four sons and at least three daughters (*Matthew 13:55-56*). How did those other children cope with Jesus? He must have seemed too good and one who had a special relationship with their mother and Joseph. He was also an extremely bright young man. Such sons do not usually fit in easily with the rest of the children of a family. They may not have always liked him because of his being different. When they did something wrong, Jesus's brothers and sisters would quickly know their parents annoyance. Jesus seemed to avoid this. If he did something that Mary and Joseph did not like he seemed able to negotiate with them.

The Gospel writer who best knew about the family life of Jesus confirms this. His cousin John, son of Zebedee, gives us a few helpful insights. In *John 7:3-8* there is a conversation between Jesus and his brothers. They were all getting ready for the Feast of Tabernacles[12] but Jesus is hesitant. His brothers tell Jesus that if he is to be taken seriously he ought to go. The tone of the conversation clearly lacks warmth and affection. *'For even his own brothers did not believe in him' (verse 5)* is the reason John gives for their attitude. This unbelief may have been affected by his not being the most popular of older brothers.

---

[12] The Feast of Tabernacles was a harvest celebration held late in the year. It is sometimes called 'the Feast of Booths' or in Hebrew, *Sukkot.*

It is true that the New Testament fails to give us the kind of background that we modern readers would wish to have. In spite of this, we do have a wealth of detail, which would fill a lifetime's study.

As we have seen, some scholars with a very sceptical outlook have tried to separate the events of the life of Jesus, as taught by the New Testament, and tried to find Jesus elsewhere. If we take away the importance of the life that Jesus lived then we are left with a shell. The Church has kept its beliefs and doctrines largely intact since the Church councils of the fourth and fifth centuries. If it had not been anything more than an ethical religion then it would have compromised far more than it has. Churchmen would have found or invented reasons to justify such things as slavery, child labour and such like. [13] In fact, would the Church exist at all?

Historically and continually committed Christians have gone through all manner of suffering for their faith. Would they have been willing, as so many were during the early years, to lay their lives on the line for merely a system of ethics? No, there had to have been a far deeper reality behind their faith. There was and there still is!

So we see that there is much more to Jesus than his moral teaching. In fact, Jesus was unique in that he

---

[13] Unfortunately, initially some Christians did support such attitudes until more enlightened minds won them over and convinced them that these things were socially and morally evil, unchristian standards that even the kindest slave owner or child employer could not accept.

asked not just that his followers obeyed his moral teaching and pleased God, although this was vitally important, he also called his followers to a personal commitment to him. We shall be looking at this later in the book.

Chapter 2

JESUS – THE EARLY YEARS

Galilee would not have been many people's first choice for a region in which to bring up Jesus and Nazareth would have been an unlikely hometown. Let's face it, most people who succeed in life begin with social advantages. That is not to say that Galilee was in any sense an economically deprived area. No, it was reasonably prosperous, belonging as it does to the most naturally fertile part of the Holy Land. As well as farming, many people would directly or indirectly have benefited from the fishing industry around Lake Galilee.

Trying to trace the childhood and early years of Jesus is a difficult but not entirely impossible task. We know of one visit to Jerusalem (refer to Chapter 1), although there would probably have been several. We are told that Joseph and Mary, as devout Jews, *'went to Jerusalem for the Feast of the Passover'* (*Luke 2:41*) and for the devout this would have been a yearly duty.

We know that Jesus would, almost certainly, have benefited from the local synagogue school and had a formal education probably as good as in any other part of the Roman Empire. Boys would have been considered as ready for schooling from five years of age. Class sizes at this stage would ideally have been twenty-five, which is rather large by modern thinking. The reason for education would have been to make boys good Jews, with knowledge of what we now call the Old Testament, Jewish history and traditions. At thirteen years of age he would have become a *Son of the Law* through the ceremony of *bar mitzvah*. At fifteen he would have learnt about legal judgements on the Law of Moses. This would be influenced by whether the boy was able to cope and whether or not his labour was needed on the land. Most children would have begun work at twelve. At eighteen they would have been thought of as having reached marriageable age.

JESUS THE CARPENTER

Like all Jewish boys Jesus would have learnt a trade. The usual route for this was to follow in the footsteps of the father or a suitable male relative and to become an apprentice. This happened in the case of Jesus, who is called a *'carpenter'*[14] (*Mark 6:1–6*) and also *'the carpenter's son'* (*Matthew 13:53–58*). This we see from the comments that followed this later visit (refer to last quotation) back to Nazareth. It is not likely that small town Nazareth would have offered Joseph and Jesus a very good living. However, during the early boyhood of Jesus, Joseph could well have benefited from living near Sepphoris.

---

[14] 'Carpenter' is certainly an accurate translation of the New Testament Greek word *tekton*, but because much stone was used in that region it would be wrong to assume that Joseph and Jesus would not have had some general building skills.

Sepphoris was one of the important cities of Hellenistic[15] Galilee and lay about three miles north-west of Nazareth. Although not mentioned in Scripture it was an important town. It was rebuilt and fortified after Galilee came under the rule of Herod Antipas[16] who was the son of evil King Herod the First (Herod the Great), mentioned in *Matthew 2* as the killer of male infants, one of whom he correctly thought was a prince with a better claim to be *King of the Jews* than he had. Sepphoris[17] was both the administrative centre of Galilee and was where Antipas had his official residence when not in Jerusalem. It was certainly a comfortable and pleasant cultural location, having a 4,000-seat amphitheatre.

Herod Antipas was the second son of the fourth of Herod the First's ten wives. Antipas made Sepphoris his capital until he built the city of Tiberias on Lake Galilee in AD 19. As Sepphoris was high in the hills it commanded views of the region of Lower Galilee and was cool in summer. Its high position would have made it of value to a garrison of Roman troops. Although it would have been an attractive place for Gentiles to live in, it seems more likely to have been lived in by moneyed Jews. Some scholars believe that Joseph and Jesus may have helped in the reconstruction of Sepphoris. Much of the work was done before AD 19

---

[15] 'Hellenistic' refers to those Jews who had accepted the values and much of the lifestyle of Greek culture and language.

[16] Please refer to **Herod Antipas** in *Supporting Cast*.

[17] Sepphoris was renamed Autocratoris, which in Greek means 'Emperor'.

so it seems likely that Jesus, probably with Joseph, had some work there. Even after Herod built Tiberias and moved his capital and residence there, Sepphoris continued to be a prominent and influential city so the young Jesus could well have gained some working skills there.

Although the New Testament gives no details about Mary, the teenage girl who became the wife of Joseph, there is a fairly reliable tradition to link her with the town of Sepphoris. According to this tradition her parents, named as Joachin and Anna, lived there. So it would be quite possible, if we assume the tradition accurate, that it was while he was working there that the craftsman Joseph from nearby Nazareth met the devout girl whom he married.

Let's put aside this interesting tradition and get back to the New Testament because it was at Nazareth that Mary learnt of God's unique plan for her life. '*God sent the angel Gabriel to Nazareth, a town in Galilee, to a virgin pledged to be married to a man named Joseph, a descendant of David*' (*Luke 1:26–27*).

If Mary had come from Sepphoris this would have meant that Jesus would have gone to that city to visit his grandparents. Then again, this is a tradition from a document dated during the second century and so we cannot be sure. If Jesus did work in Sepphoris then he is likely to have had to learn some Greek to understand his clients. No doubt the negotiations would, if they were Jews, have been in Aramaic or

Hebrew but if they were Gentiles or in some cases Hellenised Jews, then knowledge of Greek language would have been useful.

Jesus would have continued in the trade of Joseph until he began his full-time ministry which started so we are told when he was about thirty. It is likely that Jesus put himself under the part-time instruction of a teacher, or rabbi.

It was during this time, before Jesus began his ministry, we cannot be sure when, that Joseph disappears from the Gospel story. It was not very long after Jesus began his full-time preaching and teaching that he returned to Nazareth. Mark's Gospel reports that he was referred to as *'Mary's son' (Mark 6:3)*. From this it seems likely that Joseph had died.

By tradition, Joseph has been thought of as a much older man than Mary, which might account for his early death. However, the building trade during the first century may not have been a very safe one by today's Health and Safety standards. If Joseph did die early this could have delayed Jesus becoming a full-time rabbi. He would have had to wait and to train one of his brothers in the trade of carpenter and builder to ensure that the family had sufficient income. Having said this, in the society of the time, a man of thirty would have been considered as having reached his full vigour so it may have been for this reason that Jesus began his ministry at that time.

A PROPHET FROM GALILEE

However, in spite of nearby Sepphoris, Galilee as a region had a poor reputation and Nazareth did not excite people. When invited to come and meet Jesus, Nathaniel, an acquaintance of one of Jesus's disciples, asked, ' *"Nazareth! Can anything good come from there?"* ' (*John 1:46*). Perhaps this was a little unfair on Nazareth, which was classed as a town although hardly more than a village but not a very go-ahead place. But it was Galilee itself that caused reactions! To the Romans it had a history of rebellion and had to be kept an eye on. To the socially superior in Jerusalem it was a backwater where people had a very provincial accent that produced a spate of jokes based on misunderstanding but which were told to make Galileans appear stupid.

Fairly or unfairly, Galileans had a reputation for being quarrelsome and aggressive with one another and certainly this might account in part for Jesus referring to his disciples James and John as the '*Sons of Thunder*' (*Mark 3:17*).

To the religious authorities in Jerusalem's Temple, a rabbi from Galilee did not, when they first heard of him, seem a challenge to their religious life. These provincials had practices that were not approved of. The region had been called '*Galilee of the Gentiles*' by the Prophet *Isaiah (9:1)* and with good reason. It had been an area where foreigners had been settled without regard for local people.[18]

---

[18] The Assyrian Empire did this during the eighth century BC.

That had been some centuries before and by Jesus's time that had started to change but there was still a suspicion about Galilee. For their part, Galileans would not have been very concerned with the opinions of Jerusalem especially on matters religious. This was because they were likely to be among the religious conservatives.

Recent research about Galilee has painted a rather more flattering picture than we see from the prejudices of the Judean Temple authorities. There is good evidence that the level of education in Galilee was superior to that of Jerusalem, with more teachers of higher quality.

DISCIPLES

It was the usual practice for teachers, during, after and before the time of Jesus, to gather a group of disciples, or as we might say today 'students'. Unfortunately, our word 'student' does not capture the degree of total commitment that was expected of disciples. University students away from home are not expected to leave home without a guarantee of accommodation. Students are allowed relaxation. Students usually get some assistance to help them pay their expenses. When I became a full-time student, which was during easier times for those wanting higher education, I had the guarantee of having my fees paid, an allowance for living expenses and a home with a wife where I would go at the end of each day's studies. I also had holidays and I could and did earn money when away from college. It was a very pleasant, secure existence!

However, we need not be too sorry for Jesus's disciples. They knew what they were taking on and Jesus left them in no doubt if they needed career guidance. Jesus told them that they, like he, would have ' *"nowhere to lay (their) head"* ' (*Luke 9:58*). The man who wanted to follow Jesus had to be prepared to drop everything he was doing – and go![19] ' *"I will follow you, Lord; but first let me go back and say goodbye to my family."* ' This was said by one man who tried to negotiate special terms! *'Jesus replied, "No one who puts his hand to the plough and looks back is fit for service in the kingdom of God"* ' (*Luke 9:61–62*). As this man's family were probably large this would have taken time. Besides this, if he had been that serious, he would have said his goodbyes before.

Jesus and the other sages or teachers of his age were unpaid. Remember, this is before the age of professional clergy. In fact the Jewish Law (Torah) forbade accepting payment for teaching. The giving of hospitality, a thoroughly eastern habit, was all that could be accepted. Certainly, there were many supporters who were able, and very willing, to help a teacher and his disciples, especially one of Jesus's calibre. In fact, some of these people were very well placed as *Luke 8:3* tells us: *'Joanna the wife of Chuza, the manager of Herod's household, Susanna and many others. These women were helping to support them out of their own means.'* This was no small matter because at one stage Jesus

---

[19] More about the life of a disciple can be found in the article on **John** in the section *Supporting Cast*.

had a school of about seventy followers. In *Luke 10* he sent them out to heal and teach and to announce that he was going to visit their town or village. This was their instruction about the offer of hospitality (*Luke 10:7*). ' *"Stay in that house, eating and drinking whatever they give you."* '

Yes, it was a tough life and Jesus lost some of his disciples who could not stay the course. Some of Jesus's teaching was not always easy to accept. *John 6:66* tells us that after a session of instruction *'many of his disciples turned back and no longer followed him'*.

JESUS – A FIRST-CENTURY PICTURE

As I typed this heading I realised that it was being rather ambitious. I will not be able to give more than a sketch but I will try to be as close to the first-century rabbi that Jesus was. A 'picture', in these days of digital photography is usually an accurate portrait. I do not think that I can get as close as that.

Let's begin by thinking about how Jesus dressed. My memories take me back to the visit I made to the home of an Afro-Caribbean pastor in east London. This was for a paper I wrote as part of my degree. I was shown into their home and made comfortable but the pastor was busy and so kept me waiting for just a few minutes. This gave me time to study a picture on the wall. My guess was that it was from a much earlier age because it seemed rather sentimental. It was of Jesus – but a very blond Jesus. He was so blond that he could have been Scandinavian, perhaps a Finn. The robes on Jesus were beautifully white and freshly laundered. Naturally, in that setting I had to smile at a very white Jesus in a black household. The picture had nothing to say about his being Jewish, neither in his looks nor about the kind of clothing he wore! However, I do not seriously imagine that if I had asked the pastor and family they would have said that it was a good likeness.

So, what kind of garments would a first-century Jewish teacher have worn? Jesus would have had tassels (*tsitsiyot*) at each corner of the rectangular robe that he wore. We see this in *Matthew 9:20–21*: *'Just then a woman who had been subject to bleeding'* (almost certainly menstrual) *'for twelve years came up behind him and touched the edge of his cloak. She said to herself, "If I only touch his cloak, I will be healed." '*

Dressing in this way was normal for any Orthodox Jew of that period and was in accordance with regulations in the Jewish Scriptures. *Numbers 15:37–38* says that the *'LORD said to Moses, "Speak to the Israelites and say to them: 'Throughout the generations to come you are to make tassels on the corners of your garments, with a blue cord on each tassel.' " '* It is believed that the sick woman actually touched the tassels (*tsitsiyot*). *Numbers 15:39* gives the reason for this mode of dress, *'You will have these tassels to look at and so you will remember all the commands of the LORD, that you may obey them and not prostitute yourselves by going after the lusts of your own hearts and eyes.'* It was a constant reminder to Jews that as such they were called upon to be upright and moral as God's people. The length of your tassels depended on the particular religious school to which you could belong. Unfortunately, certain people wore extra long tassels in order to appear extra devout, Jesus complained about some attention-seeking devout teachers, who made the *'tassels on their garments long' (Matthew 23:5)*. In fact, there was a rabbi, who wishing to be considered very pious, had tassels so long as to trail on the ground.

Jesus would have worn two garments, an outer cloak and a lighter tunic, which was worn underneath[20] and usually of woven linen. The tunic that Jesus wore when he was arrested was extra special by being seamless. Out and about it was not considered correct dress to be seen in your tunic. Inside the home or when doing hot work it was permissible to be seen in this. The outer robe would be woven from wool.

Neither of these garments can be compared to the shawl that we can see today in pictures of Jews praying at the Western Wall, also called the 'Wailing Wall', in Jerusalem. This is a modern adaptation to cope with the invention of trousers. The modern shawl has two things in common with the cloak of the time of Jesus; it has tassels but is much shorter, and it

---

[20] The cloak was called a *talit* while the tunic was called a *haluk.* Jewish friends tell me that there are variations on how the word for the modern *talit* is pronounced. It can be called a *tallies* and although usually short can be as long as in New Testament times.

also has the same name. Here the differences begin, for the cloak that Jesus would have worn would have covered his ankles.

As an Orthodox Jew, Jesus's apparel would almost certainly have included phylacteries. When we use the word 'phylactery' we usually mean a good luck charm but what Jews of Jesus's time wore was not to ward off harm. In parts of the Middle East we often see, attached to clothing, a blue oval eye that is made of glass. This is believed to protect from the 'evil eye' but the phylactery of Jesus day had a different purpose. In these tiny leather capsules, the Hebrew name is *Tefillin*, were contained four parchments with the most important promises and instructions of God from the Jewish Scriptures; what we call the Old Testament.[21] The most well known of these is called the *Shema*, which begins: *'Hear, O Israel: the LORD our God, the LORD is one. Love the LORD your God with all your heart and with all your soul and with all your strength'* (*Deuteronomy 6:4–5*). This has become a statement of faith for all Jewry. Christians would call it a creed although it still is a commandment to them. It is not possible to say from reading the four Gospels that Jesus wore these but it would be very strange if he had not because he would have wished to obey the command. *'Tie them as symbols on your hands and bind them on your foreheads'* (*Deuteronomy 6:8*). Today Orthodox Jews tend to wear these during prayers but in the first

---

[21] These capsules or *tefillin* contained sacred writings from **Exodus 13, Deuteronomy 6** and *11*.

century they would have been worn throughout the day unless the wearer was working or had gone into a ritually impure area. For example, he would remove them when attending to a corpse.

These are useful facts that give us help in forming a sketch of what Jesus looked like. When it comes to the personality and moral character of Jesus we must turn to the Gospels.

JESUS, THE GOSPELS AND THIS BOOK

We have to face the fact that the Gospels are really all that we have to go on to build a portrait of the authentic Jesus. It is true that sometimes history can be useful in helping us to pin a time scale to the events that the Gospel writers, also known as the Evangelists, are telling us about.

Josephus, the Jewish historian, has been useful in confirming details. We should be grateful to him for the background information he supplied on Pontius Pilate, to give just one example. Unfortunately, historians, especially those living close to the events, cannot always be relied upon to be entirely objective and certainly this charge of bias has been laid at the door of Josephus who lived shortly after the time of Jesus but whose attitudes may have been formed by his parents, family and friends.

It can sometimes be very useful to look at the traditions of the time and see what others were doing during that period. It is interesting to know that Jesus and John the Baptist were certainly not the only rabbis living in the Holy Land[22] during that time. Some of these were, no doubt very sincere but some would have been no better than beggars. This is of course going into the realms of guesswork, which can at times be valuable. However, we cannot say for sure that because a certain situation existed in Jerusalem (Judea) that it would have been the same in the northern province of Galilee or the eastern province of Perea. Galilee was certainly very culturally different to Judea.

So, it is to the Gospels we must turn to gain a picture of the real Jesus. In past years I delved into black-and-white photography. I well remember images from an enlarger gradually beginning to form on photosensitive paper. Perhaps this may be a similar experience for you. The one difference will be that with that process the photograph had to be 'fixed' (process stopped) or it will go black. The difference, with our image of Jesus, is that it will only grow clearer. It will never need to be stopped.

Before we look, fairly briefly, at each of the Gospels, one final word of explanation: Mark, Matthew and Luke are sometimes called the Synoptic[23] Gospels. This is not a phrase I will use very often but readers will come across it elsewhere in more academic books.

---

[22] Please refer to notes on **Holy Land** in the *Short Dictionary*.

[23] This is a Greek word, which means: *'common view'*. Mark, Matthew and Luke had a synopsis – *a general view*. This is rather different to our modern meaning of a brief account.

MARK

I have just opened my Bible to the first chapter of Mark's Gospel and there at the top of the page is the name 'Mark'. This is fine unless we ask the question: 'Mark, who's Mark?' We will need to do a little probing. If you or I receive a letter or a document and the identity of the author is not immediately clear we will often spend a few moments discovering whom it is from before we read on. The whole Gospel of Mark gives us no direct help whatsoever on this question.

By contrast the Letters of the New Testament are often very helpful in this respect. The Apostles Paul, Peter, James and Jude all write their names at the very beginning. *The Letter to the Hebrews* (Jewish Christians) is an exception as are some short letters, towards the end of the New Testament, which are ascribed to John. For reasons that are not known and can only be guessed at, Mark and the rest of the Gospel writers do not reveal their identities. This may not have been necessary to the first people to read them but in our age of openness we find this irksome.

Do we have a problem? Well, not a very serious one. We have some documentary help given by Papias, Bishop of Hierapolis, a city that is now sited near Pamukkale in western Turkey. He reported about AD 140, having been told on excellent authority, '*Mark became the interpreter of Peter and he wrote down accurately ... as much as he [Peter] remembered of the sayings and doings of the Lord.*' The word 'remembered' could also be translated *'related'*. This, almost certainly, gives us the identity of the writer as being John Mark.[24] From the words *'interpreter'* it seems that Peter may have had some help from the younger man with translation from his natural Aramaic, or Hebrew, into Greek for although Peter seems to have been a speaker of Greek this would not mean that his ability to write that language would have been perfect. This also helps us to date the Gospel of Mark to no later, and probably some years earlier, than AD 70. It is believed that Peter died during the persecutions against Christians that occurred during the reign of the unstable Roman Emperor Nero, around AD 64–65.

Mark's Gospel begins with Jesus going to his cousin, John the Baptist, during that prophet's ministry at the river Jordan. The ministry of Jesus began after that event. Mark's Gospel moves on quickly to the calling of the first disciples. The Gospel seems to concentrate on the actions of Jesus and although there is teaching, there is not the same emphasis as in Matthew and Luke. As John Mark takes time to explain Jewish customs it is likely that Mark's first readers were mainly Gentiles.

MATTHEW

When we come to Matthew's Gospel we face the same problem over its ascription. As with Mark's Gospel there is nothing here to tell us who wrote it. Fortu-

---

[24] Refer to fuller details on John Mark. These are found under **Peter** in *Supporting Cast*. See footnote 150.

nately, we again get some help from Papias. This is what he tells us: '*So then Matthew recorded the oracles in the Hebrew tongue, and each interpreted them to the best of his ability.*' It is not totally clear whether it is the Gospel that is being referred to and why the 'oracles' were not written in Greek, a language known around much of the Mediterranean.

There is one other source worth looking at and it is of a similar date to that of Papias. Irenaeus (AD 130–200) became Bishop of Lyons (France) and tells us: '*Matthew published his Gospel among the Hebrews in their own tongue, when Peter and Paul were preaching the Gospel in Rome and founding the Church there.*' This would put his Gospel during the time, which led up to Nero's persecution of the Church. It would seem that it was, like Mark's Gospel, circulated before AD 70 because Matthew would surely have made some reference to the destruction of the Temple that occurred during that year had it been written later.

Matthew used the Gospel of Mark as one of his sources but there is so much new material that it is clear that he, and also Luke, had at least one other source[25] apart from personal experience from which they drew information when they compiled their Gospels. There are ten parables and a number of incidents that are not found in any of the other Gospels.

---

[25] This source of notes or the memories of one or more person has been called 'Q'.

LUKE

If, as many believe, Luke was a Gentile, that would make him unique among the Gospel writers! This would seem to us quite unremarkable today but during the first century that was not so. From its beginning the Church was a very Jewish organisation and its first converts would have been almost entirely Jews or those Gentiles, called proselytes[26] in the New Testament, who had adopted Judaism. Those who ran the Church, such as Peter, in overall charge, and James, who pastored the Jerusalem Church, were both Jews. The man who gave it so much of its teaching, Paul, was also a Jew. It was Paul who made the Church more accessible to Gentiles.

Finding the identity of the writer of the third Gospel is only slightly easier. Firstly, we begin in *Chapter 1, verse 3* and see that it was sent to *Theophilus*. Now if we turn over a few pages in our Bibles, skipping John's Gospel and getting to the book of Acts, we read, in the very first verse the same name: *Theophilus*.

From this we can safely conclude that the same hand wrote *Luke's Gospel* and the *Acts of the Apostles*. Later in the book of *Acts* the word *'we'* (*16:10–13, etc.*) begins to occur. The writer of *Acts*, the *'we'* had clearly joined Paul and his party. However, in *Acts 16:7* the writer uses the word *'they'*. Luke is mentioned in Paul's letters three times in all and is valued as a faithful

---

[26] Proselytes: see *Acts of the Apostles 2:10* (some translations of the Bible, i.e. the Revised Standard Version, use this word; the New International Version does not).

companion. Paul also indicates that he was a doctor of medicine (*Colossians 4:14*). There is also a mention of Lucius at the end of The Letter to the Romans when Paul is bringing his letter to an end (*16:21*). Included with his own greetings are the good wishes of those with him. Lucius is another form of Luke's name and although we cannot say for certain it may well be Luke. This same form of the name appears in *Acts 13:1* but Lucius was a common first name in Roman society.

Although many New Testament scholars are happy with the view that Luke was a Gentile some, quite naturally, have wondered about this. They point out that Luke has a very good knowledge of the Jewish (Old Testament) Scriptures. Others, taking a different view say that Gentiles may also have had an equally good knowledge. As well as this, he was with the Apostle Paul for long periods and that would have certainly helped his understanding of these Scriptures.

What is seen in the *Gospel of Luke* is that its author has a concern for the lower orders of society. He takes care to mention those who were at the lower end of first-century humanity. Let's take one or two examples. The shepherds in the Christmas story to whom the angels appear (*Luke 2:8-20*) would have been considered as being, as far as the Jewish Law of Moses was concerned, ritually unclean. This was due to the fact that in caring for sheep and dealing with ewes during lambing they came into contact with the animals' blood and afterbirth, which was considered unclean.[27] This would have put them at the bottom of the social pile. Their situation would not be totally unlike the '*dalits*', the 'untouchables'[28] of Indian society.

To use another example *Luke* quotes Jesus telling the parable (a story with a moral) of a '*good Samaritan*' (*10:29–36*) who came to the aid of a man who had been mugged and badly beaten by a group of bandits. Jesus would have not made himself popular talking about Samaritans. They had been a cause of tension to the Jews but, far worse, they practised a form of worship that Jews considered totally corrupt and unmention-able. None of the other Gospel writers mention this and it is quite possible they were not entirely comfortable with it. Luke has no such problems with this subject, mostly because Theophilus and his circle were probably Gentiles.

It is generally reckoned that to best understand the New Testament a working knowledge of the original languages is needed. This is not always necessary because as a careful reader we can see there are changes in style in *Luke's Gospel*. Scholars comment on the precise academic Greek used as Luke addresses Theophilus (*1:1–4*) to whom this Gospel was first sent. Then there is a change of style to a

---

[27] Not in our modern sense of bacterial infection but unclean of itself.

[28] To be fair to modern India, making a distinction on the basis of caste is now prohibited, but unfortunately old attitudes can still be found among the population.

rather different Greek that seems to have a more Jewish influence. This change could be explained by the fact that Luke had been sent documents from various eyewitnesses, whose Greek or Aramaic he had to translate.

It has been suggested that Luke gathered the material for the Gospel while Paul was imprisoned in Caesarea, on the coast of Judea, pending his appeal to the Emperor in Rome[29] (*Acts 21:27–26, 32*). I used to imagine that Luke, apart from visiting Paul, would have had plenty of time to meet people like Joanna who would have been able to give him first-hand accounts of the Resurrection. Such a view was rather mistaken. Many of the original believers had been driven from Jerusalem by persecution. Had Luke been able to speak to these people in person, possibly with a translator, his style would have been more uniform.

From the time of Irenaeus, the Bishop of Lyon, who lived at the latter end of the second century, the author (compiler) of the *Book of Acts* was generally thought to be Luke, a Syrian from Antioch, a doctor by profession, who had been a pupil of the apostles and who had accompanied Paul until that apostle's martyrdom. Paul is thought to have died during the Emperor Nero's attack on the Church.

---

[29] Paul had been born a Roman citizen and had the right to appeal. It also gave him the opportunity of proclaiming his faith to the top man. It also could have made clear Paul's right, and that of the Church, to be Christian.

We have a tradition regarding the last days of Luke who is said to have died unmarried in Boeotia in Greece, well advanced in years.

JOHN[30]

It does not take the reader of *John's Gospel* very long to realise that he or she is dealing with a document that is very different to the other Gospels. Whereas the first three have taken what seems to be an historical approach following the events of Jesus's life from its beginning to its end, John is concerned to set out the life of Jesus more as a series of signs. He wishes us to consider the meaning of the events or as he calls them the *'signs'*. Another difference between the first three Gospels (called the Synoptics) is that they are chiefly concerned with the events of Galilee, while John concentrates on Jesus's attendances at the Jewish festivals in Jerusalem. He also reports on Jesus paying a visit to Sychar a town in Samaria (*John 4*) an event about which the other three Gospel writers are silent.

In fact, John's reason for publishing his Gospel is spelt out very clearly: *'that you may believe that Jesus is the Christ, the Son of God, and that by believing you may have life in his name' (John 20:31)*. His Gospel is quite clearly an evangelistic treatise aimed, it is believed, primarily at the Jews and proselytes living abroad in Greek-speaking communities around the eastern Mediterranean. Does this mean that John's thinking

---

[30] There is a profile on **John** in the section *Supporting Cast.*

had been influenced by Greek culture? There has been much scholarly discussion in the past but current thinking is that this is a thoroughly Jewish Gospel.

The evidence, most of which is indirect, shows that there is no real reason for challenging the Christian tradition that John Zebedee is the author of this Gospel. This is strengthened by the fact that the author used the word *'we'* (*1:14*).[31] Here John in his prologue says: '*We have seen his glory, the glory of the One and Only, who came from the Father, full of grace and truth.*'

He also shows on many occasions that he was an eyewitness and a member of the inner circle of 'twelve' close disciples, later called apostles, who were being trained for leadership. See the testimony of *19:35–37* when he reports on the later stages of the crucifixion, reporting on the death of Jesus. It is also shown that Jesus often chose to select John, his older brother, James, and Peter as a threesome who Paul, speaking of a visit to Jerusalem, refers to as being '*pillars*' of the Church in Jerusalem (*Galatians 2:9*).

Once we have read this Gospel we may be left with one question: why doesn't the apostle name himself but only hint at his presence in such phrases as '*the disciple whom Jesus loved*' (*21:20*). The most likely answer is that the person who wrote the Gospel of John was not the Apostle John himself but was doing so as John

---

[31] Another '**we**' is found in *21:24* but this could be the influence of John's scribe or secretary.

dictated. In fact, this appears to be the most popular and widely accepted view.

At the end of *John 20,* as we have already noticed, John gives his readers his reason for writing the Gospel and this was clearly intended to be the end. Then we find that tacked on is a further chapter. The main reason that this 'afterthought' was written was the fact that the Apostle John needed to correct a rumour. People were saying that Jesus had predicted that John would not have to die. It has been suggested John may have been near the end of his life and felt that this would cause the faithful to have serious doubts. John or his scribe needed to set the record right:

Jesus did not say that he (John) would not die; he only said, 'If I want him to remain alive until I return, what is that to you?' (John 21:23).

THE EVENTS THAT LED TO JESUS'S ARREST

Only once in his life did Jesus the rabbi from Nazareth seem to have had an easy relationship with the Temple authorities. This, as we have already seen, had been when, as a young lad of about twelve years of age he had been taken to Jerusalem for the Feast of Passover. He had got into a discussion with the learnt teachers, enjoying their instruction and asking very pertinent questions. These men were very impressed; in fact, Luke tells us they were *'amazed at his understanding and his answers' (2:41–52).* This seems to have been a high-water mark.

Jesus, as we have seen, began a full-time teaching ministry at about thirty and, in reading the Gospels, we become aware that a tension quickly begins to surface between him and the religious establishment.

Early on, Jesus's keeping of the Sabbath (Saturday), the special day for worship during which no work could be done, brought about conflict. It would be possible to find several instances of this sort but let me just mention one. On at least one occasion Jesus had healed a man on the Sabbath day. That counted as work. Not unnaturally, he had been challenged about his action and gave them this answer: *'The Sabbath was made for man, not man for the Sabbath' (Mark 2:27)*. If this was the case then any good action for the benefit and alleviation of suffering was lawful. After all, opportunities for doing good to the needy could not always be put off to the next day. The opportunity might never be repeated.

Jesus, from early on during his ministry, showed an uncompromising attitude towards religious double standards as the two examples below will show. This caused much discord and actual hatred. This was what he taught about prayer:

And when you pray, do not be like the hypocrites, for they love to pray standing in the synagogues and on the street corners to be seen by men. I tell you the truth, they have received their reward in full. But when you pray, go into your room, close the door and pray to your Father, who is unseen. Then your Father, who sees what is done in secret, will reward you (Matthew 6:5 & 6).

He was just as scathing about pretence in fasting which was an integral part of orthodox Jewish religious observance. ' *"When you fast, do not look sombre as the hypocrites do, for they disfigure their faces to show men they are fasting. I tell you the truth, they have received their reward in full. But when you fast, put oil on your head and wash your face, so that it will not be obvious to men that you are fasting, but only to your Father, who is unseen; and your Father, who sees what is done in secret, will reward you"* ' *(Matthew. 6:16–18).*

Then there were the pronouncements of Jesus, which hinted that he had a unique relationship with God. This aspect is dealt with in another part of this book. Furthermore, he offered to share its benefits with those who followed him. He called for his followers to be totally dedicated to him – as of first and major importance. After that came as close second – what he taught.

This was completely different to the religious teachers of his time who usually only claimed the say-so of others. Jesus claimed his own. This made Jesus a marked man; he was very often completely different. One word sums up the personality of Jesus – authority! He had an abundance of it, which showed in his teaching but even more in the things that he did. He forgave a man his sin. This outraged the watching religious teachers but then, some were there to see what he was doing and to find fault. He made good his case for having authority to forgive by sending the forgiven man away healed (*Matthew 9:1–7*).

The Jewish religious authorities, beginning with some ordinary synagogue officials right up to the High Priest in the Temple, found Jesus a threat. The Temple staff had to carefully look over their shoulders to make sure that Rome was not unhappy with them but Jesus seemed to have no fear of anyone. Many ordinary Jews saw in Jesus a man who was familiar as a rabbi. He used parables. This was a familiar form of teaching for a rabbi to use and his Jewish hearers would have seen that before. His teaching was to all but he took a special interest in the poor, sinners and social outcasts. What the Temple authorities could not cope with was that he was unafraid to touch people like lepers. Also he took food with tax collectors who collaborated with the hated Romans. No, they could not accept his ways!

THE CLEANSING OF THE TEMPLE

Matthew 21:12–17; Mark 11:15–19; Luke 19:45–48; John 2:13–22

The final affront to the religious establishment in Jerusalem was when Jesus entered the Temple and drove out the traders from this area, which was dedicated to the worship[32] of God. This event took place soon after the entry of Jesus into Jerusalem in the days leading up to Passover and to the week that would lead to his betrayal and death.

---

[32] Refer to note on **Annas** in *Supporting Cast* for further particulars on the misuse of the Temple.

In the Temple courts he found men selling cattle, sheep and doves, and others sitting at tables exchanging money. So he made a whip out of cords, and drove all from the Temple area, both sheep and cattle; he scattered the coins of the moneychangers and overturned their tables. To those who sold doves he said, 'Get these out of here! How dare you turn my Father's house into a market!' His disciples remembered that it is written: 'Zeal for your house will consume me' (John 2:14–17).

(I imagine that John is referring to what the *'disciples remembered'* later and not at that exact moment.) Mark's Gospel also adds:

...and he would not allow anyone to carry merchandise through the Temple courts. And as he taught them, he said, 'Is it not written: "My house will be called a house of prayer for all nations"? But you have made it "a den of robbers" ' (Mark 11:16–17).

From this event some have suspected that Jesus was in direct rebellion against the Temple and all it stood for. The simplest explanation is the more likely. Jesus, along with many pilgrims to the Temple, was deeply upset that profit from selling animals for sacrifice had taken first place from sacrifice itself. It looked as though the offerings that were to be made by the pilgrims were of secondary importance. It is true that only the best animals would do. Human nature, being as it is, meant that lame or diseased animals might have been offered in sacrifice for the person's wrongdoings. Yes, there had to be some safeguards, but the Temple administration were making money and that had become too important to this organisation.

The large crowds in the Temple precincts would have either witnessed personally or heard very soon afterwards what had happened. Some would have been pleased; others rather confused by the violence of this action and some would need time to evaluate what they saw or had heard about.

The Temple officials seethed with anger. The Temple stood for law and order and they realised that they were in a very difficult situation. Not only had their authority been set aside but it had been done by a provincial rabbi! And, even worse, it was from that despised area in the north *'Galilee of the Gentiles'* (*Matthew 4:15; Isaiah 9:1*).

Then there was the fear of Rome. They would not let things get out of hand in the Temple. The Romans always suspected that trouble was just under the surface there. They could well have questions about this day's disturbance or worse – they could send in troops! That, in the past, had resulted in the shedding of Jewish blood. There is an insight into Pilate's treatment of Jews in *Luke 13:1* where we are told about *'the Galileans whose blood Pilate had mixed with their sacrifices'*. We cannot be sure of the exact circumstances but we can safely assume that they were pilgrims who on arriving in Jerusalem somehow upset Roman soldiers. Whether it is totally fair to blame

Pilate for this atrocity we will probably never know. He was of course the commander and the responsibility was naturally his. However, only a riot or something equally serious in the Temple precincts would bring in Roman troops.

' "By what authority are you doing these things?" they asked. "And who gave you this authority?" ' (Matthew 21:23). The question itself is interesting; because I wonder whether it was a spontaneous 'knee-jerk reaction' or did it come later after the Sadducees had been informed? A direct answer would have brought an earlier arrest than Jesus was prepared for. He knew it was coming but had other matters to do before he had to face that. In the event he also asked them a question knowing that an honest direct answer would embarrass them. As Jesus foreknew they declined to commit themselves with the answer, saying that they could not be sure. Jesus had asked them whether the baptism practised by John the Baptist had been purely human or had it had the authority of God (refer to *Matthew 21:23–27*).

There are some people who have a natural 'authority' and where it comes from is not always obvious. We meet them in the office and in the classroom and in many of life's situations. They may be male or female, large or small but they and their point of view usually gets respect if not final agreement. They also find it easier to get their way – they are assertive. Most teachers, the ones with this 'charisma', seem to have little problem with class discipline.

Jesus obviously had this kind of authority; at times people were frightened of him. As an example, note the reaction of the party sent to arrest him. ' *"Who is it you want?" "Jesus of Nazareth," they replied. "I am he," Jesus said. (And Judas the traitor was standing there with them.) When Jesus said, "I am he," they drew back and fell to the ground'* (*John 18:4–6*). This is not the 'Gentle Jesus, meek and mild' of the children's hymn.

This is in no way to deny those warm qualities of a thoroughly balanced human being that made him so very approachable. However, it was his authority set against that of the Jewish High Priesthood that was to be a major factor leading to his arrest.

When Jesus arrived in Jerusalem, speaking with a Galilean accent, there may have been a number of smiles. This changed quickly because behind the accent there was clearly a man of very sharp intelligence and one that seemed to be able to spot the verbal 'ambush' being set by clever legal minds. Many Pharisees and Sadducees challenged him to public debates and got an answer that caused them to end up having to stop and think. These men resented the fact that Jesus's hearers had been impressed. The chief priests knew that he had gained a strong following locally in Galilee and they feared that they would lose influence in the face of some of the criticisms he made against them.

THE TRIUMPHAL ENTRY INTO JERUSALEM

Matthew 21:1–11; Mark 11:1–11; Luke 19:29–44; John 12:12–19

One thing that caused the Sanhedrin problems was when Jesus rode into Jerusalem on a donkey. This was a few days before his arrest. The people went wild with ecstasy and it seemed as though the Kingdom of God was about to come. Jesus was fulfilling the prediction of the Old Testament prophet Zechariah.

Rejoice greatly, O Daughter of Zion! Shout, Daughter of Jerusalem! See, your king comes to you, righteous and having salvation, gentle and riding on a donkey, on a colt, the foal of a donkey (Zechariah 9:9).

This people's expectation was that the *Messiah* King would enter Jerusalem to bring in a reign of peace. Then, those Jews scattered among other nations would be able to return and a golden age would begin.

During the time of Jesus many Jews were scattered around the Mediterranean, in what has been called the *Diaspora.* Now with the hope of these Jews returning to a renewed Israel, the crowd were elated with the prospect that the hated Roman occupation would be brought to an end.

To us living in the twenty-first century the idea of a man sitting on a donkey does seem incongruous and hardly kingly. We would expect a king in waiting to appear on a strong white horse. But no! When King

David, some ten centuries before, was near to the end of his life he spoke to religious officials and *'he said to them: "Take your lord's servants with you and set Solomon my son on my own mule and take him down to Gihon.*[33] *There shall Zadok the priest and Nathan the prophet anoint him king over Israel. Blow the trumpet and shout, 'Long live King Solomon!' "'* (*1 Kings 1:33–34*). So we see that there was a very good precedent for this procedure and a mule is a cross between a horse and a donkey.

The people obviously recognised Jesus's right to the title *Son of David* (*Matthew 21:9*) that means he is of the line of King David and only someone from the royal family of David has such a right to be considered *Messiah* and King. Let us be perfectly clear about this, the Herod dynasty had no right to the title King of the Jews except through the political power of Rome. The descendents of King David had lost the power of ruling but their right to reign remained absolute and eternally backed by God's promise.

The LORD swore an oath to David, a sure oath that he will not revoke: 'One of your own descendants I will place on your throne – if your sons keep my covenant and the statutes I teach them, then their sons shall sit on your throne for ever and ever' (*Psalm 132:11–12*).

---

[33] The Gihon was one of the springs that supplied Jerusalem's water supply. It was because of this source of water that David, the King, had not built his capital on the mountaintop but on its eastern slope.

But note! This promise is conditional and, unfortunately, David's descendents had not always kept the regulations and so the covenant[34] was not kept and the kings of the house of David ceased to be rulers in the sixth century BC.

Let us look at what the people cried out in their enthusiasm at seeing this prophetic sight: ' *"Hosanna to the Son of David!"* ' ' *"Blessed is he who comes in the name of the Lord!"* ' ' *"Hosanna in the highest!"* ' *Hosanna* means 'save now' but these people were not swayed by merely patriotic fervour, they realised that God was in this event because they said, quoting *Psalm 118:25*: ' *"Blessed is he who comes in the name of the Lord!"* ' (*Matthew 21:9*). *John's Gospel* informs us that some of those who witnessed Lazarus being raised from the dead (see section below) were present there and then *'went out to meet him'* (*12:18*). As Matthew tells us: *'the whole city was stirred'* (*21:10*). As part of their rejoicing the citizens spread their cloaks and branches from trees on the road. The people sensed a winner and went in front of and also followed the donkey on which Jesus rode. At this moment Jesus seemed unstoppable.

There was another group of onlookers who were not so happy, in fact, the majority of these people were deeply unhappy; these were the Jewish religious establishment. They soon made their feeling known: ' *"Teacher, rebuke*

---

[34] For a biblical meaning of **Covenant** please see the *Short Dictionary* at the end of this book.

your disciples!" ' Jesus tells them that he cannot, will not, do any such thing. ' *"I tell you," he replied, "if they keep quiet, the stones will cry out" '* (*Luke 19:39–40*). Clearly the Pharisees, who are mentioned as the group present, feel that their position is being weakened. So *'the Pharisees said to one another, "See, this is getting us nowhere. Look how the whole world has gone after him!" '* (*John 12:19*). Luke also gives us some further information on what Jesus said to the Pharisees: ' *"If you, even you, had only known on this day what would bring you peace – but now it is hidden from your eyes. The days will come upon you when your enemies will build an embankment against you and encircle you and hem you in on every side. They will dash you to the ground, you and the children within your walls. They will not leave one stone on another, because you did not recognise the time of God's coming to you" '* (*Luke 19:42–44*).

These predictions of Jesus were to be fulfilled during the Jewish War of AD 66–70. This revolt against Rome ended with the destruction of the Temple in AD 70. This was the end of the rising except for the pocket of resistance at Masada, that hilltop fort overlooking the Dead Sea, which came to an end in AD 73.

What shall we say about the apostles, how did they see things? Like most of the crowd, they were caught up in the excitement of the day as they placed their cloaks on the animal's back to make some kind of saddle. They quickly got into the spirit of the thing. John, looking back, says quite clearly that the disciples would not realise the meaning of these events until after the Resurrection. '*Only after Jesus was glorified did they realise that these things had been written about him*' (the words of the prophet Zechariah, quoted above, p.76) '*and that they had done these things to him*' (*John 12:16*). It is certain that this 'high' stayed with the apostles until the Last Supper. Only during that evening did these feelings change.

What about Jesus; how did he feel? Certainly, there was sadness because earlier: '*As he approached Jerusalem and saw the city, he wept over it*' (*Luke 19:41*). He knew the corruption and lack of real devotion to God. So many of the people there were not concerned with the values and standards of conduct of the Law of Moses.

Then there was the crisis that Jesus knew was coming. He knew he was provoking the anger of Caiaphas,[35] the High Priest, also of Annas and the majority of the Sanhedrin and that anger would lead to death. The Jews did not have the right to impose the death penalty, so then, it would be Rome. A Roman execution could only mean crucifixion! ' "*Now my heart is troubled, and what shall I say? 'Father, save me from this hour?' No, it was for this very reason I came to this hour*" ' (*John 12:27*).

Yes, Jesus, through this action, is confronting the issue of religious authority. The chief priests considered that they

---

[35] See note on **Caiaphas** in *Supporting Cast*.

were the final authority and that day's work displeased them deeply but at this moment they felt powerless. As they saw it, the advantage had passed to Jesus.

THE RAISING OF LAZARUS – a crisis point

The Temple authorities, also known as the Sanhedrin,[36] would not have been happy with the ministry of Jesus but reports that he had brought back a man from death after he had been dead four days really galvanised them into action (*John 11:1-44*). From their point of view Jesus the rabbi was bad news.

True, there had been earlier reports of other people raised from death but these seem to have been less spectacular and, one at least, could be explained away. There had been the young girl, a daughter of Jairus, a synagogue leader, she had been 'apparently' restored to life (*Mark 5:22-43*), but that had been a rather private affair with the parents and a few disciples around the child's sickbed. They could argue that that had been a mistake or even a fraud.

Then there had been a much more public event at Nain, a village in the north (*Luke 7:11-17*). This rabbi, Jesus, had stopped a funeral cortege, spoken to a widow's dead son and the dead man sat up. That had caused much too much speculation about who this miracle man might be and there had been large crowds about. That was bad!

For the Jewish religious establishment worse was to happen. Lazarus, the brother of Mary and Martha,

---

[36] See separate note on **Sanhedrin** in the *Short Dictionary*.

residents of Bethany just a couple of miles from Jerusalem, was called out of his tomb, four days after being buried. There had even been a smell of decomposition. To have things happening just outside their own city could not be tolerated. Four days dead! People were beginning to believe in this Jesus as *Messiah*. Others had returned to Jerusalem to give an eyewitness account of what had happened. There was fear in the Sanhedrin that the Romans would take action against '*both our place and our nation*' (**11:48**). It was then that Caiaphas the High Priest made his chilling prophecy, '*that Jesus would die for the Jewish nation*' (*v.51*). A course of action was decided upon. '*So from that day on they plotted to take his life*' (*v.53*).

A question that has intrigued many scholars is the fact that only John reports such a vitally important miracle from the ministry of Jesus. This has led to the suspicion among some that the story is a fabrication. Surely Mark, Matthew and Luke knew the facts. The explanation for this omission may well be that the life of Lazarus was also in danger ('*the chief priests made plans to kill Lazarus*', *John* **12:10**) and that while he lived he was protected by the silence of the other Evangelists who feared reprisals against the man and his sisters. John, when he wrote his Gospel towards the end of the first century (85–90),[37] may not have been

---

[37] There is an interesting theory that John's Gospel was written before the Jewish Wars (AD 66–70) and not at the end of the first century. To be accurate, the main conflict of the Jewish War finished in AD 70. Certainly, if John had written his Gospel after the destruction of Jerusalem then it is rather surprising that he did not mention the fulfilment of the prophecy of Jesus about the Temple being flattened.

inhibited by the fact that Lazarus was still alive and was consequently able to give a full account that earlier Gospel writers considered to be a danger to Lazarus.

From these events we see that the entire ministry of Jesus led from its beginning to its end with an increasing friction which was to end with the events that we call the Passion.

Chapter 3

THE LAST SUPPER

It may seem strange that before we can think about the Last Supper we have to go back into the history of God's people, the Jews, because the Last Supper had developed from the original Passover many, many centuries before. Jesus and his closest disciples were going to celebrate Passover. There is the thought that this may not have been the usual celebration of orthodox[38] Jews but we will think about that later.

THE FIRST PASSOVER

Passover, as we know, was, and still is, a yearly celebration by the Jewish people of God's rescue of them from the land of Egypt. This celebration can be dated from about the thirteenth century before Christ.

How did they get to Egypt? It is a very long story so let's shorten it, shall we?

In brief: Joseph, a tactless young fellow, had fallen out with his brothers and been sold by them as a slave.

---

[38] Readers will note that I spell 'orthodox' with a small letter 'o' and not with a capital. Today, the name 'Orthodox' means a special group within Judaism. The meaning used above refers to the usual devout Jewish person of that time.

Very cruelly, his brothers explained his disappearance to his father by claiming he had been killed by a wild animal. Joseph was sold by the slave traders to one of Pharaoh's officials in Egypt. Unfortunately for Joseph his master had a lusty young wife who took a fancy to Joseph. He decided that adultery was wrong. This spelt trouble because by being loyal to his master he was falsely accused by the wife – 'a woman scorned'! Joseph was thrown into prison.

After some bad experiences he was able to make himself useful to Pharaoh, the ruler of Egypt. Joseph had a God-given gift of being able to interpret dreams. Pharaoh had been having some bad ones. Joseph explained that the dreams were warnings about future events. There were going to be seven years of good harvests followed by seven years of famine. If Pharaoh acted now all would be well. Joseph suggested to Pharaoh that he needed a first-rate administrator.

Pharaoh became quiet and was rather thoughtful then, in effect, Pharaoh asked Joseph: *'Do you want the job?'* Although I believe that we see the hand of God at work in Pharaoh's offer, there are other factors in the Egyptian ruler's thinking. Joseph came from the region north of Egypt, then known as Canaan, and that excited interest. The people of that region had invented writing that made Joseph special. He had had some education.

Well, this did mean a career opportunity and, as Joseph was a slave who had been thrown into gaol on the false charge of getting too 'amorous' with his master's wife, it did seem promising. He must have thought rather quickly because Pharaoh was not used to being kept waiting. What have I got to lose, he thought; so he happily and most politely accepted the appointment. 'Thank you, your majesty!'

It was because of the famine that Joseph's family, including his brothers, came to live in Egypt. They settled down following reconciliation between Joseph and his brothers.

About four hundred years later things were different. The Egyptian rulers had changed and the descendents of Joseph had become very successful and very numerous. The Egyptians realised that they would make a great work force and turned them into building labourers. Better still they would not have to pay them!

God's people, who were, at this time called Hebrews, prayed to him. He later provided a national leader, Moses,[39] who tried to negotiate with the new Pharaoh. Unfortunately, this was not successful; in fact, Pharaoh seemed to take a perverse delight in making things more awful than before. Then God allowed a series of catastrophes, ten in all, to come upon the land of Egypt but only the Egyptians were affected. Nothing happened to change the Hebrew's plight. Pharaoh was not going to change his mind because of plagues of frogs and gnats, etc. After all, said and done, in his

---

[39] Readers who would like further details on this period should look at the article on **Passover Meal** and also the **Holy Land** in the *Short Dictionary*. Go to the subsection called 'Canaan'.

palace Pharaoh was probably only moderately inconvenienced.

Then, as nothing else was going to work, God allowed all the firstborn sons of Egypt to be killed. This would happen at about midnight on a certain night. The Egyptians would then let them go and they were to be prepared to leave very quickly.

But the Hebrews would need God's protection. They were to kill and eat a lamb, prepared in a special way and would spread the blood of the animal upon the doorposts. This sacrifice was to happen on the fourteenth day of the month of Nisan (this is close to Easter). On seeing the blood on the doors of Hebrew homes God's Angel of Death would pass over or spare them from death. The story of Joseph can be found in the Book of *Genesis 37* and then *39–50*. For anyone unfamiliar with the events leading up to the first Passover, or wishing to refresh their memory, then read the second book of the Bible, *Exodus 3–12*.

The idea of sacrifice, here and later, is that the animal would be a substitute. The main idea in the Jewish Scriptures (Old Testament) was that national or individual wrongdoing would be cancelled by the death of the animal instead of the guilty person.

This showed the people that God was offended by their misdemeanours and as they paid for their wrongs they realised the seriousness of their deeds. The priests at the Temple had the practical benefit of some meat from the animal as payment for their services because they received no monetary reward for their hard work, especially at times such as Passover.

JESUS AND PASSOVER (*PESACH*)

Jesus, being thoroughly Jewish, would have valued Passover and our reading of the Gospels will show that there is an eagerness to celebrate this with his closest disciples (refer below on section The First Lord's Supper). Things for this group of men would never be the same and Jesus wished to make the most of this day and evening.

It would, as we know, have involved a sacrifice of a one-year-old lamb (a kid would have been sacrificially acceptable but lambs were preferred), whose blood would have been smeared around the doorpost. It centred on a meal where the lamb/kid would have been roasted and eaten without any of its bones being broken. Bread, which had not risen by the adding of yeast, accompanied the meat. That first Passover meal, in Egypt, would have been followed wherever possible in every detail. After the meal the carcass of the animal would have been burned in the fire.

Passover, as a Festival, lasted seven days (its Hebrew name is *Pesach*) and, for visitors to Jerusalem, booking a room during the time of Jesus was essential (*Matthew 26:17* & *18*). The lateness of these arrangements does seem strange although perhaps Jesus felt that it was wiser to have people ignorant of his movements so that he could have undisturbed quality time with his disciples. The focus of the Festival of Passover was the special meal that Jews ate in commemoration of their deliverance and there would have been an atmosphere of celebration.

The only people who would not have been looking forward to this yearly event were the Romans. Pontius Pilate had a command of about 5,000 men, which for most of the time was adequate. However, with Jerusalem bulging at the seams with so many pilgrims, merchants, beggars and the general run of its population, maintaining peace was a greater problem. Then there were the *Sicarii*, the Jewish national freedom fighters, who were also popularly known as Zealots.[40] They could well be around. This group were audacious enough to operate in daylight during the festivals and some who they classed as collaborators were quickly dispatched with a *sica*, the name of the short sword they carried. Pilate looked forward to getting away from Jerusalem as soon as possible after the festival and returning to the more tranquil city of Caesarea on the coast from where he administered Judea.

'SEDER',[41] THE CELEBRATION MEAL

For a Jewish man of this period it was essential that he

---

[40] The Sicarii are often confused with Zealots but appear to be a separate group. They were thought of as Zealots because of their fanatical hatred of Rome and those who were prepared to collaborate.

[41] 'Seder' is a name that is fairly contemporary and would not have been used by Jesus.

celebrated this festival and, if at all possible, to get to Jerusalem for an act of identification that commemorated his Jewishness and freedom from the slavery of Egypt many centuries before.

In every generation a man must so regard himself as if he came forth himself out of Egypt. The Mishnah[42]

Some readers may have seen a re-enactment of a *Seder*, or Passover meal, and may be a little confused with my detail of a lamb being on the menu. Over the years local variations have crept in. This may depend on whether the celebrants are Liberal, Progressive or Orthodox Jews. It also depends on local custom. To give some examples: many Jews in Europe will shy away from using lamb. This is because the Jerusalem Temple has ceased to exist and so they feel that it would not be right to eat lamb during their Seder; others are happy to be reminded of the ritual, which was conducted in the Temple before AD 70. Chicken or fish may be the main meat on many Jewish meal tables for this celebration these days.

One thing has not changed since the first Passover meal and that is the fact that leaven (bread dough containing yeast[43]) in every form has been removed from the house. In fact, in some Orthodox Jewish households

---

[42] The Mishnah [Pesahim 10.5] is a Jewish writing dating from about AD 300.

[43] The use of leaven was totally prohibited with animal sacrifices (***Exodus 23:18***). The presence of yeast was thought of as being a corrupting influence.

special crockery and cutlery may be brought out of store once a year for this one special dinner. But we seem to be straying from our subject because we have been thinking about how things are now. Our main subject was how it was during the time of Jesus.

IN JESUS'S DAY

As has been already stated the one thing that has not altered from the very beginning of the eating of Seder is the fact that all yeast products are absent and should be excluded for seven days. Wine, although it is the product of yeast and fruit, is excluded. This is because the yeast has done its work and is no longer active. It would be safe to say that the *Haggadah* (the telling), which also gives an order of service, has not changed which means that *Kiddushim* (the blessings), which we would call them prayers or 'grace', have not been altered either. Jesus's inner group would have looked forward to a great celebration.

With the end of daylight, the Passover meal begins with the special *Kiddush*, the prayer asking God's blessing on the meal and thanking him for the occasion. This is performed over the first cup of wine. Then the leader, usually the head of the house, washes his hands. Next, the household, in some cases more than one family will have come together, receives a piece of unleavened bread or *motzah*. The second cup of wine is drunk at this point. Then following the *Haggadah*, someone present, normally the youngest child, asks four questions on the theme of why this night was different from all others. This part of the meal has remained unchanged but today, in our more equal society, a daughter may ask the four questions as long as she is the youngest child. Dorothy L Sayers wondered whether at the Last Supper the Apostle John was the one to take this part in the ceremony.

JESUS'S INNER GROUP

What did the Twelve disciples feel as they gathered with Jesus? It was likely that there had been a feeling of expectancy following the triumph of their teacher's entry into Jerusalem. They must have had the expectation that the kingdom was about to be established very soon. Having such a feeling could account for the fact that they began to argue about their own status as we see from *Luke 22:24–30*. The reason for the argument was probably the seating arrangement. The argument about seating was in spite of the fact that Jesus had earlier given them some clear teaching on status seeking and that they should not assume that the higher seats, with more prestige, were theirs but should wait to be invited to *'move up to a better place' (Luke 14:10)*.

It is worthwhile spending a few moments thinking about the Last Supper and the places that the disciples occupied in the room. An understanding of the positioning will help us make greater sense of the events that took place on that momentous evening.

There will be the temptation to imagine that the guests sat around a modern style table. In fact our minds may recall Leonardo's picture of the *Last Supper* with Jesus at the centre, and the others sitting upright around a table. Clearly da Vinci had not understood the furnishings of a Jewish home in the first century. Many more recent, even relatively modern painters have made the same mistake imagining a conventional table with chairs placing the diners' stomachs at table level. Not so!

What then should we imagine? How were they seated? A traditional seating would have been just above floor level with the diners resting on low couches, mattresses or similar and eating their food from low tables. Often a U-shaped pattern of bodies would be formed. Each person would be lying with his feet alongside the tables, not under them. Normally, he or she would recline on their left elbow, leaving their right hand to pick up food. Some might be lying on their backs with their heads propped up.

As we follow **John's Gospel Chapter 13** we are told that next to Jesus on the floor was '*the disciple whom Jesus loved*' (**13:23**). This arrangement around the tables throws light on the behaviour of Peter and John during that evening. Jesus had told them ' "*one of you is going to betray me*" ' (*verse 21*). This caused a stir and a great deal of disquiet. Who was he referring to? Which one of them was the traitor? Characteristically, Peter was the one to take a lead. Quietly he whispered to John: ' "*Ask him which one he means*" ' (24). Being next to Jesus, John was the obvious person to ask this question.

'Leaning back against Jesus, he asked him, "Lord, who is it?" ' (25). Jesus then told him: ' *"It is the one to whom I will give this piece of bread when I have dipped it in the dish." Then, dipping the piece of bread, he gave it to Judas Iscariot, son of Simon.'*

Britain's Archbishop William Temple, writing many years ago, produced a seating plan of the last supper which placed Judas, as the treasurer for the disciples, next to Jesus and able to receive the special piece of unleavened bread, that Jesus had dipped, possibly in the bitter herbs, before giving it to his betrayer (**13:26 & 27**). Judas had heard what had been said about betrayal and realised that Jesus knew what he intended doing. Whatever we think of William Temple's theory, we see from this that Judas was clearly within easy reach of Jesus. Perhaps Archbishop Temple was correct. Judas might have been reclining next to Jesus on the opposite side to John. As treasurer for the Twelve he had some status.

We might be disappointed, even shocked by the thought that Jesus had favourites but there were special circumstances. Jesus, John and James Zebedee can be, almost certainly, regarded as first cousins and John could probably have regarded Jesus like an older brother having known him for much longer than the others.

THE FIRST 'LORD'S SUPPER'

From its beginning some strange events begin to change the feeling of the evening. Jesus washes the disciples' feet. That act was bad enough – their teacher doing such a menial task! But it got worse as the evening grew older. ' *"One of you will betray me"* ' (*Matthew 26:21*). This statement shocks members of the apostolic group! Then comes yet another shock. ' *"My children, I will be with you only a little longer. You will look for me, and just as I told the Jews, so I tell you now: where I am going, you cannot come"* ' (*John 13:33*). That sense of happy expectancy must now have gone and the disciples are left with a feeling of puzzlement if not dread. Then there is another shock!

' *"This is my body. This is my blood"* ' (*Mark 14:22-3*). The other Gospels add to our knowledge of this moment. *Matthew 26:28* says: ' *"This is my blood of the covenant,*[44] *which is poured out for many for the forgiveness of sins."* ' Jesus is clearly informing them that God is doing a new thing. In fact, *Luke 22:20* calls it *'the new covenant'*. It is unlikely that in the shock of that moment the disciples realised that Jesus was announcing that the Old Testament prophecy of *Jeremiah 31:31-34* was about to be fulfilled.

Now, instead of their seeking to find God by outward ritual, he would wish to be directly at work within the inner nature of their lives. Instead of God's people needing intermediaries such as Moses, who had brought them the Covenant called the Law of Moses, to help them know about the Eternal. The Holy Spirit of God would enable them not just to know about the

---

[44] Please refer to note on **Covenant** in the *Short Dictionary* section.

Lord but to begin to know and experience him at a personal level. All of this is unlikely to have percolated through to the shocked listeners. It would have been later once they had discussed this that they made the connection.

The words must have struck terror into the hearts of the diners around the table. Jesus is saying that he is a sacrifice. This is both frightening and confusing when compared to what they, as Jews, would have known about the ritual of the Temple with its daily, weekly, monthly and very special yearly sacrifices of animals and the Passover rites. Here was their leader with whom they had shared food, humour, fears and joys and their very lives. Was he saying that he was to be a sacrifice? The answers to their questions did not come immediately, in fact, they would only begin to grasp at solutions to these matters with the passing of time and in the light of the events to which they were moving.

It would be a mistake if we did not look at the meaning of 'cup' which had a symbolic meaning to Jews at this time. The 'cup' could stand for your life.[45] Your personal 'cup' might contain good things. The writer of the Psalms, recalling all the many good things in his life wrote, *'my cup overflows'* (23:5). Then there is the *'cup of God's wrath'* on the wicked (***Revelation 14:10***). When Jesus told the Twelve that his cup contained his ***blood*** he then passed it around and we are told that

---

[45] The word 'cup' can be used in English in the same way but it is rare and poetic.

'they all drank from it' (**14:**23). It was a sign of that group of disciples' solidarity with Jesus. They could not, at that stage, have known what this would entail but they were willing to trust him. Their lives and their service belonged to Jesus. Even strong-willed, assertive Peter took and drank from the 'cup' of the sufferings of his rabbi. Although it cannot be proved I think that at this point Judas would have left the supper party and not partaken of the cup. The whole mood of what had begun as a celebration had changed. A feeling of uncertainty and dread had come down on the group.

THE ROLE OF JUDAS

So far we have not thought very much about Judas Iscariot.[46] After all, he is not in any sense a sympathetic character. In fact, as we know, his name is a byword for treachery but shall we consider his part? It is reasonable to conclude that he would have had an open door at the palace of the High Priest; assuming that something of importance had happened that his paymaster ought to know about.

It seems rather strange that the Jewish High Priesthood, after paying Judas Iscariot a modest sum for information, did not ask him to testify in any of the hearings of the case against Jesus. Perhaps it was Iscariot's suicide that curtailed this option. We cannot be certain

---

[46] Although there is a profile on **Judas Iscariot** at the back (see *Supporting Cast*), in short, his reason for betrayal was because of an act of homage, which he did not like (***John 12:5–6***). We read about his actual betrayal in ***Matthew 26:14–16***.

of the exact timing of these events. Then again they might have considered him an unreliable witness well before his change of heart, following the arrest of Jesus, when he threw down his paltry thirty silver coins in front of Caiaphas and declared, ' "*I have sinned, for I have betrayed innocent blood." "What is that to us?" they replied. "That's your responsibility"* ' (*Matthew* 27:4). And indeed so it was!

A question that has intrigued many is – did Caiaphas really need Judas? After all, the movements of Jesus were not a closely guarded secret. Lots of ordinary people knew his movements so that the chief priests should have had no trouble in knowing where to find him. There was little need to send out a member of the Temple police to keep him under observation. Almost without doubt they knew, or suspected, that he and his inner group stayed at the home of Lazarus and his two sisters in Bethany a couple of miles outside Jerusalem. He spent several evenings at this house during the few days after his triumphal ride into Jerusalem on the day we now call *Palm Sunday*. Yet they did nothing to arrest him. They may not have known where he was having supper with the Twelve on the evening of his arrest until the second meeting with Judas.

Clearly the main reason for the lack of action by Caiaphas was that he and his immediate group feared the reaction of the people. Jesus, they decided, was to be arrested when '*no crowd was present*' (*Luke* 22:6). However, reading between the lines, there do seem to be other factors at work. After Jesus had ridden into Jerusalem there is a clear tone of desperation in the words of his enemies: ' *"Look how the whole world has gone after him"* ' (*John 12:19*)! They did not know what to do. Jesus seemed to be unstoppable! Then there had been the incident in the Temple, after Jesus had turned out the market traders and he had been challenged about his authority to do this.

Jesus replied, 'I will also ask you one question. If you answer me, I will tell you by what authority I am doing these things. John's baptism – where did it come from? Was it from heaven, or from men?' They discussed it among themselves and said, 'If we say, "From heaven," he will ask, "Then why didn't you believe him?" But if we say, "From men" – we are afraid of the people, for they all hold that John was a prophet.' So they answered Jesus, 'We don't know.' Then he said, 'Neither will I tell you by what authority I am doing these things' (Matthew 21:24–27).

They were frightened of the answer but they were also frightened of Jesus. As they met his gaze that day in the Temple they felt the full power of his authority. They never doubted that he had extraordinary powers of healing. They had seen him at work clearing the Temple and although emotionally moved he was in full control of his actions. They did not comprehend what was happening and the person who does not understand something is often more afraid of it. This was most probably the reason for their inaction.

Judas Iscariot has, I believe, the key to this question. His first interview together with the offer of betrayal must have occurred only a few days before Jesus's arrest. Certainly, we learn that Caiaphas and company were all *'delighted'* (*Mark 14:11*) with this unexpected offer of help. But did they really think that he was going to get them results? Those who change sides for a trifling sum of money do not usually inspire confidence.

If we read between the lines, it is Judas's second visit to Caiaphas that seems to be more interesting. Why was this? We remember that he had been in the Upper Room with other members of the twelve, had shared the meal and listened with interest as Jesus had spoken very personally of his deepest feelings. Judas had heard Jesus say: ' *"One of you will betray me"* ' (*Matthew 26:21*). Then later he had heard Jesus say: ' *"I have eagerly desired to eat this Passover with you before I suffer. For I tell you, I will not eat it again until it finds fulfilment in the kingdom of God"* ' (*Luke 22:15–16*).

Judas's instincts told him that things were changing and that it was time for him to show he was worth his pay. As he left Jesus and the rest he must have wondered whether it was going to be possible to finalise his deal with the High Priesthood.

After this second meeting with Judas there is a 'sea change.' Suddenly, we move from a state of inertia to a state of hyperactivity, certainly from no later than midnight, if not rather earlier. So, what changed this? As Caiaphas heard this report his sense of powerlessness began to lift. The man Jesus was frightened – he was thinking the one thing that Caiaphas thought was impossible; he was thinking, so Caiaphas reasoned, that he would fail! Judas had said, with certainty, that Jesus would not resist being arrested. The meaning of some of the earlier sayings of Jesus had begun to make sense to Iscariot. He had heard Jesus say, for surely no prophet can die outside Jerusalem! ' *"O Jerusalem, Jerusalem, you who kill the prophets and stone those sent to you"* ' (*Luke 13:33–34*). Then Jesus had said, and Judas had thought it strange at the time, ' *"the Son of Man did not come to be served, but to serve, and to give his life as a ransom for many"* ' (*Mark 10:45*). Yes, Judas was convinced and told the High Priest, there would be no struggle. After all, Jesus had given him the choice piece from the meal and then said, ' *"What you are about to do, do quickly"* ' (*John 13:27*). Did Judas then realise that his work could be accomplished? Yes, and suddenly he realised that Jesus not only knew his intentions but also had seen through him. This knowledge spurred him on and hardened his heart.

THE THINKING OF CAIAPHAS

It is likely that Caiaphas, as soon as possible, called in his father-in-law. After all, Annas was unofficially the power behind him and shared the news that Judas had brought. Perhaps it was Judas who retold it but whatever happened I cannot imagine that Judas would have heard their discussions. I am sure that he would have been asked to wait outside ready to be recalled in case there were more questions for him. As Caiaphas thought it through he realised that if Jesus was talking about *suffering* then he had realised that it would lead to his death. The man Iscariot had to be correct.

Joseph Caiaphas, the High Priest, realised that he had what seemed like a narrow window of opportunity. He knew where Jesus would be when his men went to make the arrest. He had double-checked that with Iscariot and yes, there was no doubt! The Sanhedrin Council could be got together. Some might be in bed but never mind that. Witnesses – getting them to a hearing might be a problem but he knew of enough men available in Jerusalem for a guilty verdict and, after all, Jewish law only needed two in full agreement to get a conviction.

Then there was Pontius Pilate – he had better be notified to authorise the death sentence. They would have to be very careful in the way he was handled – Romans had some strange ideas. They would have to ask the Governor (Procurator[47]) to be ready to hear the case against a particularly dangerous agitator and explain about the festival, if that was needed and it might well be, because although he was the Governor he had not been well advised about Jewish matters in the past; and finally to ask him to kindly be prepared to hear the case well before his normal office hours.

---

[47] It was only later, well after Pilate had left office, that the office of Governor was called 'Procurator'. At this time Pontius Pilate was called a Prefect.

What a pity the charges against Jesus were not clearly on matters of treason but for religious offences, which could create unrest. Had the security of the Roman occupation been in any way threatened, then Pilate himself would have been the judge. In no way would he have left it to the Jews. However, the charges against Jesus were not on matters of sedition but for religious offences.

A successful Roman trial would have saved a great deal of trouble. Proving that Jesus had said anything against the Romans would be a problem. He would probably need an expert in law from among the Temple staff, one who understood the Roman mentality. If only he had had more warning.

For just a moment Caiaphas thought about the possibility of arresting Jesus and dealing with him after the festival – he immediately rejected that idea. The Passover would create a week's delay. Holding Jesus in prison was far too dangerous as his enormous popularity could create dissent among local people and other pilgrims. Also the Roman garrison would be on high alert and could quickly overreact. It would be touch and go regarding timing but he had no choice, they had to get rid of this Galilean rabbi before the Feast!

Then, deep in his memory, Caiaphas remembered a report about Jesus saying something about taxes and Rome (*Matthew 22:15–22*). He made a mental note to check on that. It may not have been incriminating, otherwise he would have remembered it. At that moment dealing with his fellow Jews seemed to be the immediate need. He felt that the Sanhedrin could, and indeed should, be able to get a conviction. That would give him great personal satisfaction. However, if he could persuade Pilate that there had been any encouragement not to pay taxes it could help with getting the death penalty.

Charges of sedition against Rome would hardly be a misdemeanour in the eyes of the Sanhedrin. Something more anti-Jewish would be required to persuade them that the death penalty was needed to deal with this rabbi, Jesus. The trouble was that several believed in the goodness of Jesus.

He, as the High Priest, could not possibly believe in Jesus's powers coming from God. No, the source of his power was clearly evil. In short this Galilean practised something like witchcraft. He had been heard to claim that he had the power to destroy and rebuild the Temple in three days (*Matthew 26:60–61*). Anyone who claimed that was either mad or had evil powers at his disposal. Caiaphas preferred the second possibility and this man Jesus was too controlled and rational. He wondered how strong a case he could make to the rest of the Sanhedrin. He had suspected that some of them were partial and might even want to protect this Galilean prophet. Oh well, time would tell.

DID CAIAPHAS PREPARE PILATE FOR THE TRIAL?

Although there is no direct mention of it in the New Testament it is very likely that a deputation from the Sanhedrin visited Pontius Pilate late on the evening of the Last Supper after learning the news from Judas Iscariot that Jesus was talking about death. They had to get his compliance. They would have no doubt told him that a dangerous political prisoner was about to be arrested. They would have stressed that this was a difficult time with the Feast about to begin. They may have had to explain that the condemned man would have to be dead before sunset so that the Law of Moses would be obeyed.[48] They may well have mentioned that, because of Passover, they would not be able to enter his residence. Therefore, would he kindly come out to them? Yes, we have to consider the fact that Pontius Pilate had been forewarned about this trial.

This theory was very well argued in Frank Morison's book, *Who Moved the Stone*, and while there are arguments against, it does make sense. The best argument in support of Morison's theory is that there was a lack of time between arrest and the carrying out of the death sentence. Any delay would mean that the scheme would have to be abandoned. If they arrested Jesus and then had to release him they, the High Priests, could be finished! The population would probably take Jesus's

---

[48] Readers wishing to know more should read the section **Crucifixion and the Cross** in the *Short Dictionary*.

side and the Sanhedrin would lose prestige. It might have taken many years to recover.

The only really strong arguments against this theory are to do with the character of Pilate. He was a man who has already shown that he had little if any sympathy for the Jewish nation. He preferred giving orders to negotiation. So, why would he give Caiaphas and a select few High Priests an audience at an hour that we would call unsociable? It could not have been much earlier than ten o'clock that evening, maybe rather later. Caiaphas was probably the only non-Roman who would be able to call on the Governor at this hour. The reason for this is that Caiaphas, because of his position, had to be listened to. Then, if Caiaphas had mentioned possible trouble during the Feast, Pilate would have been very anxious to hear of it. Finally, we have evidence from the conversation between Pilate and Caiaphas, during the trial of Jesus that the High Priest had pressure, which he could bring to bear. We have to remember that there had been complaints about Pilate to Rome. He had to be careful in the way he dealt with these people. Later we shall see that the chief priests hinted that they would use another complaint to Caesar in order to force Pilate's hand and get Jesus sentenced to death.

In brief this is Morison's main theory: the High Priests would not have arrested Jesus without an assurance from Pontius Pilate that he would, with minimal delay, endorse the verdict of the Great Sanhedrin so that this political prisoner could be quickly executed. We have to believe that the Jewish clergy left the Governor's Palace happy that their 'prey' would shortly be able to be taken and by sunset the next day would be dead. This is Morison's first argument. We shall look at Morison's second argument in the next chapter.

The next morning, as we shall see, matters did not seem to go to plan for Caiaphas and the rest of the chief priests. From his known personality, Pilate would probably not have been happy to automatically *rubber stamp* the verdict of this Jewish court. So, it is likely that he had reservations. Did he consult with his advisers on this situation? Did he double check on this 'political threat' he had been hearing about? Did these discussions lead him to the conclusion that Jesus was not so much a threat to Rome as to the Jerusalem Temple authorities?

THE DIFFERENCE OF A DAY

As I promised at the beginning of this Chapter, we need to consider another factor that could greatly affect our thinking about the Last Supper. Was it, in fact, an orthodox celebration of the *Seder* (I use the modern Jewish term for the meal) or were there other matters for us to think about? Well, what exactly am I hinting at?

A casual reading of Mark, Matthew and Luke regarding the events leading up to the Last Supper would lead us, modern readers, to the conclusion that the Seder had been taken on the usual day which marked the start of Passover. Working with time in the New Testament is complicated by the fact that days begin at sundown and end with the next sundown some twenty-four hours later.

If we look at *John 13:1* a different day is indicated – *'just before the Passover Feast'*. We can assume that he means at the very least a full twenty-four hours. This would put the date back to 13 Nisan. This was the day when all leaven (dough which had risen by the addition of yeast) had to be removed from Jewish households.

As the Last Supper, according to John, was not eaten on 14 Nisan (the conventional day) then it is possible that there was no roast lamb on the menu. On a practical level, such was the demand in Jerusalem that any departure from the norm with local supply could cause difficulties. More to the point, none of the Gospel writers mention a lamb. Perhaps this was *an anticipation of the Passover Meal.*[49]

So, is John at variance with the other Gospel writers? No! The problem for us is that we do not know the culture of that day. We look at these events with a twenty-first-century mindset. The members of the Church who first read the Gospels of Mark, Matthew or Luke would have understood much more of the

---

[49] R T France, *The Man they Crucified*, Inter-Varsity Press, 1975, p.136.

background. This was largely due to the fact that these believers were, for the most part, Jewish. When Matthew mentions the *'first day of the Feast of Unleavened Bread'*, he can only mean the day when leaven had to be removed from Jewish homes. Matthew continues with the disciples' question: ' *"Where do you want us to make preparations?"* ' (*Matthew 26:17*).

As any housewife knows, a special meal requires special preparation. Purchases had to be made: unleavened bread, bitter herbs and the sauce. In an era before refrigeration some things would have had to have been ordered in advance and collected nearer the time. 'Preparations' is the key word and that required time. The disciples of Jesus were thinking of at least a day ahead.

There are other indications from John's telling of the Passion event that confirm that it is a different day. Let's take for example the moment during the meal when Judas left the supper room. Jesus had just told him that he knew of his intended betrayal.

Since Judas had charge of the money, some thought Jesus was telling him to buy what was needed for the Feast, or to give something to the poor. As soon as Judas had taken the bread, he went out. And it was night (John 13:29–30).

John's mention of *'night'* is not just a note of drama – he is telling us that the new day had begun. The day we call Good Friday!

Even a casual reading of *John 13:31-2* reveals that Jesus experienced a sense of relief once Judas had left. Evil had been present and Jesus may well have felt a sense of oppression as the betrayer went through his final charade. Now Jesus feels free to instruct his followers but first he gives vent to his feelings: '*When he was gone, Jesus said: "Now is the Son of Man glorified and God is glorified in him. If God is glorified in him, God will glorify the Son in himself, and will glorify him at once. My children, I will be with you only a little longer. You will look for me, and just as I told the Jews, so I tell you now: where I am going, you cannot come. A new command I give you: love one another. As I have loved you, so you must love one another. By this all men will know that you are my disciples, if you love one another."* '

But let's return to the moment that Judas left. Please note that '*some*' present, in the room, thought he was going to get something '*for the Feast*'. Then next day, after his arrest, John tells us that '*the Jews led Jesus from Caiaphas to the palace of the Roman governor. By now it was early morning, and to avoid ceremonial uncleanness the Jews did not enter the palace; they wanted to be able to eat the Passover*' (*John 18:28*). Finally, if this matter needed any further clarification, John has given us this piece of information about the death of Jesus:

When he had received the drink, Jesus said, 'It is finished.' With that, he bowed his head and gave up his spirit. Now it was the day of Preparation, and the next day was to be a special Sabbath. Because the Jews did not want the bodies left on the crosses during the Sabbath, they asked Pilate to have the legs broken and the bodies taken down (John 19:30–31).

These two verses would have been full of meaning for John's Jewish readers. The only meaning they could take was that Jesus had died when the lambs to be eaten during the Passover meal that evening were being sacrificed in the Temple.

John the Apostle is so insistent about the day that he may have been seeking to get rid of an error or misunderstanding in the mind of some Gentile believers. It seems likely that he is making sure that Christians understand the significance of the day of Christ's death.

So, there is no disagreement between the other Gospel writers and John. Matthew and Mark mention disciples (*Luke 22:8* tells us that they were *Peter and John*) being sent off to book the room '*to celebrate the Passover*' (*26:18*). We are not told anything about the conditions of hire but from the words we can assume that Matthew (writing of this event about thirty years later) thought of it as a booking for the keeping of the Passover meal.

One further thought on this difference. Luke mentions Jesus speaking about a ' *"guest room, where I may eat the Passover with my disciples"* ' (*Luke 22:11*). As we know, Luke is a Gentile and as such may not have had the official view on the days of Passover. For instance, the lamb for the meal was chosen on the 10 Nisan and many people, even Jews, may have thought of this as within the Passovertide period.

The Apostle John is, as we know, very well schooled in matters of Jewish religious tradition and practice and he would have used precise language, whereas his fellow Gospel writers would not necessarily have been so exact. So, in short, I am not greatly troubled by these minor differences between John and his fellow Gospel writers. It is my opinion that they really are thinking about the same day and that there is really no disagreement.

The first three Gospel writers are viewing this Jewish Feast in a different way. John, in spite of having a slightly different emphasis, would be in agreement with them. The Passion of Jesus has overtaken the Passover and everything has changed. Yes, many of the Jewish traditions, particularly of the synagogue have been kept. Many other things have changed. The Jewish Saturday Sabbath was to become, for the Christian community, Sunday. The Passover meal became the celebration of Christ's death. It is known by several names: the *Lord's Supper*, *Breaking of Bread*, *Holy Communion* and *Eucharist*.[50] It began with a meal although this is not often practised nowadays. Yes, many Jewish customs were taken over and often

---

[50] Readers who would like to know more about the vitally important subject of Holy Communion are strongly advised to look at, Steve Motyer's book, *Remember Jesus*.

changed by the early Church. They seem remote from us in the twenty-first century but some are still worth looking at once again. In fact, the preparation and studies for this book have strengthened my appreciation of the Jewish traditions of the Christian faith.

THE FUNDAMENTAL CHANGE

In the paragraph above I made the statement that with the Passion of Jesus 'everything has changed' for the early Church as indeed for today's Christian. Let me explain. Paul the Apostle, writing to the Church in Corinth during the early 50s of the first century wrote this: *'For Christ, our Passover lamb has been sacrificed'* (*1 Corinthians 5:7*).

Before the coming of Christ the Passover lamb was a yearly Jewish sacrifice. During his ministry Jesus made it clear that he wanted other nations to be blessed by his coming.

I have other sheep that are not of this sheep pen. I must bring them also. They too will listen to my voice, and there shall be one flock and one shepherd (John 10:16).

Paul was to realise that God's work for him was to take the message to those Gentiles and this is his message. Christ, *the new eternal Passover lamb*, is 'a once for all offering', eternally valid for all believing peoples, Jews and Gentiles. With the Jewish Passover the benefit of the Feast was temporary and was celebrated yearly with a new sacrifice.

The Lord's Supper is the new Passover. Like the original Passover it celebrates freedom but not just the historical freedom from bondage when the Hebrews escaped from Egypt. No – the liberty for the genuine Christian is the spiritual and continual freedom of daily deliverance from the bondage of wrongdoing. The Bible calls this sin. Then to be free to serve Christ in this world! It is to enter into our full humanity.

THE FINAL HOURS

How did Jesus spend those final few hours after the meal with his disciples before he left the house to go to the Garden of Gethsemane? Certainly it was a special valuable time. For Jesus there was the certainty of arrest, trial and execution. Perhaps for the eleven remaining disciples there was the hope that it might not be so bad, although as they looked at Jesus's face they dreaded that it was.

There is the large block of teaching that *John's Gospel* gives us in *Chapters 13–17* but I think that this took place earlier, perhaps well before the meal. What we do have is the prayer of Jesus for his disciples and for those who, through their teaching, would become his followers (*Chapter 17*). It is not always immediately obvious where every event on that final evening occurred and it is easy to confuse events, for instance, at one point in my life, early on, I sincerely believed that the prayer of Jesus for his disciples occurred in the garden where he was later arrested. It occurred before they left the house.

Then it was time to leave the privacy, security and comfort of that room and ascend to the Garden of Gethsemane. *'When they had sung a hymn, they went out to the Mount of Olives'* (*Matthew 26:30*). The Hymn that they sang was one of the set Hallel Psalms for the Feast of Passover (*Psalms 113–118*).

On the way to the Garden there is some more bad news for the Eleven.

Then Jesus told them, 'This very night you will all fall away on account of me, for it is written: 'I will strike the shepherd, and the sheep of the flock will be scattered.' But after I have risen, I will go ahead of you into Galilee.' Peter replied, 'Even if all fall away on account of you, I never will.' 'I tell you the truth,' Jesus answered, 'this very night, before the cock crows, you will disown me three times.' But Peter declared, 'Even if I have to die with you, I will never disown you.' And all the other disciples said the same' (*Matthew 26:31–35*).

On reaching the Garden of Gethsemane the full impact of what Jesus is about to suffer is felt and he has a crisis, as he is *'overwhelmed with sorrow'*. He asks for the support of Peter, James and John and for them to *'keep watch'* while he prayed. *'Going a little farther, he fell with his face to the ground and prayed, "My Father, if it is possible, may this cup be taken from me. Yet not as I will, but as you will" '* (*Matthew 26:38 & 39*). When Jesus got up and went to the three he found that they had fallen asleep. It had been a long day and as Luke, a physician by profession, tells us, they were *'exhausted by sorrow'* (22:45). It is recorded that, in all, Jesus prayed this prayer three times. Luke also gives us further details of the psychological stress Jesus was experiencing. Not surprisingly he was perspiring with beads of sweat falling to the ground. *'An angel from heaven appeared to him and strengthened him'* (22:43 & 44). This time of prayers may have, altogether, have taken about an hour or longer.

*****

From the City of Jerusalem, guided by Judas Iscariot, a group of men were trudging down the hill and across the valley towards the Garden. They were Temple officials and behind them, to make sure that there would be no trouble, a group of Roman soldiers. Their flaming torches would have created an eerie light at a time when most men and women would have been in bed asleep waiting for the beginning of the daylight of the busy Day of Preparation. This group's orders were to arrest Jesus – they arrived just after he had finished praying. Jesus anticipated events because he warned his disciples. ' *"Rise, let us go! Here comes my betrayer!"* ' *(Matthew 26:46)*.

Let us now turn to the arrest of Jesus and of the hearings before his own fellow Jews, but that is for Chapter 4.

Chapter 4

THE ARREST AND TRIAL

It was the noise of the gate to the garden[51] being forcibly pushed open that made the Eleven disciples and Jesus turn their heads to see a group of men entering. At the head of them was Judas, his face illuminated by a flaming torch. A feeling of dismay came over them as they saw the group come in looking rather uncertain. It was difficult to know how many there were, as the olive trees seemed to be hiding some of them. One thing was certain, the group was large and armed. The action of Judas in going to Jesus and giving him a kiss of greeting has gone down as one of history's most infamous acts.

THE ARREST

There is a question that may occur to you with regard to the arrest of Jesus and the answer is not immediately obvious. We will need to think about it. Jesus had been in Jerusalem for about a week prior to his arrest so why did he need to be identified by the kiss of the traitor Judas? At least some of the Temple police must have seen Jesus earlier that week and would have been able

---

[51] We cannot be entirely sure that there was a gate to the garden, but it is fairly likely that there was as this was a private grove.

to make the arrest without Judas being present. It is unlikely that it can be explained by poor light because, as Haim Cohn points out, there would have been a full moon at this time of the month. In spite of this the Temple guard were carrying torches and lanterns as well as being well armed (*John 18:3*). So, was there any strong likelihood that they would not recognise Jesus in the murky conditions of Gethsemane? It does not seem a strong possibility but perhaps they wanted to be doubly sure with this important arrest. But the answer to our question remains illusive.

The answer may lie in the fact that those acting as the Temple police were unused to the task. It could be that they were priests living well away from Jerusalem who had been brought in to help during the frenziedly busy time of the Feast and could not recognise Jesus. On that fateful night they had been asked to act as police and had to rely on Judas to positively identify the man to be arrested. Certainly this group of men seemed to be ill at ease.

This could also explain their reaction to Jesus's lack of fear as he approached them. ' *"Who is it you want?" "Jesus of Nazareth," they replied. "I am he," Jesus said. (And Judas the traitor was standing there with them.) When Jesus said, "I am he," they drew back and fell to the ground'* (John 18:4–6).

This does not seem like the reaction of experienced Temple police. However, it could well be the reaction of those who had been hastily deputised for a job they were not entirely happy with. One imagines that regular policemen, those who had seen Jesus, would have stated that they had a warrant for his arrest and apprehended him without hesitation.

Again it seems to be the personal authority of Jesus that they were up against. It seems that if he had told them to go and leave him they might just have considered going; certainly their confusion would have been even worse. However, the arresting party were under Roman control, a detail of soldiers was there as back-up, so that, if the matter were still in doubt, that fact would have forced their hand. So, Jesus was arrested, bound and taken to Annas.

It was at this point that the Eleven, and others with them, ran off. Most, we believe, headed for Bethany and the security of the home of Lazarus and his sisters. This was about an hour's walk away. However, these nine men must have covered the distance much more quickly. After running for a while, John the son of Zebedee and Peter decide that they ought to return and watch what was going to happen to Jesus. It is possible that they could have gone back into the city as the rules over closing the gates were relaxed during the Feasts. Officially the gates would have been guarded until sunrise but with so many pilgrims about it is likely that the gatekeepers saw a number of people other than John and Peter enter Jerusalem.

As the arresting party began their return to the city they noticed that someone was following them. Only

Mark's Gospel mentions this incident. *'A young man, wearing nothing but a linen garment, was following Jesus. When they seized him, he fled naked, leaving his garment behind'* (*Mark 14:51 & 52*). That is all that is said and the identity is not revealed. John Mark, I am sure, knew the identity and the likely person is John Mark himself, who using Peter's memories was to write *Mark*, the earliest of the Gospels. He had reported on his own escape from the clutches of the group sent to arrest Jesus. The garment covering him that was snatched by a policeman or Roman was nothing more than a bed sheet or blanket.

THE FIRST HEARING

This hearing, which was held before Annas, was informal, in the sense that the Great Sanhedrin had not been brought together. The purpose seems to have been to gather evidence to be used later that morning. The questioning was about Jesus's disciples and what he had taught. He replied that what he had said had been in synagogues and in the Temple and not done secretly. Jesus remarked that those present during these occasions would be able to give full details. Jesus was not drawn into saying anything about his disciples. Galileans had a reputation for being rebellious so perhaps Annas's questions are aimed at stopping any trouble before it got started and also finding other possible charges against Jesus.

When Jesus said this, one of the officials near by struck him in the face. 'Is this the way you answer the High

Priest?' he demanded. If I said something wrong,' Jesus replied, 'testify as to what is wrong. But if I spoke the truth, why did you strike me?' Then Annas sent him, still bound, to Caiaphas the High Priest (John 18:22–24).

Striking a suspect before he was proved guilty was quite contrary to the Law of Moses but Jesus bore it with quiet dignity.

THE SECOND HEARING

As the questioning is not proving to be of value, Annas brought it to an end and sent Jesus, still bound, to his son-in-law, Caiaphas the High Priest.[52] Although I shall be referring to Caiaphas, it is to be remembered that Annas, his father-in-law, was probably close to him during the hearings and could well have offered advice and support.

The Charge Sheet in the trial of Jesus changes quite distinctly from his hearing in front of the Sanhedrin to

---

[52] What would Jesus, Peter and John have seen at the house of Caiaphas? As we know, the First and Second Hearings were held at private houses and Peter and John Zebedee were witnesses to the Second Hearing at the home of Caiaphas. We know a little of what a house of a well-to-do family would have looked like during New Testament times. It would, when viewed from above, have been clearly seen as a square or rectangular block. It would have had living quarters, storage, possibly winter shelter for animals, all around a courtyard. There would usually have been a well and maybe, if room allowed, a tree for shade. At ground level the floor would have been made up of mud or loose stones. Where there was another floor above, it would have had wooden boards on the floor. It was here that the family would live. Just before New Testament times, pitched, tiled roofs began to be built. These replaced the flat roofs and had a wall to protect family members from falling off.

the later hearing before Pilate. Firstly it has to do with spiritual power. Later the emphasis will be on earthly power.

PETER'S LAPSE

Meanwhile Peter, in the company of John Zebedee, must have been keeping watch outside and followed their rabbi once they saw him leaving and thought that they would not be seen. Their journey was a short one and led them to the residence of Caiaphas. Through being known to the household John is able to get in and arranges for Peter also to be allowed in.

Peter could not keep his identity a secret; for one thing he was probably recognised as a disciple. He denied it. However, his body language may have given the game away but if that had not, his provincial Galilean accent would have. No, he stood out as a follower of the rabbi Jesus. Three times he denied being Jesus's disciple. Then, as Jesus had predicted, a cockerel crowed.

This incident shows the honesty of the Gospel accounts. Each Gospel writer records Peter's cowardice as he stood in front of the fire or moved away from its light. Peter, had he wished, could have tried to excuse his denials in the Gospel of Mark, over which he had some influence, but the fact that he did not do so shows courage and openness, which is not normal.

THE THIRD HEARING

We are told that the Sanhedrin came together about daybreak. Although fairly confident of their informant, there could have been a slight doubt as to whether Jesus would be found, let alone arrested, so I imagine that the members of the Council were on standby in their homes awaiting a call.

In spite of a parade of witnesses, Caiaphas is frustrated that he cannot find two that are in total agreement and the chance of a conviction begins to look poor. All he needs are two in complete agreement. Then he brings in two other witnesses whom he feels are better. *'This fellow said, "I am able to destroy the temple of God and rebuild it in three days" '* (*Matthew 26:61*). Even here these two are not in agreement. The lack of testimony seems to fail on only one word. One witness says that this was what Jesus *'will'* do to the Temple (*Mark 14:58*) while another states that he was *'able'* (*Matthew 26:61*) to do it. We must remember that the trial of Jesus does not take place before a Sanhedrin who is all united against Jesus. We shall see that at least two members of the Sanhedrin were later, after his death, to very bravely show solidarity with his cause.

For a successful indictment not only must there be at least two witnesses in agreement but the entire Sanhedrin, a council of seventy-one members including the High Priest, had to be in agreement. In fact, this legal system, when properly administered, was nothing if not very fair to the accused, especially in capital charges when a man's life might be forfeited.

It is worth remembering that being a witness in a Jewish trial was no small matter. To begin with false witness was a breach of the Law of Moses, as a look at the Ten Commandments will show. *'You shall not give false testimony against your neighbour'* (*Exodus 20:16*). This offence was punishable if the witness proves to be a liar, giving false testimony against his brother, *'then do to him as he intended to do to his brother'* (*Deuteronomy 19:18–19*). I wonder whether any of the witnesses against Jesus had been told, by Caiaphas, that these regulations would not be too strictly enforced. They could well have been told that, in view of the importance of keeping Rome happy, and in these exceptional circumstances, the means justified the end.

The line of Caiaphas's mouth must have hardened as he realised that he could well fail and be seen as a complete incompetent. Even more galling was the fact that the prisoner does not seem to be cowed and beaten. He is not bothering to answer the charges against him. He remains silent and composed. ' *"Are you not going to answer?"* ' Caiaphas demanded (*Matthew 26:62*). As the High Priest had failed to make a case no response was necessary, except to inform the court that they had failed. However, Caiaphas's question is met with a quiet look and no verbal response. Certainly, at this point, Jesus was entitled to give evidence in his own defence. But for Caiaphas it is useless and the prospect of defeat and humiliation begins to look likely.

THE OATH OF TESTIMONY

There is, in almost all legal codes, the right of an accused person not to incriminate him or herself. The prosecution has to make a sound case against them on which their guilt will be judged. As the American Constitution puts it in the Fifth Amendment, no person *shall be compelled in any criminal case to be a witness against himself.* Readers will remember TV courtroom dramas with witnesses refusing to answer on the grounds that they *might incriminate themselves.* Also the Law of Moses, under which Jesus was tried, had this provision. As witnesses had failed to make such a case and indeed there was a tradition that witnesses ought to bring the case themselves, other options had to be considered. Such an option was open to Caiaphas, it was rather irregular and members of the Council might object but he felt that no other course of action was open to him.

He had risen from his seat some moments before – he now took a deep breath and looked Jesus fully in the face. Caiaphas played what he knew was a trump card. Such was the solemnity of the *Oath of the Testimony* that it could not be avoided. An attempt to do so would mean that any credibility that Jesus, as a pious Jew, had would be lost. Caiaphas, as the President of the Court of the Sanhedrin, knew it and he knew that it would be known to the accused.

' *"I charge you under oath by the living God: tell us if you are the Christ, the Son of God." "Yes, it is as you say," Jesus replied. "But I say to all of you: in the future you will see the Son of Man sitting at the right hand of the Mighty One and coming on the clouds of heaven" '* (*Matthew 26:63–64*). The Gospel writers vary a little from one another in the way this is reported and this is important as it shows that there must have been some discussion on Jesus's answer in the Sanhedrin. In no way would this jury have received this affirmation in silence, there would have been a united intake of breath. Then some discussion would have followed. Not only had Jesus answered the question with a 'yes' he had then quoted two Old Testament scriptures, which all knowledgeable Jews knew referred to the *Messiah*. ' *"Sit at my right hand until I make your enemies a footstool for your feet"* ' (*Psalm 110:1*). Then, as if to make the point even clearer, Jesus said he was: ' *"one like a son of man, coming with the clouds of heaven. He approached the Ancient of Days and was led into his presence"* ' (*Daniel 7:13*).

The words of Jesus, ' *"it is as you say"* ', are worth looking at for a moment. Another version of the Bible translates this in a rather strange way: ' *"You have said so"* ' (i.e. the words are yours) which seems as if Jesus is trying to evade the issue.[53] But this is a very Jewish way of speaking, which Jesus often used and it is found in other writing of rabbis of this time. It appears to mean that Jesus is saying something like, *I would not express it like that*. After all, the word *Messiah* had far too many political meanings. Caiaphas, to use other words, had asked Jesus if he was the *Messiah*, the one from the royal family of King David, who would deliver Israel. Jesus knew that by 'deliverance' they were thinking of freedom from Rome.

---

[53] The Revised Standard Version (*Matthew 26:64*).

The real deliverance Jesus wished to see and bring in was freedom from sin, in other words being under the control of God. But by nature humankind is controlled by its imperfect character. The plan of God is that by experiencing freedom from wrongdoing we are able to become more human, free from our own nature. We are then free for serving God. This kind of freedom is highly unlikely to have been in the mind of Caiaphas.

Luke's Gospel does give us further particulars that are worth looking at. ' *"If you are the Christ," they said, "tell us." Jesus answered, "If I tell you, you will not believe me, and if I asked you, you would not answer. But from now on, the Son of Man will be seated at the right hand of the mighty God." They all asked, "Are you then the Son of God?" He replied, "You are right in saying I am." '* That set the whole Sanhedrin talking excitedly! Their discussion may have lasted for quite a while.

'Then they said, "Why do we need any more testimony? We have heard it from his own lips" ' (*Luke 22:67–71*). The stress must have immediately lessened and there would have been a note of triumph in his voice as Caiaphas heard these words. Witnesses had not done it, Jesus had in fact, delivered his own death sentence. Caiaphas had hoped to convict Jesus for dabbling in witchcraft and using it as a threat to tear down the Temple. An indictment for blasphemy was much better. There was now only one action that Caiaphas, as High Priest, had to do. As required by rabbinic law he

'*tore his clothes*' (***Matthew 26:65***) and that part of the hearing came to an end.

The charge was blasphemy and the Law of Moses required that those proved guilty would be put to death by stoning (***Leviticus 24:14***) but this was not permitted, especially for the Temple authorities in Jerusalem. No, Rome kept control of capital punishment. Besides this, Jesus of Nazareth was too public and popular a figure for the Sanhedrin to deal with alone – if he died then the Romans would be seen as those who killed him. So before any execution could be authorised, Jesus would have to be taken before Pontius Pilate. For a moment Caiaphas's feeling of control lessened. He knew he had some influence but the last word as to whether he could get the prisoner executed lay with the Governor. This Jesus was a man full of surprises so what effect would he have on the Governor? Caiaphas would have to stress and explain that *Messiah* also stood for king. That ought to make Pilate take matters seriously. The charge of blasphemy would produce nothing more than blank looks from Pilate and his advisers but if this Jesus could be shown as a threat to Rome then he and the hazard he posed to the Temple establishment would be finished.

WAS THE TRIAL BEFORE THE SANHEDRIN LEGAL?

Many who, over the years, have written on this subject have raised questions over the legality of the trial of Jesus and have raised serious questions. Some of these cannot be answered in a definite way.

If we look at the failure of two witnesses to agree, and they had to be in total agreement, then we have to say that there had been a mistrial and that the case should at that moment have collapsed. According to the Old Testament, God could be called upon to act as a witness[54] in the absence of a human but that was a very solemn matter. It was one that would not be done lightly. When Jesus was arrested, his being taken into custody was the job of those who would be witnesses in his trial. The Gospel writers leave this detail out of their records although some might have been witnesses who were present in the arresting party. But then why was Judas Iscariot needed to make a formal identification of the accused? It is just possible, that at some stage, the High Priest had intended to call Judas as a witness. If the thought had crossed his mind he was soon to reject it.

In a Jewish execution the witnesses against the accused would, to show their confidence and good faith in their testimony, lay their hands on the head of the victim before taking part in his death by stoning.

The most flagrant injustice is the lack of impartiality shown by Caiaphas as President of the Sanhedrin. As

---

[54] In ancient times, going to the High Priest or Judge of Israel disclosed God's wishes. A man with a decision to make would ask a question to which a 'yes' or 'no' answer would settle the matter. The Judge (a religious official) would take two consecrated stones, Urim and Thummin, from his robes and use them to discover the wishes of God. This practice did not seem to be used very much in New Testament times, but it was available to Caiaphas as High Priest. Exactly how they were used is uncertain but they may have been pulled from a bag after being shaken.

we have noted, Jewish justice in matters of capital offences was weighted in favour of those whose lives were in danger from injustice. Caiaphas ought not to have cross-examined Jesus after the failure of the witnesses. Not only was the President of the Great Sanhedrin hostile it also seems that most, if not all, the members were guilty of abuse. *'Then they spat in his face and struck him with their fists. Others slapped him and said, "Prophesy to us, Christ. Who hit you?" '* (*Matthew 26:67–68*).

All this is fairly certain but there are several matters that we cannot be sure of as far as their legality is concerned:

1. Only trials over money could be held during the hours of darkness,

2. Capital offences could not be held on a feast day or the day before,

3. With capital offences a death sentence could not be pronounced by the court on the same day as the trial began.

The greatest source of knowledge about Jewish legal procedures comes from the Mishnah. This is a collection of legal practices, which was to become a code, but it was published some 200 years after Christ so we cannot be sure of how many of these regulations were in force during the life of Jesus.

I have a feeling that it was because of the bad press that the trial of Jesus received, that many legal practices were later 'tidied up' and made to be more just, especially to the Gentile world. It would have taken time but the Jewish Community, always aware of anti-Semitism, would have wished their excellent laws (when properly administered) to be beyond reproach.

Caiaphas and his supporters now had exactly what they wanted. The next difficulty was Pilate. He hoped that the Roman had got himself ready, as requested for this dangerous agitator. His interview before the Governor had not been easy. Firstly, Pilate had pointed out that there were set hours, even for the business of the Empire and that this *had to be* very important. Then, when they had mentioned the name Jesus of Nazareth, Pilate and his adviser had not looked totally convinced.

THE FOURTH HEARING – BEFORE PILATE

The distance between the High Priest's residence, and the Governor's residence, called the *Praetorium*, was short, probably about one kilometre or half a mile. There is some discussion as to exactly where it was. The Palace of Herod has been mentioned but the favourite is the strongly fortified Tower or Fortress of Antonia. This was built on a high point, which allowed an oversight of Jerusalem and being next to the Temple had the advantage of allowing the Roman garrison to be next to a potential trouble spot.

We are told that the *'whole assembly'* (*Luke 23:1*) went with the High Priest. They obviously believed in strength in numbers. Clearly, before they left to see the

Governor, there would have been a very rapid conference on how the High Priests were to handle this stage of the trial. They had to stress the claim of Jesus to be the *Messiah*, a Jewish king and ruler; they had to get Pilate to take this seriously.

They would normally have entered his quarters but because of their religion and their wishes to celebrate the Passover meal that coming evening, when the new day began, they did not enter. The main problem for them was that the Romans, like the rest of the Gentiles, did not observe the regulation regarding unleavened bread; so in case they might unknowingly come into contact with breadcrumbs or dust with a trace of yeast, they stayed outside.

John's Gospel tells us that Pilate asked to know the charges on which Jesus was appearing before him. ' *"What charges are you bringing against this man?"* ' The answer he received does seem to be rather abrupt. ' *"If he were not a criminal," they replied, "we would not have handed him over to you"* ' (*John 18:29–30*). Pilate then asked them if this is something that they could deal with themselves. They replied that a real crime had been committed and that they did not have the power to sentence execution (*18:31*). We are told *'they began to accuse him'* (Jesus) *'saying, "We have found this man subverting our nation. He opposes payment of taxes to Caesar and claims to be Christ, a king"* ' (*Luke 23:2*). This does look very much like pressure being applied and Pontius Pilate is not the kind of man to try to compel. Whatever he has been told he seems intent on maintaining the appearance of Roman justice.

Pilate, on hearing this, entered into his residence to interrogate the prisoner. Under Roman law there had to be a charge or charges (*accusatio*,[55] which we see that Luke has given us, set out above). Then the judge, in this case Pilate, would interrogate (*interrogatio*) the prisoner. Finally the prisoner would be given leave to make a defence (*excusatio*). This would have been the normal procedure in any Roman trial. If we follow Luke and John we see this pattern in the way the hearing develops.

Although, on the surface any opposition to Roman taxation would seem to be a crime against Rome, it would not have carried any weight. Pilate would have known what was happening locally and his spies and informants would have taken great interest in a preacher able to command large, enthusiastic audiences. It must have occurred to Jesus that there was a strong possibility that he might have to persuade Pilate that his 'kingdom' was not a direct threat to Rome. Pilate, not known for his liking of the Jewish establishment, is astute enough to know that the threat of Jesus is not so much to the Roman Senate and people, as to the Sanhedrin and that they are bringing these charges *'out of envy' (Matthew 27:18)*.

---

[55] The three words in brackets would have been the Latin phases used during the first century in Roman law.

Pilate's interrogation of Jesus took place in his official suite, the *Praetorium*, and would not have been within earshot of his accusers. *'So Pilate asked Jesus, "Are you the king of the Jews?" "Yes, it is as you say," Jesus replied'* (*Luke 23:3*). Pilate is both in awe of Jesus but exasperated by him but has to get to the truth or as much of it as possible. Pilate suspects that he had missed something, something that Caiaphas is not telling him. He asks Jesus: *' "What is it you have done?" '* (*John 18:35*). Jesus tells him that: *' "My kingdom is not of this world" '* and it is because he has no army or supporters to fight for him, he adds that: *' "my kingdom is from another place" '* (*18:36*). Pilate does not find this interrogation going as expected; he is beginning to find this is a more complex matter than he anticipated. *' "You are a king, then!" '* said Pilate. Jesus informs him that this is the reason for his birth and speaks of *' "truth" '*. As he is feeling rather confused Pilate asks his famous question: *' "What is truth?" '* (*18:33–38*).

Following Luke's Gospel we learn that once more Pilate goes outside to face the *'chief priests and the crowd, "I find no basis for a charge against this man." '* Pilate's treatment of their charges brings yet more complaints: *'they insisted, "He stirs up the people all over Judea by his teaching. He started in Galilee and has come all the way here" '* (*Luke 23:1–5*). Pilate is impressed with the accused who is both composed and silent. This Jesus was amazingly dignified and he commanded Pilate's admiration.

Frank Morison's second argument is the one we must now consider. It is that Pontius Pilate's wife influenced him!

Before we come to that we should consider a few facts about this lady. As the history books tell us, the marriage was an unusual one, in as much as Pilate had won the hand of someone who was far above his social status. Perhaps it was because of this that he had obtained special permission to take her with him. It would appear to be a close marriage and in close marriages things are naturally shared. It would not be an unreasonable assumption to believe that after the departure of the priestly deputation, on that Thursday evening, the Lady Claudia asked something like: *'What did they want?'* On learning the facts she may have expressed reservations then and there, but their conversation, that evening, was to lead to events changing the next day.

This second idea of Morison's theory is that it was Claudia's disturbed night that coloured Christian history to some small extent. Pilate, possibly to have a quiet life, was prepared to use his influence to allow a rapid sentence of the accused followed by as quick a crucifixion as possible. It was the message from Claudia that he received early the next day that changed that. *' "Don't have anything to do with that innocent man, for I have suffered a great deal today in a dream because of him"'* (*Matthew 27:19*). In Frank Morison's view, it was because of this message that Pilate had a change of heart and tried to free Jesus from the death sentence. Although, Morison is trying to extract clues from a two-thousand-year-old mystery it is difficult to fault his thinking.

Sometime during his interrogation of Jesus, Pilate received this message from home and we may surmise that this happened very early on. It is likely to have been even before the priestly deputation bringing Jesus had arrived. Feelings of superstition welled up inside him, as there was something about this accused man that was unreal. Also he did not look forward to dealing with his wife's terrors.

THE FIFTH HEARING – BEFORE HEROD ANTIPAS

Luke's Gospel tells us that Pilate finds that he has what seems to be a way out of this dilemma. The chief priests have mentioned Galilee and Pilate discovers that Jesus came from there (*Luke 23:5*). This means that this matter is not under his authority but comes under that of Herod Antipas[56] who was no friend of Pilate's. Nevertheless, Herod is in town and has the authority of settling this matter and can authorise an execution, which means that Pilate's wife will not blame him for what happens in this case. Pilate, therefore, sent Jesus to Herod Antipas.

The opportunity of seeing Jesus is one that Antipas was very happy about. He had long wished to satisfy his

---

[56] See separate note on **Herod Antipas** in *Supporting Cast.*

curiosity over this rabbi from Nazareth. He had at one time thought that Jesus was John the Baptist who had somehow risen from the dead and come back to afflict him, *'he said,'* on a much earlier occasion, *'to his attendants, "This is John the Baptist; he has risen from the dead! That is why miraculous powers are at work in him" '* (*Matthew 14:2*).

However, that was the thought of that moment and Antipas does not come across as one of history's more stable characters. He had hoped that Jesus would entertain him with one or two miracles but in this he was disappointed. Moreover, Jesus refuses to speak. During the course of his time with Jesus, Antipas finds out that Jesus had been born in Bethlehem. This means that he has no jurisdiction in this case so, after allowing his men to abuse the prisoner, he sends him back to Pilate who does have the authority.

BACK TO PILATE – THE FINAL HEARING

The Governor's heart must have sunk at the news that Herod had no authority. Pilate's attempt to pass the buck had failed. There is just one more thing that Pilate could do that could save this man from the horrors of crucifixion. In order to keep populations happy, the Romans would allow them a concession; a prisoner could be released by popular demand during Feasts. *Mark's Gospel* tells us: *'The crowd came up and asked Pilate to do for them what he usually did'* (*Mark 15:8*). In custody at that time was a rebel, a man called Barabbas, who had committed murder in a rising against Rome. He was not the kind of person that Pilate really wanted to set free. Barabbas had only recently been arrested. He really thought that the crowd would not want him released either. Men like that only caused problems for Rome; surely the Jews did not want that. Addressing the crowd that had gathered he gave them the stark choice of choosing Barabbas or Jesus.

Unfortunately for Pilate, he had not understood either the crowd or Jewish thinking. Something over 100 people in this gathering were members of the Sanhedrin and their staff and supporters. We can be sure that the crowd had grown much larger but the people in the front had made up their mind what they wanted. Mark also tells us that the *'chief priests stirred up the crowd to'* choose *'Barabbas' (15:11)*. Those who had arrived later, even had they been neutral, would have been either confused or very suspicious of Pilate's backing Jesus and proposing that he be released instead of Barabbas. To have the hated Roman authority trying to make them go a certain way was strange and their suspicions would have been aroused.

Pilate is horrified and seems genuinely surprised by their decision. Didn't they know what would happen to Jesus? He tried again. ' *"Which of the two do you want me to release to you?" he asked. "Barabbas," they answered. "What shall I do, then, with Jesus who is called Christ?" Pilate asked. They all answered, "Crucify him!"* ' *(Matthew 27:21 & 22)*.

Pilate, for all his faults, is Roman, and law and justice are personally important. It was part of the system of values that Rome prided itself upon. It was, overall, a good one, for today the legal codes of many European countries are based on Roman legal values. Disregarding the clamour Pilate states that he had found nothing that warrants a charge against Jesus (*Luke 23:4*). The result is more shouts of ' *"Crucify!"* ' and Pilate realises that a riot could develop. Certainly he has enough troops on hand to deal with this but not at this time. The spilling of more Jewish blood would not help his reputation in Syria, with his immediate commander, nor in Rome.

We cannot be certain of all the reasons why Pilate had Jesus flogged. ' *"Therefore, I will punish him and then release him"* ' (*Luke 23:16* see also *v.22*). He might have hoped that this action would placate the chief priests and that they would not insist on the death penalty. If this was the case his hope was misplaced. There was also the chance that the prisoner would die under the Roman lash and spared the awfulness of the cross. Pilate's soldiers then took charge of Jesus.

The soldiers twisted together a crown of thorns and put it on his head. They clothed him in a purple robe and went up to him again and again, saying, 'Hail, king of the Jews!' And they struck him in the face (John 19:2–3).

To his credit Pilate tries again and repeats the fact that he cannot justly pronounce the death sentence on Jesus. Jesus is then paraded in front of them with the crown of thorns and wearing a borrowed purple robe – one that its last owner had discarded or 'lost'. The sight causes the heartless crowd into another chant of ' *"Crucify!"* ' Pilate again states that there is no charge worthy of death. The Jews insist that, according to Jewish law, he is worthy of death. Then, without realising its effect, they make a statement that turns Pilate's feeling of being anxious into cold fear: ' *"he claimed to be the Son of God"* ' (*John 19:7*). To a Roman, whether he was devout or not, 'a son of the gods' is a possibility. Pontius Pilate would have had instruction in the religion. Traditions that the gods came down to earth were quite commonplace. Was he dealing with a supernatural being?

Pilate then went back inside the *Praetorium* to question Jesus more fully. ' *"Where do you come from?"* ' (*John 19:8*). His state of mind is not helped by the fact that Jesus *'gave him no answer'* (*John 19:9–10*). Pilate is both offended and made to feel uneasy by this silence and tries to assert his authority. ' *"Do you refuse to speak to me?" Pilate says. "Don't you realise I have power either to free you or to crucify you?" Jesus answers, "You would have no power over me if it were not given to you from above."* ' The authority passes back to Jesus and Pilate's terror is confirmed. Then Jesus brings up the subject of guilt. ' *"Therefore the one who handed me over to you is guilty of a greater sin"* ' (*19:10* & 11).

Pilate summons up his best effort to set Jesus free. John tells us that Pilate's final attempts are answered by the *Jews* telling him that if Jesus was released he would be *'no friend of Caesar. "Anyone who claims to be a king opposes Caesar" ' (John 19:12)*. We are not told more than that it was the 'Jews' who said this but it would be likely to have been at the instance of Annas and Caiaphas. We can also guess that it was said in front of some of Pilate's staff officers and men. So, two utterly unscrupulous men have forced the Governor's hand. He has no room to manoeuvre.

Pilate has to contend with two fears: the Emperor and that this man who he has tried to save is a divine being. Then there is the Lady Claudia, his wife. What will she say about this day's work? That message he had received from her about a *'dream'* concerning the accused, which had greatly disturbed her, also troubled him. With a dull feeling of dread he realises there is nothing else he could do.

Against his will he orders the release of Barabbas. He then ceremonially washes his hands in front of them all declaring that this is not his will and he is not guilty of the blood of Jesus. The responsibility was theirs he tells them. *'All the people answer, "Let his blood be on us and on our children!" '* (27:24–25).

Pilate's final act was to hand Jesus over to be crucified.

Chapter 5

THE TAKING UP OF THE CROSS

Was it some strange coincidence or deliberate fore-knowledge that made Jesus use the word picture of the Cross as a symbol of discipleship? The cross as a symbol was a strange one and the meaning for those who would follow was not a soft option. His listeners would have realised that the unfortunate man who carried his cross would bear it until he died tied or nailed to it. In spite of this Jesus chose to use this despised symbol when he said to various people that a man (or a woman) should *'take up his* [or her] *cross'* (*Mark 8:34*).[57]

In the time of Jesus it meant that those under sentence of death would carry their crosses until they reached the scene of their execution. It was part of the death sentence and Jesus would have known this and yet chose this as an image of service and discipleship.

☩   ☩   ☩

Frustrated by his failure to control the course of events Pilate decided on a snub to the Jewish establishment.

---

[57] For further details on how the Cross was viewed in New Testament times, refer to **Crucifixion and the Cross** in the *Short Dictionary*.

Condemned men usually carried around their necks the charge for which they were being executed. This would have been on a piece of board covered with gypsum and on this white background the charge would have been written in black lettering. Pilate chose wording that would anger the chief priests. He had had the charge, which would be attached to the cross, written with these words: *'The King of the Jews'*.[58] And so that no one would be in any doubt Pilate had used three languages, known and used by everyone in Jerusalem for the Passover. He used *Aramaic, Latin and Greek*.[59] Not surprisingly the Jewish clergy, there to witness the death of their enemy, objected, saying, ' *"this man claimed to be king of the Jews"* '. They sent a messenger to Pilate but he answered, ' *"What I have written, I have written"* ' (*19:20–22*). As well as pointing to the evil jealousy of the chief priests the notice did serve another purpose. It was a reminder of the power of Rome and the folly of seeking to challenge it.

However, this is to move ahead of the story because Jesus had to get to the scene of his execution carrying the cross. At least, that was the way it began. John tells us that Jesus set out carrying his own cross (*19:17*). It is not surprising that after the flogging he could not cope with its weight.

---

[58] There are variations in the accounts of each Gospel on the exact wording of the charge, which was placed over Jesus's head. All the Gospel writers agree that it included the words 'King of the Jews'.

[59] Please refer to notes on Hebrew, Greek and Latin in the *Short Dictionary*, see **Languages**.

There is a tradition that Jesus fell three times under the burden of it but the New Testament does not help us on this. All that the other Gospel writers tell us is that the Romans, who had the power to commandeer the services of able-bodied men, asked Simon from Cyrene to carry Jesus's cross.[60] Mark's Gospel adds some interesting details by telling us that he was '*the father of Alexander and Rufus, and was passing by on his way in from the country, and they forced him to carry the cross*' (*Mark 15:21*). It is likely from these details that this man or members of his family became believers. There is a Rufus mentioned in the **Letter to the Romans Chapter 16** among the greetings at the end of this letter. Simon was, judging from his name, a Jew living in North Africa who had come to Jerusalem for Passover. Artists have portrayed him as a Negro. This is a nice idea but there is no evidence for it.

WHERE DID JESUS DIE?

They came to a place called Golgotha, which means the 'Place of the Skull' (Matthew 27:33).

It has been suggested that there were skulls lying around. This ancient explanation is not so popular today with modern scholars. There is also an ancient tradition that the skull of Adam was buried at Golgotha. We also have the name 'Calvary' which is adapted from the Latin word for skull (*Calvaria*) found

---

[60] The Roman could order a man to carry things for a mile. Jesus mentions this in **Matthew 5:41**.

in a fourth-century translation of the Latin Bible known as the Vulgate. It is also possible to call it *cranium*. This translates a New Testament Greek word that sounds almost exactly the same when spoken in Greek or English.

We cannot be sure of the exact location of the execution, but we do know the following. The execution took place outside the walls of Jerusalem – *'the place was near the city'* (*John 19:20*). Another New Testament writer tells us that it was *'outside the city gate'* (*Letter to the Hebrews 13:12*). Matthew's Gospel indicates a public place and some further suggest that it was near one of the main roads into the city (*Matthew 27:39*). Mark's Gospel indicates that many were able to see the crucifixion so we assume that it was on a hill, or at least on raised ground (*Mark 15:29*).

JESUS'S CRUCIFIXION

There they offered Jesus wine to drink, mixed with gall; but after tasting it, he refused to drink it (Matthew 27:34).

There has been some discussion by New Testament commentators as to the reasons this drink was given to Jesus. Some have suggested that the bitter taste was myrrh and this would have had a sedative effect by dulling the pain. Some believe that some kindly women in Jerusalem had prepared the concoction for the benefit of Jesus. If this were the case then they would have had to bribe the guards handsomely to administer the drink to the man on the Cross.

Just recently I have come across another view by Professor Geza Vermes who, in his book *The Passion*, has suggested that the purpose was completely different. In his view it could have enabled Jesus to stay alive or alert rather longer for the entertainment of the crowd. In either event Jesus was to refuse the drink.

With what appears to be total callousness the Roman guard divided Jesus's clothing. This would have been all Jesus's garments – everything! Oh yes, the Romans would have enjoyed totally humiliating the victims of a crucifixion. One item of Jesus's clothing was quite a treasure, a tunic undergarment,[61] woven without seams. The soldiers threw dice to see which one of them should keep that (*Mark 15:24*). Normally the only people who wore garments of this quality were the priests but these would have been vestments for ceremonial use, not everyday clothing.

Only one man, the senior non-commissioned officer, was moved by the plight of the condemned victim. This centurion witnessed the concern for the other victims being slowly put to death by Jesus's side. One had asked Jesus to *'remember him when'* Jesus had *'come into'* his *'kingdom. Jesus answered him, "I tell you the truth, today you will be with me in paradise" '* (*Luke 23:42–43*). Then he had noticed the prisoner speaking

---

[61] The tunic is called a *haluk*.

with a man regarding an older woman, who the centurion realised, was the condemned man's mother. Jesus was giving his mother into the care of one of his disciples (*John 19:25*). This does seem strange until we remember that John's Gospel had told us that *'his own brothers did not believe in him'* (*John 7:5*), but where were his brothers? In the course of time they would come to believe (*Acts 1:14*) but for their own reasons they chose to be absent.

How much of the conversation this Roman soldier understood would depend on his understanding of Aramaic, which was almost certainly the language used in these conversations! However, he realised that the concern and compassion for others was something that he had never experienced before. This man Jesus was amazing! It is likely that the centurion would have had given permission for Mary and other family members to be at the foot of the cross. No doubt many in charge of crucifixions would have found grieving relatives a nuisance and a possible hazard, likely to get in the way.

What the centurion would not have known, unless an onlooker had explained it to him, was that there was a family connection. John, the Beloved Disciple,[62] and Jesus were cousins. Mary, the Mother of Jesus and Salome, wife of Zebedee and mother of John and his elder brother (who we call James),[63] were almost certainly sisters.

---

[62] Please refer to the article on **John** called *the Beloved Disciple* in *Supporting Cast*.

[63] The given name of James Zebedee was 'Jacob'. James is an anglicised form of Jacob.

After being given the responsibility for his aunt, we are told that: *'From that time on, this disciple took her into his home' (John 19:27)*. This took effect almost immediately and we can easily imagine John taking the distraught mother of Jesus to his home, almost certainly with his mother, Salome, and possibly with Mary, wife of Clopas.

John would have been away from Golgotha for some considerable time and would not have witnessed much of the crucifixion. In fact, he tells us that this is the case by using the word *'later'*, in *John 19:28*, when he returns to be with his rabbi for the end.

We cannot be certain who, among Jesus's friends and family, were present. John's Gospel tells us that very few allowed themselves to get close enough to be identified as his friends or family. Those who were close enough to hear his weakening voice were *'his mother, his mother's sister'* (Salome) *'Mary the wife of Clopas, and Mary Magdalene' (John 19:25)*. Both Mark and Matthew mention that *'many women were there, watching from a distance. They had followed Jesus from Galilee to care for his needs' (Matthew 27:55)*. Luke mentions *'those who knew him' (Luke 23:49)* referring to male acquaintances all fearfully standing away from the cross.

At midday, even the callous soldiers began to wonder. There was an eclipse, a total one, but something was wrong![64] The soldiers knew about this phenomenon but it usually only lasted a few minutes before daylight returned. But no, daylight didn't return, it stayed dark and they had to bring in torches. They all began to experience fear.

The afternoon wore on and the darkness continued, and the orders of the centurion were that this execution had to be followed by a swift burial. These three men had to be dead and buried before the sun went down. The next day was a Jewish religious feast and bodies could not be left around. It was not decent for these Jewish priests. It was necessary to bring a quick death. Once they were off the crosses they would be dropped into a common grave for criminals and the day's work would be over.

About 3 p.m. there was some activity that excited the onlookers. Jesus called out in Aramaic asking, ' "*My God, my God why have you forsaken me?*" ' (*Matthew 27:45*).[65] Many who heard this thought that he was calling to the Old Testament, miracle-working prophet Elijah for deliverance but Jesus was quoting *Psalm 22:1* a Scripture that describes the horrors of death by crucifixion. Although Jesus fulfilled the Scripture about

---

[64] The strange darkness was known about and there is independent evidence for it. Julius Africanus writes quoting from Thallus the Samaritan: '*Thallus, in the third book of his history, calls this darkness an eclipse of the sun, but in my opinion he is wrong.*' This means that the darkness was known about around twenty years after the crucifixion.

[65] The actual words: '*Eli, Eli, lema sabachthani*' (*Mark 15:14*).

himself there can be little doubt that he did very deeply feel on his own. He felt totally forsaken! A little later Jesus gasped, ' *"I am thirsty"* ' (*John 19:28*).

At last, some of the guards began to feel some compassion and offered him some wine vinegar, a drink that the soldiers would have taken to quench their thirsts. Luke then records that Jesus said a prayer committing himself into God's keeping: ' *"Father into your hands I commit my spirit"* ' (*Luke 23:46*). John also records that Jesus finally said: ' *"It is accomplished!"* ' (*John 19:30*).[66]

Also we remember that later that afternoon when the soldiers came to kill Jesus, this was about 3 p.m., they smashed the legs of the criminals on either side of Jesus before trying to carry out this same act on Jesus. The Latin name for this act was *crurifragium*.

As to why Jesus was dealt with last of all we cannot be certain but it could be explained by the fact that Jesus's cross, the central one, was above the other two and the soldiers would have had to climb a few steps further up the slope. John's Gospel gives us the facts about *crurifragium* but makes it clear that it did not happen to

---

[66] Although the New International Version translates this as '*It is finished*', the New Testament Greek word carries the meaning of 'completion, something concluded'. Jewish scholar Professor Vermes suggests that the word 'fulfilled' is a better translation than '*finished*'. R T France suggests that it could be translated as '*I have done it*'. In the Greek of the New Testament, the word is *tetélestai.*

Jesus. When they had ceased to be amused by the suffering of the victims or if there were a reason to shorten the execution they would apply a heavy hammer to the victim's legs. The result was both a shock to the victim but with his legs broken he was unable to lift his body to breathe and death would follow within a very few minutes. Anywhere else in the Roman Empire the soldiers work would have been simpler – victims would have been left on their crosses for the birds to feast upon.

Certainly, the man on the central cross looked lifeless but the Roman soldiers could not assume that Jesus was dead; they had to be sure. Failure to follow orders would lead to dire consequences. They knew that Pilate did not suffer fools gladly especially among his own men. There was another test they could apply to ensure that the man was really dead. Taking his spear one soldier thrust it into the side of Jesus. This would have been enough to kill him by itself but if he had lapsed into unconsciousness then there would have been some reaction. There was nothing and the soldiers knew that their work had been done and that the spear thrust had been unnecessary. John the Apostle, whose Gospel records this act, tells of *'a sudden flow of blood and water'* (*19:34*).

John also has another point to make and he wished his readers at the end of the first century and those at the beginning of the twenty-first to understand its vital importance. Jesus had already been called *'the Lamb of*

God who takes away the sin of the world' by John the Baptist (*John 1:29*). Yet, lambs were being sacrificed every day so John Zebedee explains which *'Lamb of God'* Jesus represented. Jesus is the new Passover lamb and as the yearly Passover lambs were kept whole it would have been totally wrong for an orthodox Jew to break any of the bones of the yearly Passover sacrifice. John drives home his point, which his first-century Jewish readers would have quickly grasped. His thinking is, for us, not so accessible. *'These things happened so that the scripture would be fulfilled: "Not one of his bones will be broken," and, as another scripture says, "They will look on the one they have pierced"'* (*John 19:36–37*).[67]

Some medical practitioners have been rather mystified as to why Jesus died so early when for many healthy victims death could take two or three days. Some have even tried to work out the pathology – the actual cause of death. Theories such as a ruptured heart have been put forward but the most convincing of these is that the stomach of Jesus became dangerously enlarged with fluids and that the upward spear thrust of the Roman soldier penetrated the stomach and then the heart. The soldier had seen symptoms such as these before and knew that, as far as Jesus was concerned, no further punishment need be inflicted. The actual reason for the death of Jesus is not explained by medical science. Luke's Gospel gives us the answer. *'Jesus called out*

---

[67] John is not alone in seeing Jesus in this way. Compare the words of the Apostle Paul in *1 Corinthians 5:7–8*.

with a loud voice, "Father, into your hands I commit my spirit." When he had said this, he breathed his last' (**Luke 23:46**).[68] Jesus, having completed his sacrifice, ended his own life by his own act of will.

While this was taking place, other strange events are recorded in Matthew's Gospel: *'At that moment, the curtain of the Temple was torn in two from top to bottom. The earth shook and the rocks split. The tombs broke open and the bodies of many holy people who had died were raised to life'* (**Matthew 27:51–53**).

JOSEPH OF ARIMATHEA AND NICODEMUS

With the death of Jesus, two covert supporters decide to take action. They sought the permission of Pontius Pilate to give the deceased a decent burial. Not for him the common grave where the other two criminals' bodies were to be thrown. No, he deserved something far better. This was a good opportunity to get away and speak to Pilate without any of the chief priests noticing. They were all in the Temple dealing with the Passover lambs. So heavy was the workload that every priest, including Caiaphas, would be busy with the ritual sacrificing of the animals or felt duty-bound to be present. Besides this, they had had their way – Jesus was dead!

Joseph of Arimathea, a prominent member of the council, who was himself waiting for the kingdom of

---

[68] Also see **John 10:18** where Jesus said he had power over death and life.

God, went boldly to Pilate and asked for Jesus's body. Pilate was surprised to hear that he was already dead. Summoning the centurion, he asked him if Jesus had already died. When he learnt from the centurion that it was so, he gave the body to Joseph. So Joseph bought some linen cloth, took down the body, wrapped it in the linen, and placed it in a tomb cut out of rock. Then he rolled a stone against the entrance of the tomb (Mark 15:43–46).

It is John's Gospel that tells us Joseph *'was accompanied by Nicodemus'*[69] who *'brought a mixture of myrrh and aloes, about seventy-five pounds'* (*John 19:39*). This was a very expensive offering as myrrh was imported and highly valued.

Without wishing to read too much into the Passion narrative it seems likely that while Joseph made his way to see Pilate and to get custody of the body of Jesus, Nicodemus, his fellow member of the Sanhedrin, stayed to make sure that the soldiers did not dispose of Jesus body in the way that they feared.

The sculpture called the *Pietà* by Michelangelo[70] showing Nicodemus supporting the body of Jesus sees the Passion in the same way. It also captures the indignity of crucifixion with Jesus's lower abdomen being covered with a hastily placed cloth. Naturally, artists down the ages have not been able to portray

---

[69] To learn more about Nicodemus see *John 3:1–12*.
[70] This piece of art is displayed at the Museo dell'Opera di Santa Maria del Fiore (OPA), Florence, Italy.

the total nudity of the victims of this vile death sentence.

Obviously getting the body of Jesus off the cross presented no problem for Joseph and Nicodemus. The soldiers would have been anxious to finish their duty. They could have probably had to pay to get these men to move the bodies to the tomb in the nearby *'garden'* (*John 19:41*) had that been necessary and it is likely that it was. Matthew's Gospel tells us that the tomb belonged to Joseph (*Matthew 27:60*) and had been excavated for the use of him and his family. Although the rock of this region is relatively soft it would still have needed great effort to excavate but the cavity would not have needed to be large.

THE LAST RITES

The Jewish custom, among families or individuals, was that at the end, when life had passed, the body would naturally be buried but this usually occurred on the same day as death. This was for reasons of cleanliness and for fear of defilement. In fact, so strong was this notion of defilement, that tombs were whitewashed so that no one would blunder into them at night and so be defiled. Contact with dead bodies was held to be a source of defilement and priests were only allowed to have contact with their deceased next of kin but no other.

The duty of preparing a body for burial would normally fall upon the next of kin. This would by custom be the task of women. Failing Jesus's mother, who was obviously too distressed to do it, this task should have been the responsibility of his sisters or brothers. The oldest remaining brother would have made sure his eyes were closed. Then normally the women would complete the washing, anointing with spiced ointment and finally wrapping the body. In the case of Jesus's burial, his brothers and sisters had distanced themselves from any connection that could cause them to be interviewed by the Sanhedrin.

Spices and ointments were used for purification and in no way in order to prevent, or slow, the body's decomposition. Naturally, in an age before refrigeration, such rapid burials made sense, especially in warm climates.

This seems very foreign to non-Jewish westerners who expect to be able to see the body as part of the process of bereavement and, in many cases, to come to an acceptance of the death of the loved one. However, even today in Orthodox Jewish circles, the deceased are buried as soon as possible and this is, in the view of the religious authorities, ideally within twenty-four hours.

Normally the body would have been washed, anointed and then put into a shroud. Unlike in the west, no coffin would be used. The dead would have been conveyed to the grave on a bier. Once inside the burial chamber the corpse would be placed on a shelf or a suitable area on the floor when no shelf had been cut out. The body would stay for years until all that remained was the skeleton then the bones would have been placed into a container of wood, stone or plaster called an ossuary. We can assume that Joseph had little or no thought about this stage. We can safely suppose that he was of mature years so it would have been most unlikely to have become his problem, nor that of his family, for many generations. His one concern is about the remains of Jesus, to save his body from the dishonour of a common grave, burial among criminals.

Both Joseph and Nicodemus would have been very aware of time and would have realised that with the changing of the light as the afternoon wore on their time for giving the body of Jesus its last rights would be limited. Then with sunset came the Sabbath and this year it coincided with the Passover. For Jews, no work was allowed on the Sabbath. They were greatly aware of the pressure of time from the moment of Jesus's death. Joseph and Nicodemus had only two or three hours to finish their work of getting permission to bury him, move his body to the nearby tomb, complete the last rites and leave the tomb sealed.

Did these two men have any help? It is likely that they did and two women, mentioned in *Luke's Gospel* (*8:3*) have been mentioned as possible helpers with this task. These were Joanna and Susanna. We are told nothing about Susanna except that she was a follower of Jesus. Joanna was the wife of Chuza, steward (or an official) of King Herod Antipas.

As we shall see, there were two other women witnesses to this event. It is strange that they, realising the difficulty of completing the arrangements before sunset, did not offer Joseph and Nicodemus any practical help. The explanation is likely to have been the fact that the status of women in first-century Judea was far lower than that of men and it is probable that the social position of Joseph and Nicodemus, wealthy and influential, made these two women reluctant to offer help even if they had been acquainted with them.

It is possible that John, the Beloved Disciple, may have helped to carry the heavy weight of spices to the tomb. He is the only Gospel writer to mention Nicodemus's contribution. Also it is John who gives us details about the laying out of the body. *'Taking Jesus's body, the two of them wrapped it, with the spices, in strips of linen. This was in accordance with Jewish burial customs' (John 19:40)*. The strips of linen would be intended to keep the arms and the legs together while the head covering was wound tightly around the head in order to stop the mouth falling open. As John was near kin to Jesus he would have been anxious to give a full report of what happened in the tomb to other family members, most particularly to Jesus's mother.

We get a picture of what the body of Jesus could have looked like from the description of the raising of Lazarus in *John 11:38–44*. Note these similarities: *'It was a cave with a stone laid across the entrance.'* Jesus had commanded in a loud voice, ' *"Lazarus, come out!" The dead man came out, his hands and feet wrapped with strips of linen, and a cloth around his face. Jesus said to them, "Take off the grave clothes and let him go."* '

There was also another problem for Joseph and Nicodemus or any Jew involved with the burial of a corpse. As the Law of Moses taught having contact with a dead body made them ritually unclean.[71] This meant that they would not have been able to partake in the Passover meal. In fact, their 'defilement' would have lasted for a month. Only contact with family corpses was allowed. We cannot be sure of what happened but it is possible that others did this work under their supervision without their needing to touch the body of Jesus.

There were two onlookers to what went on at the tomb of Jesus. These were Mary Magdalene and another Mary who was the mother of *Joses* (*Mark 15:47*), it is possible that she was the wife of Clopas (Cleopas), mentioned in *John 19:25*. We are told that they '*were sitting opposite the tomb*' (*Matthew 27:61*) and saw where, while *Luke 23:55* tells us that they saw '*how*' the body of Jesus had been dealt with.

This raises another question. The two women, Mary Magdalene and the other Mary, must have had a very good idea of what was happening at the tomb. In spite of this they put themselves to the inconvenience and

---

[71] Normally contact with the dead would cause them to be 'unclean' for seven days. See the fourth book of the Old Testament, *Numbers 19:6–11*.

danger of going to the tomb approximately thirty-six hours later at daybreak with their own spices. Certainly, John had been satisfied that the interment *'was in accordance with Jewish burial customs'* (*John 19:40*). However, these women who were known to John may not have seen him present at the tomb nor heard his statement regarding the final rites given to the body of Jesus. These details may have been only for his mother, Salome, and his aunt Mary, the mother of Jesus.

It is also possible that given the available time, Joseph and Nicodemus were only able to complete the necessary part of the full 'laying out' and would have had it in mind to give extra attention once the Sabbath was over. Then again there is the emotional element; these women wanted the very best for the body of Jesus.

A casual reading of this account means that the twenty-first-century reader is going to miss vital facts that the first-century believer would have understood immediately. In our society laying out a corpse is a very private matter and is dealt with in private, as it would normally have been in the days of Joseph and Nicodemus. So, what fact are we missing?

The answer is that it is a mistake to imagine that Joseph and Nicodemus, probably with help from others, wrapped the body of Jesus inside the tomb. This would likely have been impossible. It had to be done outside for observers to see. There was not normally enough room in those burial chambers. Once they had completed their temporary dressing of the body they would have, probably with some difficulty, manoeuvred the body into the tomb. The women saw everything that happened and knew exactly what they needed to bring the following Sunday morning after the Sabbath had ended. It seems that Nicodemus and Joseph and any helpers had completed the minimum so that the body could be decently buried in accordance with Jewish social customs. The watching women saw that other things still needed to be done and decided to do them at the earliest possible time. We know from Mark's Gospel that Salome was among the women who went to the tomb on the first Easter morning. As Jesus's aunt and near kin she would have felt that she ought to be involved with making sure that everything had been done and the burial of Jesus had been done properly.

THE CENTURION

The man given responsibility for the execution of Jesus made remarkable statements upon witnessing the death of Jesus. Firstly and less dramatically, we learn from *Luke* that he declared Jesus ' *"a righteous man"* ' (*23:47*). Much more remarkable is the fact that Mark and Matthew's Gospel report that the centurion declared Jesus to be the ' *"Son of God"* '.[72] We cannot say what this man meant, without knowledge of his background. It is quite possible that he was not Roman by birth. He and his soldiers and all of the onlookers had just

---

[72] Centurion: please refer to *Matthew 27:54*, *Mark 15:39*, *Luke 23:47* & *48*.

experienced an earthquake and there was a feeling of fear, amazement and awe at Golgotha. They had earlier also experienced an unnaturally long eclipse. Then, and this caused the centurion to wonder, the man on the middle cross said, ' *"Father, forgive them, for they do not know what they are doing"* ' (*Luke* 23:34). He was clearly referring to him and his men, Roman soldiers, who were hammering in the nails. The centurion may well have had to ask for a translation but he had already begun to realise that something incredible had been said. How could anyone have hatred or contempt for someone who, instead of cursing you, asked God for your forgiveness? The effect on the Jewish crowds who had come to mock was remarkable. They had then left the scene shocked and grieving at what had been done with their approval (*Luke* 23:48). This Roman would likely have begun this day's work with either contempt for Jesus, if not an actual hatred, but ended the day believing that the man on the cross was divine.

THE REPENTANT ROBBER

One of the two other victims of crucifixion on that first Good Friday afternoon deserves our attention. Both Mark and Matthew tell us that they were thieves. Matthew tells us that they both began by taunting Jesus (*Matthew* 27:44). It is left to Luke to give us the full picture of what happened later that day. One of them continued to taunt Jesus saying that if he really was the ' *"Christ"* ' then he ought to save himself and them from the cross. The man on the other side of Jesus had had a change of heart and took the other thief to task.

He reminded the complainant that they were getting fair, if painful justice but that Jesus did not deserve any of this. He then turned towards the middle cross. ' *"Jesus, remember me when you come into your kingdom."* '

It would be interesting to speculate about this man although to do so is rather dangerous and gets us away from what is I trust an objective study. However, perhaps he was not a hardened criminal. Whatever his situation Jesus had a word of acceptance and forgiveness for him. ' *"I tell you the truth, today you will be with me in paradise"* ' (*Luke* 22:42-3). To have used the words that he did, the dying thief had come to recognise that Jesus was God's *Messiah* and had real faith that he could do something for him.

HOW DID JESUS SEE THE CROSS?

It would be very easy to regard Golgotha as a low point in the ministry and life of Christ but that was not how he saw it. For him it was the fulfilment of his own understanding of being *Messiah*.

He would have taken the teaching of the Old Testament prophet *Isaiah* as the basis of his model. The passages concerning *The Suffering Servant* (**Isaiah** 53), who: '*was despised and rejected by men, a man of sorrows, and familiar with suffering*' (*v.*3) '*...was pierced for our transgressions, he was crushed for our iniquities; the punishment that brought us peace was upon him, and by his wounds we are healed*' (*v.*5)

'...This servant of God was cut off from the land of the living; for the transgression of my people he was stricken' (v.8) '...the LORD has laid on him the iniquity of us all' (v.6) '...He was assigned a grave with the wicked, and with the rich in his death, though he had done no violence, nor was any deceit in his mouth' (v.9).

Towards the end of this chapter of *Isaiah*, the note of suffering begins to give way to hope that from all this something good and even triumphant will result.

'After the suffering of his soul, he will see the light (of life) and be satisfied; by his knowledge my righteous servant will justify many, and he will bear their iniquities. Therefore I will give him a portion among the great, and he will divide the spoils with the strong, because he poured out his life unto death, and was numbered with the transgressors. For he bore the sin of many, and made intercession for the transgressors' (53:11–54:1). It was these verses and others that upheld Jesus in the belief that his death would result in forgiveness being made available to all who trusted in the Cross.

Oh yes, there was the utterly bleak time when Jesus cried with a deep feeling of total desolation, ' "*Why have you forsaken me?*" ' Both Matthew and Mark report this (*Matthew 27:46* and *Mark 15:34*). And yes, he did quote an Old Testament scripture which was about the *Messiah*'s sufferings (*Psalm 22:1*) but have no doubt he was not just fulfilling a prophecy. The feeling he was expressing was heartfelt, totally sincere.

There was an enormously strong power at work just outside the walls of Jerusalem on the day we now call Good Friday. Yes, Jesus had been at his lowest point but there was a note of triumph at the end when after asking God to receive his spirit he then declares that his work is successfully concluded.[73]

This subject is also looked into in Chapter 8, which deals with the teaching, which occurred on the Emmaus Road and readers may wish to go on to look at that.

THE CROSS – A MORAL OBJECTION

We all tend to feel uneasy or even angry when we hear about injustice. In some cases this feeling will be mild, as in the case of the person who has been found guilty of similar offences in the past, but is, on this occasion, innocent. We feel it unjust that guilt has been presumed because of a past criminal career or misleading circumstantial evidence.

When an accused prisoner, who has strongly denied wrongdoing, is cleared of any suspicion we also can feel very upset. The system of justice has not only let the innocent person down, it has, in a sense, harmed us, making us feel more vulnerable. Although the released prisoner can, in theory, hold his head high, will he feel able to do so? There will often be a victim of the crime not fully able to accept the acquittal because there is no closure of the suffering he/she feels.

---

[73] Please refer also to the *Short Dictionary* section on **Crucifixion and the Cross**.

There are, of course, people who, for reasons perhaps known to themselves or often not understood at all, are willing to 'carry the can' but they are not that many. I remember a strange case during my early days at school of a fellow pupil offering to 'take the blame'. This was so long ago I cannot now remember the offence. Naturally, the teacher was surprised and we were mystified.

Let's be clear on this point, the cross can sometimes be thought of as being a gross injustice. After all, why should a good and righteous man suffer for the wrongs of others? In the early centuries of the Church, a strange group of people called Docetists, who were very unorthodox, stated that they could not believe that a righteous God could allow Jesus to physically suffer for the wrongdoing (sin) of others. Their name comes from a Greek word that means 'to seem'. They then decided that Jesus only 'seemed' to come as a man. Docetism was of a group of beliefs, which said that you needed secret 'knowledge', not merely faith and that without this you would be less than a complete disciple. This 'secret knowledge' was only available from certain teachers!

The Docetists believed this in spite of the many references to Jesus touching things, touching people, eating, falling asleep from sheer exhaustion and doing so very many things that proved that he was not just some kind of 'apparition' but had a real physical body. This is a case of having a belief and trying to fit all the other facts around it.

Islam has a similar problem with the death of Jesus. They find it impossible to believe that a prophet of God should meet such an ignoble end as to die on a Roman gibbet. In fact, the Quran, their Scripture, goes out of its way to deny this in words that sound almost docetic: *'They did not kill him and they did not crucify him, but one was made to resemble him.'* Some Muslims believe that Judas Iscariot was the *'one made to resemble'* Jesus. In spite of this there are other passages in the Quran that indicate that Jesus did die and then was raised to life. *'I was blessed on the day I was born, and blessed I shall be on the day of my death; and ... on the day I shall be raised to life.'*[74]

Although they would strongly deny it, early Islam drew its knowledge of Christian faith from a group who were far from orthodox and it is possible that individuals who had had Docetic teaching helped form Mohammed's views.

To believe that God permits only justice for his higher purposes would need a belief in a perfect world. Christians believe that God is working towards this objective in spite of corrupt humanity intent on its own way. He is, however, using his own time scale for this. In the meantime, to believe that the good do not suffer in place of the bad or evil is over-idealistic! The life and death of Jesus is the supreme case.

---

[74] Surah, 19:33.

WHAT HAPPENED THE NEXT DAY?

The title is not often used but the day following Good Friday is sometimes known, among Christians, as *Holy Saturday*. This is, of course, our present Saturday, which begins for us in the modern world immediately after midnight and ends twenty-four hours later.

It is easy to dismiss the fact that there were at least two events during the next day that deserve a look. Firstly, the *'chief priests and the Pharisees'* thought it necessary to request another meeting with Pontius Pilate to discuss putting a guard on the tomb.

' "Sir," they said, "we remember that while he was still alive that deceiver said, 'After three days I will rise again.' So give the order for the tomb to be made secure until the third day. Otherwise, his disciples may come and steal the body and tell the people that he has been raised from the dead. This last deception will be worse than the first." "Take a guard," Pilate answered. "Go, make the tomb as secure as you know how." ' Pilate, who had grown tired of being the Sanhedrin's servant, was in fact saying, ' *"Get on with it yourselves"* '. *'So they went and made the tomb secure by putting a seal on the stone and posting the guard'* (*Matthew 27:62–66*).

This incident is very interesting. Firstly, let's note that this time it is not just the Sadducees. The delegation consists of Pharisees who were not always of the same opinion on matters religious. Secondly, they all thought that this matter was so important that they decided to forget that it was the Sabbath and a very special Sabbath too. We notice that, unlike the last visit to Pilate, they had no difficulty and walked into the *Praetorium*. We also notice that they are extra polite to the Governor. They seemed to have forgotten the rather hostile, shall we say acrimonious, arguments of the day before. Today it is ' "*sir*" ', because they need his help.

The Sanhedrin seemed to have taken more notice of Jesus's prophecy about rising from the dead than his disciples had. They also imagine that the disciples of Jesus have the courage to go and remove the body; this shows no understanding of the total depression of the disciples. It also assumes that they are together, whereas we know that they were in at least two places. But why should they want to do this – steal the body and start a deception? The truth is that the Sanhedrin and its supporters are utterly frightened by the influence of Jesus and fear that they have not stopped him – even by execution.

Pilate does not consider this request of any great importance and gives them a Roman guard. Pilate may have been made rather uneasy by talk about Jesus 'rising' again from the dead or he may just have been puzzled by the fear expressed by these Temple officials. It seemed a small matter so he agreed to let them have a guard on the tomb. The language in the above passage seems uncertain as to whether the guard is made up of Temple staff but as we shall see later in the Passion narrative there were Roman soldiers present.

We can be sure that Caiaphas would have made certain that there would be observers from the Temple staff to make sure that everything was totally secure. The only other duty for the priests to do is to set their own seal across the stone.

The second event concerns the women who have decided, or are about to decide, to visit the tomb of Jesus. There are two matters: one was dealt with as soon as the Sabbath ended at sunset. They had to go and get spices, which they would buy from merchants in Jerusalem or elsewhere.

The second is, on the surface, a problem that seemed likely to stop their anointing the body of Jesus, making this task totally impossible. How were they going to remove the stone across the opening to the tomb? They could need the help of several able-bodied men. We shall be looking into this matter more fully in a later chapter.

In the event, they decided to go as dawn was breaking. It would save them from being seen by too many people but it would mean that they might have to wait around for help to pass by. I imagine that the women who were to go to the garden tomb would have had no knowledge of the Roman guard having been posted. This could have seemed one obstacle too many!

DID JESUS REALLY DIE?

Not surprisingly a few people have sought other explanations to explain the events of Good Friday and

Easter Day and most of them are literally incredible. It seems to be a case of *'I've made up my mind; don't bother me with the facts'*. To me and to many others, these people sometimes need more faith in their own beliefs than those who believe in the Resurrection of Jesus.

Towards the end of the eighteenth century, Karl Bahrdt[75] came up with a rather odd theory.[76] He suggested that on the cross Jesus, through pain and loss of blood, did not die but became unconscious. This is usually referred to as the *'swoon'* theory. In support of his theory Bahrdt pointed to the fact that Pontius Pilate, when approached by Joseph of Arimathea and Nicodemus asking permission to bury the body of Jesus, expressed surprise (***Matthew 27:57-58***).

This is his only real piece of evidence. As to the mistake that the experienced Roman executioners made, that could be explained by lack of medical knowledge. This, said Bahrdt, was less well developed than at the end of the eighteenth century. This would seem to doubt the expertise of Roman soldiers who were well used to killing rebels with this particularly awful mode of execution. Let me say that the Roman guard knew exactly what they were doing and would not have made such a basic mistake.

---

[75] This Bahrdt is not to be confused with the twentieth century theologian Karl Barth.

[76] I have chosen to use the word 'theory' but most of these ideas are really too weak to be logically called that. A better word for an explanation of this type of idea is hypothesis.

What Bahrdt suggests is that having been put into the tomb, Jesus then recovered and struggled out of his tight grave clothes. Then, using all his strength pushed away that very heavy stone sealing the tomb and finally hobbled through the streets of Jerusalem to make contact with his disciples. But surely the noise of the stone being removed would have disturbed the Roman guard?

This theory is so preposterous that I do not intend, or need, to go through all the arguments against it. If there had been any suggestion that Jesus was alive then Joseph and Nicodemus would have sought help. If Jesus had recovered in the tomb and not died through cold and the wounds of the cross, would he have been able to convince his disciples that his was a cause that they should live and be ready to die for? Lastly, Jesus would almost certainly have contracted some infection and have died very shortly afterwards. No, a half dead *Messiah* would not have inspired his followers to create a church. They were prepared to risk their lives suffering for their faith by persecution, cold, disease and usually facing death for their beliefs.

Chapter 6

RAISED FROM THE DEAD

Many academics have, over the years, been sceptical over the prospect of harmonising the various accounts of the Resurrection given by the four Gospel writers, and yes, a superficial reading has led many to the conclusion that this is an impossible task. However, these men and women often come from a background that believes that to be anything else than sceptical is to be considered intellectually weak. Yes, there is some strength in testing things but not in assuming that the Gospel writers were like politicians putting a particular 'spin' on the events in order to gain supporters. No, that objection will not do! The men who wrote the Gospels really put their lives on the line and many died for their beliefs. Not many politicians are in danger of doing that!

I find it heartening that legal minds have applied a forensic approach to the evidence and concluded that the apparent points of disagreement can be reconciled. In 1969, Sir Norman Anderson, then Professor of Oriental Laws at London University, wrote on the life of Jesus and devoted well-argued chapters on both the trial, and on the Resurrection.

One of the first and foremost in using this approach was Frank Morison whose interest in the subject began as a determined effort to disprove the Resurrection. Over the course of time, he found that the evidence he had once wished to disparage could not be dismissed and, later in 1930, his book *Who Moved the Stone* was published.

There are many good, logical reasons for believing in the truth and reliability of the various accounts. This is in spite of some points in the Gospels, which to a casual critic look at odds with one another.

Anyone who has heard evidence from different witnesses to an accident knows how in that situation people with different interests, backgrounds and emotional make-up tend to notice and remember different elements in a composite picture.[77]

In some ways to have details that seem to mirror one another would appear suspicious. So the fact that there are variations should not be taken as a bar to belief in the historical fact of the bodily Resurrection. It seems likely that the accounts come from various sources, a fact, which, in itself, is liable to produce some degree of difference.

To this situation we must add that the three Jews and one Gentile who have given us our Gospels are from an

---

[77] David Wheaton, 'Accounts of the Resurrection', in *The Lion Handbook to the Bible*, Pat and David Alexander (eds), Lion Hudson, 1973, pp.529–30. Used with permission of Lion Hudson plc.

earlier age and have a different mindset to us. Let me give an example: their pace of life was not governed by the clock; it was governed by the sun. Consequently the exact order of events might not always be as important as the events themselves.

Besides this, had Matthew, Mark and John, who had had firsthand experience of the Passion, known beforehand that they would, many years later have had to give a written report, then, no doubt more of a sequence and fuller details would have been seen in their accounts.

EASTER DAY – the Road to Jerusalem

It was still very dark. She knew that it would not be long before things began to stir; quietly letting herself out of the house she glanced cautiously up and down the street. She sensed, rather than saw that there was no one about. She set out on her journey. It was far and would take about an hour even in the light of day. In the darkness she walked slower and that would make it seem even longer. Please God she would not meet a Roman patrol! It was unlikely but she could not rule it out.

On the outskirts of the village the road took her very close to a couple of houses. They were in deep shadow. Then, from out of the shadow she heard a noise then saw a movement! She took a quick intake of breath and her arm was flung across her heart! Then she recognised the shape, relaxed and went on her way. The donkey that had startled her was too sleepy to make any more noise.

****

Yes, this is partly fictional because we cannot be sure that any of the women began their journey from Bethany. However, it is not unlikely that one of the women to arrive at the tomb would have started from there or from outside the city. A woman on her own in the dark would, then as now, feel some fear. Many of us may have been brought up with the Easter Sunday story. If we have the main events they are of course the vitally important ones. The small dramas of people, like the two women named Mary, and the other women, may get lost, although, as witnesses these people are of untold value!

THE FIRST EASTER MORNING

It is the four Gospel accounts of the Resurrection given by Matthew, Mark, Luke and John that need to be looked at. So, let's now look at each account of what happened early on Resurrection morning and see what each Gospel writer can tell us. We will look at *Matthew 28:1–11* and will then compare the other Gospel writers dealing with this event: *Mark 16:1–14, Luke 24:1–12* and *John 20:1–9.*

John, Mark and Matthew all agree and tell us immediately that Mary Magdalene[78] visited the tomb; she is

---

[78] See article on **Mary Magdalene** in *Supporting Cast.*

almost certainly mentioned for the fact that she was already well known to the first readers of their Gospels by her reputation as a committed disciple. The apostles and those who preached the message of Jesus would have used her as an example. This happened well before the writing of any of the Gospels. It was unlikely to have been merely word of mouth; there are believed to have been written documents in existence at this time but where and how these were used we do not know. Another reason for mentioning Magdalene by name is because she may have taken the initiative in organising the women's visit to the tomb. *Luke* agrees with the other Gospel writers but also adds the name of *'Joanna'* and says that there were *'others'* (*24:10*). We will consider *Luke* more thoroughly later.

'After the Sabbath, at dawn on the first day of the week, while it was still dark' (*John 20:1*) *'Mary Magdalene and the other Mary'* (Mark's Gospel tells us that this Mary was *'the mother of James and Joses'* (*Mark*[79] *15:40* & *47*)) *'and Salome brought spices to anoint Jesus's body'* (*Mark 16:1*). Let's look at Matthew's Gospel, which tells us that they *'went to look at the tomb. There was a violent earthquake, for an angel of the Lord came down from heaven and, going to the tomb, rolled back the stone and sat on it'* (*Matthew 28:1*).

---

[79] The James in this verse is referred to as James *the younger* in *Mark 15:40*. He is referred to as the *son of Alpheus* in *Matthew 10:3*. His brother Joses' name is a form of Joseph.

The earthquake, which technically speaking might have been an aftershock from Friday's main quake, occurred at the same moment that Jesus was raised from death. *'His'* (the angel's) *'appearance was like lightning and his clothes were white as snow'* (*Matthew 28:2*). Luke's Gospel does not mention the removal of the stone. Luke's Gospel goes on to report that after finding the tomb open the women *'entered'* but *'did not find the body'* (*24:2*).

MARY MAGDALENE'S FIRST VISIT

I will try to show that it is probably a mistake to believe that all the women set out from one house at a certain time. It is far more likely that they left their homes, or lodgings, at different times having arranged to meet at a convenient address. As an alternative they may have decided to rendezvous close to Joseph of Arimathea's tomb. *John's* account says that *'it was still dark'*. John is writing about Mary Magdalene, perhaps she had a longer walk. Did Magdalene start her journey from Bethany? If so, she would have had approximately two miles to travel. She saw that the stone had been removed from the entrance (*20:1*). She was greatly shocked! This was the last thing that she had expected. What she and her friends saw changed things. Very distressed, she left the garden tomb to go into the city and tell John and Peter. ' *"They have taken the Lord out of the tomb, and we don't know where they have put him!"* ' Please notice that Magdalene says ' "*we*" '. What we cannot know is if her friends went with her or stayed at the tomb. However, does it seem likely that she would want to be alone on such a journey? As almost any man can confirm, women like to do things together. Mary Magdalene, on seeing the empty tomb was, as we have already noticed, highly distressed. She drew the worst of all conclusions. In this she was not alone; others with her were experiencing similar emotions. I think that she would have been glad of the support of her friends as she went into Jerusalem.

I also wonder how long it took Mary and the other women to find Peter and John. Let's assume for the sake of argument that the women knew exactly where to go to find both men. Their walk into the city could well have taken ten or fifteen minutes, perhaps more. Then, assuming that the two men were together, would they have been willing to go? The word of a woman was not considered of any value in first-century Judean male society. Therefore, the women may have had a very difficult task persuading John and then Peter to go and see for themselves. Plus the fact that after Peter's denials he is a very depressed, even broken individual! He is unlikely to be ready for making decisions. I shall return to Peter and John's part later.

THE OTHER VISITORS

Mark's Gospel reports things slightly differently. He mentions, as we have already noticed, *'Mary Magdalene, Mary, the mother of James, and Salome'* but here there seems to be a difference in time of day for it is *'just after sunrise'* (*Mark 16:1*). If we look at Matthew's Gospel we find that he does not help us in this matter, he says that they came *'at dawn'* (*28:1*). The expression 'light' and 'dark' are relative and have to depend on personal perception and emotional state of mind. Another factor is the time they left to go to the tomb.

Let's now turn our attention to Luke's Gospel and see what he tells us. Luke's main contribution to his first readers and to us, his twenty-first-century ones, is to tell us about the events that occurred later that first Easter Day. This is a subject almost unmentioned by the other three Gospel writers.

In his reports of early that morning Luke mentions three women by name: '*Mary Magdalene, Joanna, Mary, the mother of James*' but by talking of '*others*' (*24:10*) he means at least five. Joanna, as the wife of Chuza, an official of King Herod Antipas would, most likely, have begun her journey from the Hasmonean Palace, the royal residence in Jerusalem.

Joanna may have been Luke's main informant when he wrote his Gospel, or gathered information for it. This was at a time while he was with Paul the Apostle in Judea. It is now impossible to say exactly how many women went to the tomb. Among those not listed but whose name we could add to the list is Susanna. She was one of Jesus's supporters from Galilee (*Luke 8:3*) who had come to Jerusalem and is, by tradition rather than New Testament evidence, thought of as one of the women visiting the tomb on the first Easter day. It is probably wrong to assume that in naming the two Marys and Joanna, Luke is mentioning a group who set out for the tomb together. By giving these names, Luke may be mentioning the most important or women likely to have been known, at least by reputation, to Theophilus[80] and the early Christians who met together with him. No doubt they knew quite well of the sightings of early that Sunday morning but wished to know the names.

From this it seems that there may have been two groups of women, perhaps three, who went to the tomb separately from each other. It would be wrong to say that they did not know about each other's intention. In fact, it is likely that they had planned to rendezvous at the entrance of the garden. But Mary Magdalene and her companions, unnamed in John's Gospel had a shock, which altered their plans.

Mark and Luke mention the fact that spices had been *'prepared'* and brought to the tomb to *'anoint Jesus's body'*. It had puzzled me that the women, knowing that Joseph of Arimathea and Nicodemus had interned Jesus's body *'in accordance with Jewish burial customs' (John 19:40)*, had gone to the trouble of buying expensive spices and ointments. Then, as I thought this over, I began to realise that it was part of their dealing with their personal grief. It was part of their saying 'goodbye'. In Salome's case, as near kin to Jesus on the

---

[80] We do not know anything for sure about Theophilus. The ***Book of the Acts of the Apostles*** mentions him as the one to whom ***Acts*** was sent. It also mentions a 'former book', which is Luke's Gospel (***Acts 1:1***). Theophilus's name means 'lover of God', which means either a change of name or a name to protect his real identity.

female side, it was a formal duty. Salome may have felt that these two men had performed, or supervised, a task that she should have done herself. There is another factor in this. Joseph and Nicodemus had had limited time for this ritual and although it *'was in accordance with Jewish burial customs'* they had only done the minimum. After all, for Joseph and Nicodemus, the Sabbath had been about to begin and not just an ordinary Sabbath. It was the Passover Sabbath!

Magdalene and the other Mary (*'mother of Joses'* **Mark 15:47**) had been *'opposite the tomb'* (**Matthew 27:61**) on the Friday afternoon before and had seen the site but how near were they? Luke mentions *'women who had come with Jesus from Galilee ... saw how his body was laid in it'* (**23:55**), again we cannot be sure of the number or names. Mary Magdalene would have foreseen some of the problems in making an early morning visit. Luke mentions Magdalene rather later in his account of the empty tomb (**24:10**). This makes her seem less important to his telling of the events of early Resurrection morning. I believe, as I have already mentioned, that his main source of information was Joanna.

PETER AND JOHN'S VISIT (*John 20:3–10*)

In *verse 3* of his report, John says that *'Peter and the other disciple started for the tomb'* and, as we have concluded, we cannot be sure of when this took place except that it was rather later that morning. Once they had both learnt of Magdalene's discovery that the body of Jesus had gone and that Magdalene's story had to be checked, they both set off for the tomb briskly.

Near the end of their journey Peter and John ran to the tomb, although John got there first and then looked in *'at the strips of linen lying. Then Simon Peter ... arrived and went into the tomb. He saw the strips of linen lying there, as well as the burial cloth that had been around Jesus's head. The cloth was folded up by itself, separate from the linen. Finally the other disciple, who had reached the tomb first, also went inside. He saw and believed'* (John 20:5-8).

Luke is able to give us a valuable insight into Peter's reaction. Luke's account of what Peter had seen inside the tomb matches John's but this is what he tells us of Peter's attitude: *'and he went away, wondering to himself what had happened'* (24:12).

Is this Peter's lack of faith? Yes, it is at one level, but let's remember the state of mind of this man. He was so mentally stressed and filled with guilt at his recent failure on Good Friday that he is certainly suffering from severe depression. In this state sleeping, eating and normal mental processes are badly hindered. It is likely that he could not forgive himself for firstly being boastful and then cowardly. Men and women in this state are not always capable of working out even simple things. But the facts are asking Peter to believe the impossible!

Yet how could Peter not believe the evidence of his own eyes? The stone had been removed, the guards had mysteriously disappeared but of much more vital significance was the fact that the grave clothes lay there undisturbed! With the exception of the cloth that had been tied around the Lord's head, that *'was folded up by itself, separated from the linen'*, surely he could see that something inexplicable had occurred?

As for John's reaction, he tells us that *'He saw and believed'* (*John 20:8*). In spite of all the teaching, John and Peter had not really understood the idea that Jesus would be resurrected. It was at this stage that they, or at least John, began to make sense of this amazing teaching.

Before we move on to think about the next section let's think about the tomb itself, it will help our under-standing. As we have already noted the entrance to the tomb was low and visitors had to stoop to look in. It is obvious that the place, within the tomb, where Jesus had been laid could not be seen from directly in front; you would have needed to stoop and look to the right (see *Mark 16:5*, which tells us that when the women entered the tomb *'they saw a young man dressed in a white robe sitting on the right side'*). This means that the place where Jesus body was placed was to the right of the entrance. It might have been a space either flush with the floor or raised slightly above it.

NUMBERS – A CRUCIAL ISSUE FOR SOME!

I'm going to apologise in advance if some of my readers are irritated by what appears to be backtracking of previous material covered. My reason for doing this is that some of you, who have had a break in reading, may be happier if I repeat myself. Also there are some people who are concerned about how many women or angels there were.

We have already seen that we cannot be certain of the exact number of women who visited the tomb early on that first Easter Day. It would not be difficult to imagine that at times, around the entrance of the tomb, the garden might have seemed slightly crowded.

The question of the number of angels and their roles does seem to present some problems for those who wish to have a social science approach to the Gospels, which relies on exact numbers. However, as we have already mentioned, lawyers, in particular judges are prepared for the fact that there are sometimes variations in the testimony of truthful witnesses. Matthew and Mark mention one angel. Luke and John state that there were two of them present.

We ought to remember, as I have already mentioned, that there were at least five women visiting the tomb that morning. Because of these numbers they may have felt that it might be unwise to gather together at the tomb as a group. It could have created too much curiosity in anyone who was passing by. Some of this group may have decided to keep a look out. Then again, the space within the tomb would have been insufficient to allow a group of this size (five or more) to enter all at once. So it is possible that the number of angels seen may have been different according to each woman, or pair/trio of women. Differences in number could also be explained by the fact that although there may have been more than one angel present, only the one who spoke is mentioned. Let's look at each angelic appearance.

There was a violent earthquake, for an angel of the Lord came down from heaven and, going to the tomb, rolled back the stone and sat on it. His appearance was like lightning, and his clothes were white as snow. The guards were so afraid of him that they shook and became like dead men (Matthew 28:2–4).

As we shall see from *verse 11* of **Matthew's** account the guards had left the scene and had gone to make a report to the chief priests. At what exact moment they left we cannot be entirely sure. It is likely that they would have left after seeing the angel who had *'rolled back the stone'*. After all, there was then no reason to stay when they realised that there was no body to guard.

I am sure they had recovered from their quaking with fear and had left before the women arrived. The sight of a guard of soldiers lying around looking drunk or dead may have made the women too fearful to approach the tomb. It is possible, that they saw the guards running out of the garden as they were arriving. Would these men return? The writer Dorothy L Sayers believes that the women saw the guard fleeing on their way to the garden and very close to the tomb (*The Man Born to be King*).

The angel said to the women: 'Do not be afraid' [stop being afraid] *'for I know that you are looking for Jesus, who was crucified. He is not here; he has risen, just as he said. Come and see the place where he lay. Then go quickly and tell his disciples: "He has risen from the dead and is going ahead of you into Galilee. There you will see him." Now I have told you' (Matthew 28:5–7).*

Matthew gives us a very interesting piece of information, which John's Gospel explains more fully. Matthew reports on the angel, who after removing the stone, *'sat on it'*. Without John's help we may imagine a very tall angel sitting uncomfortably on the top of the stone. No, the angel laid it flat on the ground. Well, angels don't do things by halves! *John 20:1* confirms that *'the stone had been removed from the entrance'*. This sounds like a much more normal sitting position, even for an angel! In Scripture the act of sitting down often means that an action has been completed. When the angel sat down he was showing that what had been done would not be and could not be undone.

Let's be clear on one vitally important point, the stone was not removed so that the body of Jesus could get out. No, Jesus, after being raised found walls and solid objects no obstacle to movement. The stone was removed for the benefit of the early morning witnesses.

Now we shall look at the other accounts and see what we can learn. Luke's Gospel states, as we have already discovered, that the women arrived to find *'the stone rolled away'* and says nothing about the removal of the stone. He goes on to report that after finding the tomb open, the women *'entered'* but *'did not find the body'*.

He then deals with the angels' appearance to the women: *'suddenly two men*[81] *in clothes that gleamed like lightning stood beside them'*. Luke's angels went on to remind the women of what Jesus had taught about being *'crucified'* and then of his Resurrection *'on the third day'*. Although Luke includes Mary Magdalene in his Gospel account, it is very evident, as we shall see, that she was not present to hear the angel reminding the women of what Jesus had predicted. Suddenly these women made complete sense of something Jesus had told them earlier when *'they remembered his words'* (24:2–8).

The only explanation for Luke not mentioning the angel's removal of the stone could be that his informant was not an eyewitness to that action. We can be sure that he believed in the angel's appearance and work of removing and sitting on the stone but may not have been entirely sure of the order of events.

But where did the Gospel writers get their facts about the removal of the stone? Perhaps it was from another source. So, if it was not the women who reported seeing the angel, who was the witness or witnesses to the removal of the stone and the guards' reaction to the angel? Let me suggest that it could have been one of the Roman sentries or someone with them who later came to Christian faith.

As far as information is concerned we cannot overlook the fact that Joseph of Arimathea or Nicodemus may

---

[81] Angels do not always look like human beings (*Isaiah 6*).

have given Matthew an account of what had happened to the guard. I wonder whether they had been told this by another member of the Sanhedrin or had overheard a conversation. Remember that it is very likely that Nicodemus and Joseph would now have been known as supporters of Jesus, and although distrusted by Caiaphas, may have been given information by less hard-line members of the Sanhedrin.

This could account for Matthew being so well informed about what had happened early on that Resurrection Day and of the conversation between some of the guard and the High Priests and of the orders to these sentries. *'You are to say, "His disciples came during the night and stole him away while we were asleep"* ' (*Matthew 28:13*). Now, if these men, the soldiers on guard, saw the angel removing the stone did they also see or sense something else? Before the angel came down did they see a figure passing through the stone that covered the tomb? If so they would have begun to be highly alarmed and to discuss whether they had seen a ghost. Then to compound their fear the angel came down!

Mark's Gospel has the women wondering ' "*Who will roll the stone away from the tomb*" ' (*16:3*). This does look like a lack of planning on the part of these women. The likely answer is that they knew, or thought it probable that Joseph of Arimathea employed a gardener or that there was a night watchman who could assist them. If the night watchman was still there or the gardener had begun his day they would have had no way of knowing. This is borne out, as we shall see later, when Mary Magdalene, seeing a stranger outside the tomb, thought he was 'the gardener'.

As we now know this was not a problem. Seeing that the tomb was open they went in. '*As they entered the tomb, they saw a young man dressed in a white robe sitting on the right side, and they were alarmed. "Don't be alarmed," he said. "You are looking for Jesus the Nazarene, who was crucified. He has risen! He is not here. See the place where they laid him. But go, tell his disciples and Peter, 'He is going ahead of you into Galilee. There you will see him, just as he told you' " '* (*Mark 16:*5–7). The meaning found in *Matthew 28:*5–7 is here in these verses. Only Luke gives us the additional information that the women remembered Jesus's words (*24:*7), but he has two angels.

The fact that Mark and Matthew mention only one angel does not preclude the fact that there was another angel who took no active part in the message given to these women.

WHY IS MARK'S GOSPEL DIFFERENT?

There is one crucial difference between Mark and Matthew. The women in Matthew's account meet with the risen Jesus and the natural meaning of this encounter is that it took place very soon, if not immediately, after they left the tomb.

' *"Greetings," he said. They came to him, clasped his feet and worshipped him*' (*Matthew 28:*9). Jesus then, for emphasis, repeated the message of the angel. We notice that Jesus seemed to have no objection to be touched by these ladies. This is very different to the way he dealt with Mary Magdalene. We will consider Mary Magdalene's meeting with Jesus a little later. For these women there must have been a need to believe that he was really alive, raised from the dead and not just a figment of their imagination or that they were seeing his ghost.

It is amazing that Mark did not mention such an incredible meeting. There are a few possible answers for this. Could it be that Peter, Mark's main source of Gospel material, had forgotten? That really does not stand up as an argument. This was such an amazing event that Mark would not have forgotten Peter's memory. Jesus – who they knew to be dead and buried being seen alive. Being touched! No, he would not. He could not have forgotten that! Mark or, to give him his fuller name, John Mark may not have been a close eyewitness of much of Easter morning but he undoubtedly felt strongly the emotion of the events of the Passion and would have been aware of its full impact.

The only other explanation was that Mark's group of women, those who did not see the risen Lord, were a different group to the ones that Matthew describes. The only support that I can find for this is that Mark's group, at that stage, *'said nothing to anyone'* (*16:8*).

It would not be very surprising that these women had experienced some shock. How would you or I react to an angelic experience? It could well be that we would need some time to evaluate what had happened to us. That may well have been the reaction of these women. I imagine that after the shock had worn off the women did begin to speak about what they had experienced at the tomb. It could have taken a little time before they began to share this with others.

On the other hand Matthew's group *'ran to tell the disciples'* (*28:9*). They obeyed the angel's instruction to ' *"go quickly"* ' (*v.7*).

How long this took we can only guess although, from later in *Luke 24*, we know that it could have taken at least a couple of hours. If commentators are correct most of the Eleven had probably gone to Bethany a couple of miles outside the city. Later in the chapter (*v.11*) Luke tells us that the women were not believed. This again is another example of the unfortunate but fairly typical first-century Jewish male chauvinist attitude. In legal and other important matters you could not rely on a woman's words. Luke informs us that *'their words seemed like nonsense'*. This was probably partly due to the excitement in the women's telling of the event. The facts may well have tumbled out of them in a cascade of words, with each of them cutting across the others. Such an amazing, incredible story and delivered in a jumble of words – no wonder these already sceptical men did not believe.

Why are there differences between Mark and the rest of the Gospels? Only Peter, Mark's main informant can explain this. John's Gospel is quite definite about Mary

Magdalene telling *'Simon Peter and the other disciple'* (John son of Zebedee) (**20:2**). In fact, they may have received another separate report from the women who visited the tomb after Mary had left.

So far, I have not attempted to explain the fact that Mark seems to contradict the other Gospel writers. Let me say that I don't honestly think there is a serious problem here and I say this for the following reasons.

The women who Mark reports as not saying anything *'to anyone'* may have been different women. Who were those that they met without passing on this amazing news? These people may have been followers or sympathetic to Jesus and his work but whose commitment was not fully known. But we do not know!

The strongest reason is that Mark's Gospel was almost certainly the first to be written. This was after the death of Peter around AD 64–5, we can say fairly definitely earlier than AD 70. Mark's Gospel is certainly earlier than Matthew's. Matthew used Mark's Gospel as one of his sources and expanded the material in it.

JESUS AND HIS DEALINGS WITH MARY MAGDALENE

As we have seen Mary was quick off the mark in informing Peter and John about the disappearance of the body of Jesus. In following the events of what happened to her we will need to look carefully at the *Gospel of John*. Mary, very upset, stayed behind *'after the disciples'* (Peter and John) *'went back to their homes'*. We cannot know all that she felt. *'As she wept, she bent over to look into the tomb and saw two angels in white, seated where Jesus's body had been, one at the head and the other at the foot. They asked her, "Woman, why are you crying?"'* Without wanting to read too much into our text it is easy to imagine that there is a note of surprise in the angel's question. There is no cause for sorrow only rejoicing. *' "They have taken my Lord away," she said, "and I don't know where they have put him" '* (20:10–13).

Something made Mary turn her head away and look out into the garden. Perhaps she felt that there was someone there or perhaps she saw the angel glancing beyond her. There was someone there! A stranger was standing watching her. *' "Woman, why are you crying? Who is it you are looking for?" '* Mary assumed that this stranger was the gardener. On her own, in a quiet place with an unknown man, she might have been uneasy but she felt no fear and answered his question. *' "They have taken my Lord away and I don't know where they have put him. Sir, if you have carried him away, tell me where you have put him, and I will get him." '*

If Mary felt uneasy during this discussion it would have been at this moment. After all, this man might have been one of those who had shouted 'crucify' on that awful Friday just a couple of days before. Then she heard a familiar voice speaking to her.

'Jesus said to her, "Miriam". She turned towards him and cried out in Aramaic, "Rabboni!" (which means "teacher").' This form of address, which means in Aramaic "my master" or "my rabbi" was rarely used and only to very special rabbis.

'Jesus said, "Do not hold onto me, for I have not yet returned to the Father. Go instead to my brothers and tell them, 'I am returning to my Father and your Father, to my God and your God.' " ' Jesus uses a new name for his disciples he calls them ' *"brothers"* '.

There were several reasons why Jesus may not have allowed Mary to hold onto him. As we have seen above in *Matthew 28:9* Jesus was quite prepared to allow others to touch him. This was of course later that morning. Then, on a much later occasion, Jesus encouraged Thomas, known as the twin and sometimes as *doubting Thomas*, to touch his wounds (*John 20:27*).

So, is Mary Magdalene a special case? The answer seems to be 'yes'. Why might this be so? Firstly, we must look at the Greek and see what the grammar can tell us about this verse. *The New International Version* is quite good in translating this but the *New American Standard Bible* is better on this verse. This is how it translates *John 20:17*: ' *"Stop clinging to Me."* ' Was Magdalene trying to monopolise Jesus? It seems that she was.

Most commentators point out that Mary had to be prepared to let Jesus go. True, he would be with her and his disciples for a time, several weeks, until that stage of his work was finished and he would return to heaven. Then, at that time, his disciples would see *'him taken up before their very eyes, and a cloud then hid him from their sight'*. Then angelic figures promised that Jesus would return in the same way as he had left (*Acts 1:9*).

Mary Magdalene went to the disciples with the news: 'I have seen the Lord!' And she told them that he had said these things to her (John 20:13–19).

This time her news went to all the disciples – except one. However, that is another subject that we will come to later.

THE STONE THAT SEALED THE TOMB

There was one facet of the Gospel story that used to puzzle me and only recently during my studies have I found the explanation. Let me tell you what I mean. I had a wrong understanding about the stone. Let me share what I have discovered.

At this time there were two ways of closing the entrance of a tomb. The most common one was to cut a stone slightly smaller than the entrance, which would be pushed into the entrance and acted a little like a cork in the neck of a bottle. A much less common manner of closing the entrance to a tomb was a stone that was rolled down a slight slope in a groove and in this position lay flush against the entrance. This would have required considerably more strength to move than the first type of stone.

My earlier understanding had been that the tomb of Jesus had been sealed with the heavier type. The stone rolled down the slope in a groove. Mark, as we have noticed, has the women asking ' *"Who will roll the stone away from the tomb"* ' (*16:3*). The stone was clearly of the common type that acted like a bung in the mouth of the tomb. If it had been of the heavier type then the women would have needed a gang of weight-lifting strongmen to roll the stone up the slope. It would have been illogical and quite unreasonable to expect the night watchman or gardener to try to deal with such a task. That was who these ladies thought would help them with this problem.

DID JESUS REALLY RISE?

Again there have been others who have tried to find another answer to the events of Easter morning. Some strange explanations have been put forward that attempt to explain away the Resurrection. These people agree that Jesus died but that nothing of real importance happened afterwards. Some have suggested that a person or persons unknown stole the body. These theorists do not give a reasonable motive to say why anyone would want to do this. Suspicion might fall on the disciples but we have already thought about this and dismissed the idea.

Once *they*, whoever *they* might have been, had removed the body these grave robbers would have had to dispose of it in some manner. We have to remember that handling the dead was something orthodox Jews would only do for close members of their family. Even touching graves was avoided as making a person ceremonially unclean. This was part of Jewish culture and they would have grown up with this as a taboo.

We know that in later centuries there were thieves who stole the newly dead for primitive medical research, but that did not happen for many centuries.

The final difficulty for anyone wishing to believe in the body of Jesus being removed is the fact that a detail of Roman soldiers were in charge of the tomb. So let's forget this very strange explanation – nobody removed Jesus's body.

Hallucination is another theory put forward to explain the fact that Jesus did not really rise from the dead; that is, his followers only thought that he had. It is true that some people who have recently experienced bereavement do think that they see or feel the presence of the departed. This often happens when they have been asleep and wake to feel that they have caught a fleeting glimpse of the departed. This can often be part of the early process of learning to live with loss. But these experiences are usually transitory!

Then there is the possibility that the ghost of Jesus was very active and seen by many. Supporters of this idea will point to the fact that physical objects, like doors or the stone on his tomb, did not present an obstacle to Jesus. However, this is the only similarity. The body that Jesus appeared in could be touched and shared the supper of the Eleven disciples. On that Sunday, the first Easter day, Jesus asked them: ' *"Do you have anything here to eat?" They gave him a piece of broiled fish; he took it and ate it in their presence'* (*Luke 24:41–43*). That was not exactly ghostly behaviour. Nor, a little later, is the fact that he met them on the shore of Lake Galilee after they had had an unsuccessful night's fishing, having cooked some fish for their breakfast (*John 21:1–14*). The final fault in the 'ghost' theory is that not everyone is aware of these spirits. When Jesus appeared, everyone present was convinced that he was back, and that somehow death had been defeated.

Those who wish to disprove the death and Resurrection of Jesus by advancing strange notions of what might have happened are all, with one exception, comparatively recent. The exception is the story put out by the Jewish Council that Jesus's disciples had stolen and taken his body away (*Matthew 28:12–15*). In spite of this story, once they had met the risen Jesus, the apostles were changed men and their influence spread. Because of their preaching, many converts were made in the Jerusalem area. The apostles stated with complete confidence that Jesus had risen and been seen in Jerusalem. This message was preached within a short distance of where he had been buried and rose from the dead. Joseph of Arimathea and Nicodemus, well known in the community, were witnesses who could be consulted. So, is it any wonder that within weeks thousands of people, priests and Pharisees among them, had become believers?

Had there really been serious doubts the crowd would have laughed at them and then picked up stones to punish this insult – a blasphemy against God. There would have been a summary execution unless there had been Romans about to prevent it.

THE HIGH PRIESTS' UNBELIEVABLE STORY!

The chief priests must have been quite desperate in concocting this story. A fiction is concocted which might not please the soldiers as it made them sound guilty of a total failure of duty. However, any reservations and hurt feelings on their part are dealt with by a bribe. And so the story is put about that: *'His disciples came during the night and stole him away while we were asleep' (Matthew 28:13).*

What kind of nonsense is this? John Wenham has pointed out that anyone hearing this piece of fiction would ask how they knew it was the disciples if they were asleep at the time. Surely removing the stone and replacing it would have disturbed them (it could not have been done silently). Even if the guard had been drinking they would have been disturbed. This makes this whole story even more unbelievable. Moreover, would the Roman soldiers have confessed to falling asleep on duty? No, they would have faced the death penalty.

There must have been a great deal of fear among these priests. Another question we have to consider is why the guard of Roman soldiers went to the chief priests. After all, the two groups would not have been on easy speaking terms. The most likely explanation was that there was at least one of Caiaphas's men with them and that the suggestion came from him.[82] In addition to the money there is also a promise that should Pilate learn of this then the Sanhedrin will undertake to square matters so that the guard will not need to fear official action from the Governor. However, even with a Jewish guard it all came under Pilate's ultimate authority and they would have to answer to him. If the chief priests did have their man at the tomb then they would have known about the events of that first Easter morning at about the same time as Peter and John or even earlier.

We do not know how successful this story was and how widely it was believed. What we can say is that it was being used to explain why the body of Jesus could not be produced many years after the event. Justine Martyr, a Christian born about seventy years later in the Holy Land, knew of this story.

Let us imagine that we could go back in time and ask the chief priests some questions: *'If the disciples stole the body of Jesus where did they put it? How were they able to remove the heavy stone without disturbing the guard? What was their thinking in doing this? Don't you think that they were just too demoralised to have even considered it?'*

Clearly this was a desperate story that raises more questions than it answers. It had been thought up by desperate men.

---

[82] John Wenham, *Easter Enigma*, Paternoster Press, p.80.

Chapter 7

LATER THAT FIRST EASTER DAY

The bottom had fallen out of their lives and they were feeling desperate. They did not despair of life itself, although they must have wondered whether, as disciples of Jesus, the Temple, authorities would arrest and question them. So, it was with a great sense of relief that they left Jerusalem.

Their feelings and state of mind had to do with high hopes being dashed. It would not even have been back to square one. It was a sense of emptiness that they felt; like looking into a black bottomless pit. It may not have helped but they began to talk about the events of the previous Friday. What had gone wrong? Right up to the time he was arrested their hopes had remained alive. But then, that ghastly flogging and, far, far worse, crucifixion… Surely something was wrong. *Messiah* did not get crucified! These two knew, with every other devout Jew, *'that anyone who is hung on a tree is under God's curse'* (*Deuteronomy 21:23*). So, had they been wrong or had Jesus been mistaken and misled them? They really could not understand it. During their lives both of them had met a number of rogues and cranks but Jesus did not seem to be either of those, nor did he seem deluded, he was far too rational and self-controlled.

There was one slight hope. There were those strange rumours of angels having been seen. These angels had reported to some of the women, who had earlier that day gone to the tomb, that Jesus was alive. What had sounded rather more likely was the report by John Zebedee that the tomb had been empty. He and Peter had gone to the tomb to see for themselves. They confirmed that there was no body! But who would have wanted to remove the body of Jesus, it just did not make sense! None of his disciples would have done that, they had bolted – left Jerusalem as soon as he had been arrested in the garden in the early hours of Friday. No, that was *not* quite right; it was true a couple had remained! Peter and John were still in the city but Peter was in a terrible state of deep depression. Only John seemed to have his wits about him; he was a good man; you could rely on John.

The only other possibility was that the Temple priests had taken the body. But why, what reason would they have had? Again it did not make sense. Besides, the Temple, so it was rumoured, had asked for a troop of Roman soldiers to watch over his tomb and also included some of their own staff to make sure the guard did their duty and did not drink too much.

There had been something that Jesus had said to the Twelve disciples and they had passed it on to others. It was extraordinary, but had they understood correctly? Jesus had said that '*he must go to Jerusalem and suffer many things at the hands of the elders, chief priests and teachers of the law, and that he must be killed and on the* *third day be raised to life' (**Matthew 16:21**). He had said this, so they had been told, more than once. The Twelve had not been sure of what to make of this saying, so what hope was there for the more ordinary disciples like themselves. Was it possible that Jesus had been resurrected? Well, like many Jews brought up under the influence of the Pharisees,[83] they believed that the righteous would be brought back from death to some kind of life and that they would meet God and explain their actions during the earthly life that they had lived. No, he had surely not meant that; they must have misunderstood him. There had to be a simpler explanation.

THE TRAVELLERS ON THE ROAD TO EMMAUS

It is left, almost exclusively, to Luke to tell us of the further appearance of Jesus on the Road to Emmaus but Mark's Gospel gives us supporting evidence. '*After-wards Jesus appeared in a different form to two of them while they were walking in the country' (**Mark 16:12**). It is rather strange that Mark makes so little of this. A possible reason is that his first readers would not have known the name of Cleopas, while for some of Luke's readers this man was known at least by reputation. Only Luke gives us an in-depth report on what happened on that Sunday afternoon.

We are not told very much about the two people who had the amazing experience of discovering that Jesus

---

[83] See note on **Pharisees** in the *Short Dictionary.*

had conquered death and was alive. The beginning of this report raises other questions, which a good journalist would like to have answered. We only have the name of one of the travellers, Cleopas; the identity of the second man or woman is unknown.

Question 1: Who was it who travelled with Cleopas?

Question 2: Why were they making this journey? Were they returning to their home in Emmaus or visiting a relative?

Question 3: To which of the several places called Emmaus were they going?

So, what do we know about Cleopas or, if we wish to be formal and use his name in full – Cleopatros? To complicate our enquiry there is also a Clopas mentioned in *John 19:25*, although some scholars have said that, as Clopas[84] was an Aramaic name it is safer to assume that he was a different man but names can change according to the user. So we ought not to rule this out. If we are talking about Clopas then it is possible that he was a brother of Joseph of Nazareth, the husband of Mary, the mother of Jesus. It does seem that Mary[85] was a very common name during this time.

---

[84] It is possible that he was also known as Alphaeus, which would mean he was the father of James listed as one of the twelve Apostles in *Matthew 10:3*.

[85] Mary is a variation of the Greek form (Maria or Marium). The name Miriam first appears in Scripture as the name of Moses's sister (*Exodus 15:20*). The meaning of the name implies a 'plump' lady.

The biblical scholar John Wenham has put forward an interesting opinion about the identity of the second traveller. He believes the travelling companion is none other than the Gospel writer Luke. Although this is possible other evidence suggests that Luke does not figure in the events of the New Testament until much later. I have reached my own different conclusion but I am open to other ideas.

Should Cleopas and Clopas be one and the same then this might give us a helpful clue as to the identity of his travelling companion on that first Easter Sunday afternoon. Mary, *'the wife of Clopas'* (*John 19:25*), who stood by the Cross of Jesus, is usually thought of as his wife.[86] This could answer my first question and mean that his companion was in fact his spouse. If we assume that Cleopas and Mary were together then the most likely reason for their walk was simply to return home after Passover.

The final question is where on the map one can find Emmaus. Finding the answer to this is not easy. Most New Testament manuscripts indicate seven miles (or to use the Greek measurements of that time, 60 *stadia*) from Jerusalem. There is no village or mound of ruins that any archaeologist has claimed with certainty to be ancient Emmaus. This is not surprising when one

---

[86] It is possible that she might have been his daughter or mother. So, to say that she that was a 'female relative' covers all eventualities and, if we are to be strict with the meaning of the Greek text, it does not allow anything else. However, I personally do not have a problem with translating this phrase 'wife'.

remembers the amount of warfare that occurred after the life of Jesus. It is therefore quite likely this village, whose name means 'a place where warm springs can be found', may have disappeared for ever.

There is an interesting tradition that may be worth considering. About seven miles west of Jerusalem, there is a village called El-Qubeibeh. There are also the remains of a Roman road. In AD 1099 Crusaders found the remains of an old Roman fort named Castellum Emmaus. There are also the remains of an ancient church that could be Crusader or Byzantine.

THE STRANGER ON THE ROAD TO EMMAUS

They did not see the stranger until he had caught up with them. They then exchanged the traditional greeting 'Shalom'. After that this stranger took over the conversation. *'He asked them, "What are you discussing together as you walk along?" They stood still, their faces downcast. One of them, named Cleopas, asked him, "Are you only a visitor to Jerusalem and do not know the things that have happened there in these days?" "What things?" he asked. "About Jesus of Nazareth," they replied. "He was a prophet, powerful in word and deed before God and all the people. The chief priests and our rulers handed him over to be sentenced to death, and they crucified him; but we had hoped that he was the one who was going to redeem Israel. And what is more, it is the third day since all this took place. In addition, some of our women amazed us. They went to the tomb early this morning but didn't find his body. They came and told us that they had seen a vision of angels, who said he was alive. Then some of our companions went to the tomb and found it just as the women had said, but him they did not see." He said to them, "How foolish you are, and how slow of heart to believe all that the prophets have spoken! Did not the Christ have to suffer these things and then enter his glory?" And beginning with Moses and all the prophets, he explained to them what was said in all the Scriptures concerning himself'* (24:17–28).

Cleopas and his companion must have been quite desperate because they began to unburden themselves to a complete stranger. We can safely presume that they knew that this man was not priestly; they could tell that from his clothing. Was he a friend or a supporter of the Temple? That was something they could not know but they felt that he could be trusted.

To enable the narrative to flow I have provided a study of the teaching that occurred on the Emmaus Road to Chapter 8. People will either think me rather brave or that I have been unwise. I wrote this later section knowing that I am using a certain amount of guess-work; however, I have also looked carefully at the prophecies concerning God's *Messiah* in the Jewish Scriptures, also called the Old Testament. I have had to select some and reject others. Those Scriptures that I have chosen are ones that are going to be fairly clear to twenty-first-century Bible readers. Jesus may well have quoted some that I have left out. They may have had meaning for Cleopas and his fellow traveller but would be less clear to us. So, let's return to the narrative.

AT THE VILLAGE OF EMMAUS

They did not want this walk to end. It had started out as a chore walking those seven miles from Jerusalem. Now the cloud of depression had begun to lift from Cleopas and his companion. They slowed and came to a stop to say their goodbyes to the stranger who had it seemed, further to go.

But they urged him strongly, 'Stay with us, for it is nearly evening; the day is almost over.' So he went in to stay with them. When he was at the table with them, he took bread, gave thanks, broke it and began to give it to them. Then their eyes were opened and they recognised him, and he disappeared from their sight (Luke 24:29–31).

Some scholars have wondered how late in the day it really was. Perhaps in the way of the east this very interesting guest was asked to stay partly for the sake of hospitality and partly because they may have had more questions to ask.

As he broke the 'bread', which remember was the unleavened flour and water *motzah*, as the Feast of the Passover was only one day old, Jesus would, almost certainly, have used this ancient blessing or *Kiddush*:

Blessed are you, O Eternal God, Ruler of the Universe, who has chosen us among all peoples to proclaim your unity and to sanctify our lives by obeying your commandments. In your love you have given us rest and holidays for rejoicing, and this Feast of Unleavened Bread, the time of our freedom, in remembrance of Israel's exodus from Egypt. Blessed are you, O Eternal who sanctifies Israel and the festive seasons. Amen

There was nothing strange in these words, they were the set *Kiddush* but at that moment recognition took place. As he took the *motzah*, broke it and then handed them the two halves, they saw his hands – they had been pierced. Then they raised their eyes to his face. There was no mistake it was Jesus! Then he was gone. It was as if he had never been there – but he had been and they had the two pieces in their hands to prove it.

There was a long, long pause. They just looked at one another. Then they looked at the bread, then again at one another.

' **"Wasn't it like a fire burning in us when he talked to us on the road and explained the Scriptures to us?"** ' (*Luke 24:32*).[87] Cleopas looked at this hand; he was still holding the *motzah*. *'Let's have something to eat and drink, although I'm not sure if I'm hungry. But let's eat.'*

'Yes, let's, especially as he touched it and gave it to us. It wouldn't be right not *to eat and enjoy it.'* There was a

---

[87] This quotation is from the *Good News Bible*, 1976.

pause as they ate what they had, just a few minutes before, set out for themselves and the stranger.

'What shall we do?'

There was no immediate answer, just a shrug of the shoulders and the sound of breath being exhaled. *'I think we need to tell them.'*

'You mean...?'

'Yes, back in Jerusalem, they'll need to know we've seen him.'

Only a few minutes before when they had sat down facing the stranger they had felt a pleasant fatigue. Now that had gone, they paused for a very few moments wondering whether they would need anything from the house but it seemed impossible to think about that. Within a few minutes they had left the village and with the light turning to the rich colours of evening they set out for Jerusalem. Darkness would be with them before long.

****

We do not have details but in some way or other, Jesus's close group, originally 'the Twelve', had all been informed. Peter and John were in the city. The other nine were elsewhere. Most, if not all, had to be brought back into Jerusalem from their hideout in Bethany. It would be easy to see the hand of John Zebedee in this. He would probably have discussed this with his own brother, James, and Andrew, the brother of Peter. Peter himself would still have been too depressed to be able to make the decision about coming together again in Jerusalem. Others had to make that choice. But for Peter things were going to change!

We cannot be completely sure of where they planned to meet but the upper room, where they had met with Jesus only three evenings before, may not have been chosen. They could not be sure of how much Judas had disclosed to the High Priests.

These arrangements would, most probably, have taken place while Cleopas and companion were away from Jerusalem but it was a known place where disciples had gathered and so they went there. It was fairly likely to have been the home of John Mark, the man who later was to be Peter's secretary and to write down his leader's memories in the document known as Mark's Gospel.

It is rather strange but we have two reports of what happened which seem to be at variance. When they entered the meeting, Luke's reports that they entered the room and were told by *'the Eleven gathered together. "The Lord has risen indeed and has appeared to Simon." Then the two told what had happened to them ... and how Jesus was recognised by them when he broke the bread'* (24:34-5).

Mark reports it like this. *'They went back and told the rest, but they did not believe them'* (16:11). Now, how are we to deal with this seeming contradiction? John Wenham believes that *'the rest'* were not the *'Eleven'* that Luke speaks of, but other disciples.

Simon Peter is back with his companions and although we have no details of what took place and where and when, Jesus *'appeared to him'* (*Luke 24:34*).[88] Jesus's understanding and forgiveness had been given and Simon could move on to be Peter, 'the rock' that Jesus told him he was. I imagine that like all excellent counsellors, Jesus helped him to see and admit the weaknesses of the past and how to avoid them in the future. It was from this interview that Peter's natural gifts as a leader began to show through once again.

While Cleopas and the eleven disciples were talking together a staggering event happened! Luke reports it as a matter of fact although for the disciples gathered it must have been a breathtaking moment. *'While they were still talking about this, Jesus himself stood among them and said to them, "Peace* (Shalom) *be with you"* ' (*24:36*). Well, we can understand their reaction. They thought they had seen a ghost! But Jesus was quick to reassure them. ' *"Why are you troubled, and why do doubts rise in your minds? Look at my hands and my feet. It is I myself! Touch me and see; a ghost does not have flesh and bones"* ' (*24:37–39*).[89]

It is easy to understand the shock of the Eleven and their companions – they were glued to the spot. Jesus

---

[88] Paul also confirms this appearance in *1 Corinthians 15:5*. The New International Version uses the name '*Peter*' but look down to the footnote at the bottom of the page in your Bible and you will see the name '*Cephas*', the Aramaic word for 'rock'.

[89] Note that Jesus says nothing about 'blood'. We in English would have said 'flesh and blood' but Jesus had lost his blood on the Cross. He now has a Resurrection body.

held out his hands and let them see the nail holes in his feet. The disciples were overcome with a mixture of joy and *'amazement'* so that the request for something to eat gave them something to do. It was also a further sign that they were not having a wonderful dream and would wake up. *'They gave him a piece of broiled fish, and he took it and ate it in their presence'* (**24:40–44**).

Then, as earlier that day, he explained what the Jewish Scriptures had taught about him and that so many passages had not been fully understood.

We have to turn to John's Gospel for further details of what happened in the upper room that evening and it could be seen as John, probably the last to write a Gospel, deciding that the event needed a corrective. Yes, the facts themselves were correct but someone had been left out and ought to have been included. Firstly, John confirms that it was the same occasion and gives the same details of the appearance of Jesus (***John 20:19–23***). John adds two details that Luke does not.

<u>Firstly</u>, Jesus gives them a re-commissioning, ' *"I am sending you"* ' (*v.21*). They were given the task of telling of God's forgiveness but with that frightening job they were given the power to perform it.

<u>Secondly</u>, John tells us that there was an important absence. Didymus, called 'Thomas' (a nickname meaning 'the twin'), was not there to see the Lord appear.

Why was Thomas, absent from the upper room on that first Easter Sunday? It is fully possible that he just had to get out of the atmosphere of fear that filled the place where the remaining disciples had taken refuge. When he returned and eventually got in he discovered that the rest of the band was in a very elated state and that there was a celebration in progress. ' *"We have seen the Lord!"* ' (*John 20:25*). Thomas's reaction is scepticism and his reaction has become a byword for the honest doubter. One does wonder whether there was not just a trace of envy in his reaction with reasoning of this kind: *'if you have seen the Lord, which I doubt, why did I get left out; why didn't he include me?'* On the surface it does seem strange that Thomas was so very willing to set aside the evidence of ten other men with whom he had begun to build a deep relationship.

One week later Thomas is challenged and his own words of the previous week are quoted back at him. Thomas is shocked as the living Jesus invites him to place his *'finger' where the nails had been* and his *'hand' into Christ's 'side'* (*20:27*). Thomas had missed the blessing of that first Easter Sunday evening only to have his very own encounter with the risen Lord.

We do not know Thomas's full story but it is believed that he went to India. What is more probable is that he worked among Jews in Persia and his converts later took Christian faith to India.

Before we close this chapter it is necessary to mention some other of Jesus's appearances, which are mentioned in Paul's *First Letter to the Church at Corinth*. In *Chapter 15*, the apostle writes to the Church, among other matters, about other people who had seen the risen Christ. Paul in this same passage mentions *'more than five hundred of the brothers at the same time, most of whom are still living'* (*v.6*). In *verse 7*, he mentions *'James, then all the apostles'*. Paul is clearly talking about another James, not the elder brother of John Zebedee. The most likely man is James, the first named son of Mary and Joseph. Jesus, as we may remember, had returned to Nazareth and had had a not completely successful visit to his hometown. *Matthew* reports on this in *Chapter 13:55*, ' *"Isn't this the carpenter's son? Isn't his mother's name Mary, and aren't his brothers James, Joseph, Simon and Judas?"* '

The appearances of the risen Christ finished with his Ascension – please refer to *Acts 1:3–11*. This subject will be covered more fully in Chapter 10.

Chapter 8

THE LESSON ON THE EMMAUS ROAD

This is an attempted reconstruction of the conversation that occurred on the road to the village of Emmaus and is offered to the more experienced reader of the Bible. Any who feel that this does not describe them can disregard this chapter without losing the thread of the book.

Trying to second-guess what people were feeling in the first century is a risky undertaking for any writer living in the twenty-first but I offer it in the hope that some readers will be helped. As I have already said this is unlikely to please all but will, I hope, help some.

To avoid any confusion I have put the **words of** the stranger, who they later discover is the risen **Jesus in bold**. I have used a different type for biblical quotations.

****

'Tell me what has happened that has caused you to be so sad.'

I wonder whether there was a glance between the two travellers when they thought about this stranger. After all there was fear, shock, uncertainty in the air after the events of the previous Friday. Who were they talking to? If there had been a momentary doubt it soon passed and the floodgates opened. They were prepared to take a chance on who they were speaking to.

'It happened last Friday. Jesus of Nazareth a prophet of God, if ever you saw one, was crucified.'

'Where? Was that outside of Jerusalem?'

'Yes. There were two others with him but they were just criminals. He was placed in between them as if he were the same. Treated like a common criminal! But this man had healed the sick and was a wonderful teacher. Do you know — he had even raised the dead! The ordinary people were in awe of him but the chief priests — that was a different matter. They saw him as a threat. It was them that took him to Pilate. That meant only one thing: death on a cross. But those Romans flogged him before crucifying him. It was the kind of beating from which men sometimes die. Then they made him walk to the spot outside the city where he was to die, where he would be nailed to a cross. At least, that was how it began, but he was too weak. The Romans ordered another man to take over carrying the cross.'

'But he was different to those other two. When they drove the nails into their hands and feet they cursed the soldiers. Those Romans just laughed, of course. Jesus was completely different; he didn't say a word of complaint. Oh, you could see it was agony because what little colour he had drained away. He looked ghastly!'

'He was led like a lamb to the slaughter, and as a sheep before her shearers is silent, so he did not open his mouth.'

'Sorry, what was that you said?'

'I was quoting the Prophet Isaiah' (53:7).

'Oh yes, of course. Anyway, his ordeal was a lot shorter than we expected. He died quite quietly at three o'clock, the others had their legs broken but he was spared that. Of course, the Sanhedrin wanted it all over quickly so they could go home and celebrate the Feast. As we know, broken legs kill off the victim of a crucifixion very quickly.'

'You said he died quietly but did he say anything before the end came?'

'Oh yes, he said quite a lot. Several things I can remember immediately. He asked God that the Roman soldiers nailing him to the cross should be forgiven. At least, at the time we thought he meant the Romans, but perhaps he was speaking of others as well. The centurion asked what he had said and when it was translated that soldier looked amazed. Then later he seemed to despair and asked God why he was on the cross.'

'When you said "he" you mean Jesus of Nazareth?'

'Yes, that's right! Later still he asked for a drink and they held up a sponge. We didn't see whether he drank from it or not. Then finally, just before he died he asked God to receive him and said, "It is finished" (John 19:39). The strange thing was that he shouted it. It wasn't the whisper of a dying man.'

'Cleopas,' said his companion, *'you haven't mentioned the darkness that came over the earth from about midday. It became dark and then, just after he had died it seemed like an earthquake struck.'*

'These are remarkable signs, aren't they?'

'Yes they are but... well... we thought that Jesus was Messiah *but the* Messiah *does not end up suffering the disgraceful death of a cross.'*

THE LESSON FROM THE STRANGER

'You have understood the glory and the triumph of *Messiah* but you have rather foolishly missed so much, because there is another side of his work: struggle and suffering. From the earliest of our Scriptures there is warning of suffering. This would be, first of all for all humanity. Do you remember God's word to the snake,[90] the one who brought evil into the world?

' "I will put enmity between you and the woman, and between your offspring and hers; he will crush your head, and you will strike his heel" (Genesis 3:15).

'When evil entered the world – remember that God created a perfect world – it spread everywhere. When

---

[90] In ***Genesis***, the first book of the Jewish Scriptures (Old Testament) the ***snake*** is a symbol of evil. This symbolism is also used in the ***Book of Revelation***, the last book of the New Testament, where he is called '***the serpent***'.

Messiah came as a human he would also suffer and in the worst possible way on a cross. Like all people *"his heel"* has been hurt. But there is a difference, a vital difference! Ordinary people cannot overturn evil but *Messiah* has begun a process, which will, in the end, destroy Satan – *"he"*, Messiah, *"will crush"* his *"head"* and evil, all evil, will end' (*Genesis* 3:9).'

Cleopas thought about this and then asked, '*But we don't understand why God allows evil to triumph, can you explain it?*'

'No, the answer to that is that humans will not be given all the reasons, not in this life. Let me say that evil has, in a strange way, a part to play. Without evil we humans would not appreciate goodness. Without the problems that evil brings we humans would be weaker. Troubles make us stronger, more mature, more compassionate to the suffering of others.

'The suffering of God's *Messiah* would bring blessing to all peoples, Jew and Gentile. Remember what the LORD God promised our forefather Abraham? *"I will bless those who bless you, and whoever curses you I will curse; and all peoples on earth will be blessed through you"* (*Genesis* 12:3). This promise of blessing that is to *all peoples on earth* would only be fulfilled in God's *Messiah*, the descendant of Abraham. To make sure that faithful Abraham had really understood, the LORD repeated the message and said, *" Through your offspring all nations on earth will be blessed, because you have obeyed me"* (Genesis 22:18).

'Abraham did not live to see these promises fulfilled. Yet, with the LORD a promise is firm and is never forgotten. Many years after Abraham, King David also had this promise given to him. *"When your days are over and you rest with your fathers, I will raise up your offspring to succeed you, who will come from your own body, and I will establish his kingdom. He is the one who will build a house for my name, and I will establish the throne of his kingdom for ever"* (2 Samuel 7:12–13).[91] Remember, this was fulfilled in part by David's son, Solomon, who built a house, the First Temple. But the most important part of that promise was to be fulfilled by the *Messiah*.

'This promise, to David, was a little different to the one given to Abraham. Abraham's descendant would bring blessing to all people. To David's descendant there is also the promise that there will be both blessing and kingly rule for all earth's people. But you see the *"throne is for ever"* (2 Samuel 7:13), so whatever happens on earth the LORD's promise is firm.'

---

[91] *Psalm 132:11–12* also gives a similar promise.
'The LORD swore an oath to David, a sure oath that he will not revoke: "One of your own descendants I will place on your throne – if your sons keep my covenant and the statutes I teach them, then their sons shall sit on your throne for ever and ever." '

'But why did so few people, especially the Priests, fail to see that Jesus was Messiah?'

'Ah yes, the signs were there to be seen but so often they wished to ignore them. *Messiah* would be like Moses, a leader, a prophet and a teacher. Do you remember this promise? "*The LORD your God will raise up for you a prophet like me from among your own brothers. You must listen to him. I will put my words in his mouth, and he will tell them everything I command him*" (*Deuteronomy* 18:15 & 18).

'If only the Priests had looked at the birth of Jesus with care they would have seen that here was someone who had to be considered as being, at least, like *Messiah*. There was the place of his birth; the Prophet had foretold that some centuries ago, do you remember?

' "*But you, Bethlehem Ephrathah, though you are small among the clans of Judah, out of you will come for me one who will be ruler over Israel, whose origins are from of old, from ancient times*" (*Micah* 5:2).

'As I have said if the priests had really read and believed the Scriptures they would have seen that *Messiah*'s birth would be a supernatural one, "*the Lord himself will give you a sign: The virgin will be with child and will give birth to a son, and will call him Immanuel*" (*Isaiah* 7:14). The child to be born would be

Immanuel, God living with humanity, not just a king waiting to reign but born ready to rule.

' "*For to us a child is born, to us a son is given, and the government will be on his shoulders. And he will be called Wonderful Counsellor, Mighty God, Everlasting Father, Prince of Peace. Of the increase of his government and peace there will be no end. He will reign on David's throne and over his kingdom, establishing and upholding it with justice and righteousness from that time on and forever. The zeal of the LORD Almighty will accomplish this*" (Isaiah 9:6–7).'

'*Yes, this does make sense,*' said Cleopas and his companion nodded in agreement. '*Please continue.*'

'As we know, the Priests, well… not all but most of them, failed to realise or did not want to think that the prophet from Nazareth was of the Tribe of *Judah*, fully Jewish and so unique – fit to be the one "*to whom … belongs the obedience of the nations*" (*Genesis* 49:19).'

'*Yes,*' said Cleopas, '*we understand better but what about the suffering and all that blood?*'

THE *MESSIAH* AND THE SUFFERING SERVANT

'You have asked about the suffering of *Messiah* and I have mentioned the promise that even from the beginning of the Scriptures he would suffer. To understand this better we have to look at the Prophet Isaiah. You know, of course, that he foretold about a *"Suffering Servant"*. Then think about what this *Servant of the Lord* suffered. The *"Servant"* tells us, *"I offered my back to those who beat me, my cheeks to those who pulled out my beard; I did not hide my face from mocking and spitting"* (Isaiah 50:6). Does this sound familiar to you?'

Cleopas and his companion looked at one another. *'Yes, Jesus suffered that; we saw it with our own eyes.'*

'These sacred writings of Isaiah have much to say that you will realise speak of the one that you mourn for. Let me quote another:

"He was despised and rejected by men, a man of sorrows, and familiar with suffering. Like one from whom men hide their faces he was despised, and we esteemed him not" [we ignored and rejected him]. *"Surely he took up our infirmities"* [he endured the suffering] *"and carried our sorrows, yet we considered him stricken by God, smitten by him, and afflicted. But he was pierced for our transgressions, he was crushed for our iniquities; the punishment that brought us peace was upon him, and by his wounds we are healed. We all, like sheep, have gone astray, each of us has turned to his own way; and the LORD has laid on him the iniquity of us all"* (Isaiah 53:3–

6). So you see there is a purpose in the suffering of Messiah.'

'We know these Scriptures but never thought that they were about Messiah.' Then Cleopas, who had been listening intently, suddenly said with emotion, *'But why did he suffer on a cross? I couldn't think of anything worse! Are you sure that Jesus had to die in that way. It's a death for criminals, not godly men.'*

'Oh yes, it is an awful death but *Messiah* triumphed over even the awful death of the cross. What we consider "awful" God can accept. We have been thinking about the Prophet Isaiah, this is what he said about *Messiah*: "*See, my servant will act wisely; he will be raised and lifted up and highly exalted*' (Isaiah 52:13). Yes, *Messiah* suffered greatly but he will be honoured above every man. "*Yet it was the LORD's will to crush him and cause him to suffer, and though the LORD makes his life a guilt offering, he will see his offspring and prolong his days. After the suffering of his soul, he will see the light (of life) and be satisfied; by his knowledge my righteous servant will justify many*" [like a judge who gives a moral verdict of acquittal] "*and he will bear their iniquities*" (Isaiah 53:10–11).

'Yes, *Messiah* will have offspring – those who follow him faithfully are his children. Shall we think about other things that Isaiah said which are true of the man who died last Friday?'

'Oh, yes please! This is helping us,' said Cleopas's companion.

'Isaiah also said this of the *Messiah "He was assigned a grave with the wicked, and with the rich in his death"* **(***Isaiah 53:9***).**

'Well, that was true because Jesus was going to be quickly buried in a common grave with those others who died, common criminals, except that Joseph of Arimathea, a member of the Sanhedrin, offered his own tomb. He was certainly "rich" enough. Isaiah was certainly right on that!'

'Now, you wanted to know about the blood, didn't you?'

'Yes!' Cleopas nodded, answering for both of them.

'Think of the *Day of Atonement*[92] **when a goat is sacrificed for the wrongdoing of the people. An innocent animal is killed because of the evils that people do to each other and against God. As God is the Father of our nation and cares for every person, a wrong done against the person offends God. The blood of the animal is used to remind the people of**

---

[92] This is still celebrated in the Jewish Religion and is called *Yom Kippur* and it follows ten days after the *Rosh Hashanah*, the Jewish New Year. Since the destruction of the Temple (AD 70) and its sacrificial system there have been changes in the way this is celebrated. Between New Year and *Yom Kippur*, the ten days are a time for reflection and have been likened to the Christian Lent. This contemplative period is known as *t'shuva*.

the seriousness of their wrongs. It is presented at the Temple. Instead of the person being punished the animal dies. But you understand these things, don't you.'

'We understand this well but there is more to this, isn't there?'

'Yes, you're right. These sacrifices are a sign of what *Messiah* would suffer. His blood would be able to bring pardon to all people.'

'This helps us understand something that we were told about the evening before Jesus was arrested. After they, he and the Twelve had had their supper. In fact, it was just after. Jesus said – and it caused them quite a shock – anyway, he had broken a motzah handed it around then said, "This is my body given for you," then a little later he took a sip from his own cup then said: "This cup is the new covenant in my blood" (Luke 22:19 & 20). Some of those present did not quite know how to take his meaning. As I said, it caused quite a shock but they all drank from his cup. We, too, would like to understand it.'

'The Covenant he spoke of is the same New Covenant that Jeremiah the prophet wrote about centuries ago.[93] Remember he wrote and told the people that God would "put" his "laws in their minds and write it on their hearts". The prophet also said that

---

[93] *Jeremiah 31:31–34.*

the people "*will all know*" God and that he "*will forgive their wickedness*".

'You know, God does not really want to see the sacrifice of animals. The Psalm of David says that the sacrifices that God really wishes to see "*are a broken spirit; a broken and contrite heart God ... will not despise*" (*Psalms* 51:17). There is another Psalm, which says much the same thing: "*Sacrifices and offering you did not desire sin offerings you did not require*" (*Psalms* 40:6). But sacrifice will continue for a little longer and it does have its strong points. It helps us to remember.'

'You mean Passover?'

'I do! We have just celebrated Passover and it was like a foretaste of what the *Messiah* would experience because he is our new Passover lamb. His blood was given for all people, everywhere. What are we told about the first Passover back in Egypt? "*The blood will be a sign for you on the houses where you are; and when I see the blood, I will pass over you. No destructive plague will touch you when I strike Egypt*" (*Exodus* 12:13). So you see with the first Passover God saw the blood on the Hebrews homes and did not allow harm to come to them. Now, God sees the blood of Jesus *Messiah* on the Cross and will not allow harm to those who are his people.'

'*But a cross, it's too awful! Couldn't there have been some other way?*'

'**With God all things are possible but we have been warned what to expect in the Scriptures.**'

'*How do you mean?*'

'One of the Psalms (22)[94] tells us much about crucifixion. "*My God, my God, why have you forsaken me? Why are you so far from saving me, so far from the words of my groaning?*" (*v.*1) "*All who see me mock me; they hurl insults, shaking their heads: he trusts in the LORD; let him rescue him. Let him deliver him*" (*v.*7 & 8). **Do you also remember this? It is also in that same Psalm.**

'"*They divide my garments among them and cast lots for my clothing*" (*v.*18). **Also, I have mentioned Isaiah and what he said of God's Servant that "*he was pierced for our wrongdoing*" (Isaiah 53:5). You see the Psalmist, speaking with the voice of God's Spirit, foretold a death by crucifixion. The prophet was writing about crucifixion.**'

'*Well, we heard those things said and done as we stood near the cross last Friday afternoon,*' said Cleopas's companion. '*Why is it that in the age of* Messiah *we have been*

---

[94] I have put the Psalm number in brackets '(**22**)' because the numbering of chapters, verses and the Psalms was done much later, well after the first century. Chapter and verse, so helpful to us, would have meant nothing to Cleopas and others of his time.

looking forward to his reign and the benefits he will bring to all? That's what we have been expecting. Were we wrong in this? Only days ago we saw Jesus our prophet ride into Jerusalem and we thought that the kingdom had come. We thought of what the Prophet Zechariah had said, "Rejoice greatly, O Daughter of Zion! Shout, Daughter of Jerusalem! See, your king comes to you, righteous and having salvation, gentle and riding on a donkey, on a colt, the foal of a donkey" (Zechariah 9:9). We thought the time had come, then and there!'

'Oh no, it has only begun, the blessings that you hope for are yet to come. The full blessings of *Messiah*'s reign.'

'Yes but when will this be? That time when "the God of heaven will set up a kingdom that will never be destroyed, nor will it be left to another people. It will crush all those kingdoms and bring them to an end, but it will itself endure for ever" (Daniel 2:44). We thought we would live to see that time "when he will swallow up death. The Sovereign LORD will wipe away the tears from all faces; he will remove the disgrace of his people from all the earth" (Isaiah 25:8). We don't understand all this.'

'Ah, I see that you know these Scriptures well and indeed many others which tell of the reign of God's *Messiah*. If you do, you will know that God's Kingdom will not be set up without opposition.

' " *The kings of the earth take their stand and the rulers gather together against the LORD and against his Anointed One. 'Let us break their chains,' they say, 'and throw off their fetters' "* (Psalms 2:2–7).

'I expect that you also know this verse: *"the LORD says to my Lord: 'Sit at my right hand until I make your enemies a footstool for your feet' "* (Psalms 110:1–2).

'If you know it well you will have realised that the promise was made firstly to King David but then to *Messiah* the LORD, in other words our God says to *"my Lord"*, that is the Lord *Messiah*, that he will have the rule of all God's enemies. Now, you want to know when these things will happen, don't you.'

'Of course we do, but can you tell us?'

'No! It is not for men, even the faithful, to know these times. But live in the expectation that what God has promised he will do.'

'Would you kindly tell us what will happen once God's enemies have stopped resisting?'

' " *He will judge between the nations and will settle disputes for many peoples. They will beat their swords into ploughshares and their spears into pruning hooks. Nation will not take up sword against nation, nor will they train for war any more"* (Isaiah 2:4). Also there will come a great time of blessing upon the human race. But there is a warning to be patient, for it is still to come. Do you remember these words?

' "*Strengthen the feeble hands, steady the knees that give way; say to those with fearful hearts, 'Be strong, do not fear, your God will come, he will come with vengeance; with divine retribution he will come to save you.' Then will the eyes of the blind be opened and the ears of the deaf unstopped. Then will the lame leap like a deer, and the mute tongue shout for joy*" (Isaiah 35:3–6). Let me tell you something else; there will be work for you as believers in God's Messiah to do. "*God says, 'I will also make you a light for the Gentiles, that you may bring my salvation to the ends of the earth*'" (Isaiah 49:6).'

'We thought that that was to be Messiah's work.'

'It is, but he will use people like you.'

'Oh, that is a frightening thing to think about. I couldn't do that!'

'Do not be afraid, you will be given power from on high. It is Messiah's work but you will be given inner strength.'

'Perhaps we have never fully understood about Messiah and his power but I have not thought about this and what he may want us to do.'

'In the Book of the Prophet Daniel there is a vision, let me remind you of what Daniel reported. *"In my vision at night I looked, and there before me was one like a son of man, coming with the clouds of heaven. He approached the Ancient of Days and was led into his presence. He was given authority, glory and sovereign power; all peoples, nations and men of every language worshipped him. His dominion is an everlasting dominion that will not pass away, and his kingdom is one that will never be destroyed'* (Daniel 7:13–14). There, that tells you about *Messiah*'s power and the authority God has given him.'

'Ah yes, we remember that Jesus used to refer to himself as "the son of man", we heard him say that about himself more than once. You have told us that we will never know when Messiah will take power, but he did say there would be signs before that happened.'

Cleopas felt his fellow traveller's hand on his arm. *'Cleopas, don't you remember Jesus himself taught about the end times. He spoke about "wars and rumours of wars, famines and earthquakes and false prophets"(Matthew 24:6–7).'*

'You are right, I do remember now and he also said there would be great distress, I seem to remember he quoted a prophecy:

"...the sun will be darkened,
the moon will not give its light;
the stars will fall from the sky,
and the heavenly bodies will be shaken..." [95]

'I think that the prophecy he quoted from is from Isaiah. Is that right?'

'Yes, the first part is from Isaiah. His warnings are also like the writing of the prophet Haggai: *"This is what the LORD Almighty says: 'In a little while I will once more shake the heavens and the earth, the sea and the dry land I will shake all nations, and the desired of all nations will come, and I will fill this house with glory,' says the LORD Almighty"* **(Haggai 2:6–8).'**

'When Haggai wrote that the "desired of all nations will come", was he thinking about the Messiah?'

'Indeed he was!'

'But, surely, Messiah has come already – it's Jesus, isn't it? Oh dear, I'm getting confused.'

'Let me explain. Messiah has come and lived here among us. Messiah will return into heaven but come again at the end of the age. Did he not tell you this?'

---

[95] **Matthew 24:29** here Jesus quoted from **Isaiah 13:10 and 34:4**, although it was not a direct quotation more the inspiration for his words.

'Yes – it's making sense; although, at the time, when we first heard it, it was hard for many of us to take it in. He spoke of returning to the "*Father*" and then he said, "*I will come back and take you to be with me*" (John 14:1-4).' Cleopas stood still and smiled to himself, then to his companion. '*At last, I'm beginning to understand this.*'

'Was there anything else you heard him say or was told that he had said? Do you remember him saying anything about the way he would return?'

'Yes – he said that "*all the nations of the earth ... will see the Son of Man coming in the clouds of the sky, with power and great glory*" (Matthew 24:30).'

The conversation came to an end but the three kept walking. The stranger was the one to break the silence.

'Well, here we are, the village of Emmaus, and I must go on a little further. I have given you much to think about but we finish our discussion at a suitable place, although there is much more to say.'

'Come in, stay with us a while and have something to eat. We have been on the road for a long time.'

'Thank you, it would be good to have something to eat.'

****

A SIMPLE APPROACH TO PROPHECY

We have been looking at the prophecies in the Old Testament, which gave the people of Israel an image of the coming *Messiah*. We noticed that for them these Scriptures did not always give a clear-cut message. In fact, those verses that I have included in the section above are a great deal clearer than many others. Those I have left out were for two reasons: space and, of course, for the very reason that although hopefully having more meaning for first-century Jewry are much less clear for people, Jew or Gentile, in the twenty-first century.

There are several difficulties that we face when trying to properly understand prophecy. At a non-technical level there are three that we ought to consider: <u>language, timing and our interpretation</u> of the prediction.

<u>The language used</u> in prophecy can be poetic or obscure. We usually accept the use of poetic language when speaking or writing about ordinary events. The poet William Wordsworth wrote of seeing a 'host of golden daffodils'. Now, if we wish to be very 'picky' about language we could argue that there is no such thing as an army of daffodils. Also, how dare he use military language when describing a calm peaceable flower that would do not harm to anyone.

When it comes to the poetry of the Jewish Scriptures we have two other matters to consider. One is that there were forms used then which are different to the way poetry is written in the western world now. The other matter is that writers use analogy in poetry, which can be understood by the reader when he compares one thing with another. We start to understand because he uses familiar things. We see that he is saying that something is like something else.

The Hebrew or Israelite poet was better understood in his day than in ours. Perhaps he uses a Hebrew word in an unfamiliar way. The people of his day knew, or could work out, what he meant but sometimes we are struggling to understand him. Language, then as now, changes with the passing of time and through local usage. Fortunately for us, there are experts in Hebrew language and the Hebrew Scriptures to give us some guidance.

<u>What do I mean by 'timing'?</u> My meaning is that on some occasions what was prophesied has: (a) already come to pass, (b) was in the process of coming to pass in the life of Jesus, or (c) would be fulfilled in the future.

Let me give an example where a misunderstanding might occur: the prophet Daniel had predicted in *Chapter 11:31* that '*armed forces will rise up to desecrate the temple fortress and will abolish the daily sacrifice. Then they will set up the abomination that causes deso- lation.*' This foretelling would seem to relate to an act of religious vandalism by the Greeks who ruled Israel at that time. About the year 168 BC the citizens of Jerusalem had revolted. Antiochus their ruler, called Epiphanes, had been away and on returning decided to punish them. The worst punishment would be to disrupt their religious observance. Then, as if that was not enough, he decided to place a pagan statue of Zeus in Jerusalem's Temple. Doing this resulted in much Jewish blood being shed!

Daniel, who lived in late seventh century BC, might have been alluding to the later Roman destruction but the reference to the abolition of *the daily sacrifice* fits better. Without knowing of this outrage we would naturally think that AD 70 is the subject of Daniel's prophecy.

In *Matthew's Gospel, 24 and 25,* Jesus gives teaching on the end times. His listeners would remember from history the events of the second century BC. Jesus reminds them of that first *abomination* and of the *desolation* that resulted. Jesus himself prophesied that similar events were to happen in Jerusalem and that his followers should be ready to go quickly. This occurred about thirty years later. Yes, to understand timing is not always entirely easy.

I have, in the past, heard some rather strange things said about this prophecy. My Bible class leader said that this meant that the Temple at Jerusalem would be rebuilt only to be destroyed again, possibly during his own lifetime. It is clear that the people who stated this had little or no knowledge of the Jewish history of the first century.

In fact, the defiling of the Temple happened three times in Jewish history but the final time was the most important. In AD 70, during the Jewish war, the Roman general Titus captured the Temple and set it on fire. I cannot imagine that his soldiers did not first have a good look around – that itself would have defiled the Most Holy Place – before taking anything that was worthwhile. Visitors to ancient Rome can see a depiction of the pillaging of the Temple on the Arch of Titus on which you can see sacred objects being carried away. These items were believed to have been paraded through the streets of Rome as a celebration of the power of Rome.

There is an irony in the date on which this destruction happened. It occurred, and historians are quietly confident that they are correct, on 9 Av in the Jewish calendar (probably August). As that day in the Hebrew calendar was the anniversary of the first defilement of this holy building in 587–586 BC, it is thought of as one of the saddest days in Jewish history.

<u>Our interpretation</u> of prophecy can sometimes be very unhelpful to others and possibly ourselves! I have already mentioned my Bible Class leader and his view on a future Temple but that was a small error. Others are guilty of taking far worse liberties. The Jehovah's Witness movement, who do not actively call themselves Christian, look at *Daniel 7:13 & 14* and have taken

this to mean that Jesus was given the title 'King in Heaven' in 1914 (these verses are quoted above).[96] Jesus did not have so long to wait. Honour and the *'authority and power'* were given to Jesus after his Resurrection as he informed his disciples at the end of *Matthew's Gospel. 'All authority in heaven and on earth has been given to me'* (28:18).

This is a rather extreme example but one that we can learn from. Orthodox Christians (I am using 'orthodox' in the general sense) can also develop strange ideas. The secret may be to use caution and to compare one part of the Bible with another. This usually helps us to stay away from error.

---

[96] It is not my task to say how the *Witness* movement has arrived at this date but it involves a complex process. This movement, although often looking 'Christian', regards the Church as being in error and that they, the JWs, are separate. But this will only be revealed if Witnesses are carefully questioned.

Chapter 9

THE PERILS OF BEING A PILGRIM

Let's face it, checking in at an airport is usually uneventful and, once you are a regular flier and accustomed to it, rather boring.

Not so on my first flight to Israel. Even before I had begun my first visit to Israel or allowed to go to the departure lounge some very interesting experiences took place. It is a very well-known fact that *El Al*, the Israeli national carrier, has an enviable safety record. I was soon to learn why! Their X-ray machines seemed huge, more suitable for looking into the insides of elephants than suitcases. Then there was my passport – there were questions with that. I had a year or so before visited an Egyptian friend who lives in Alexandria. Who was he? How did I meet him? What was his profession? Eventually I satisfied the Israeli staff.

Then their powerful 'all-seeing' X-ray equipment found something in our case. At that stage neither they nor I knew exactly what. The case was of course opened and an inoffensive library book on Israel was found to be the problem. The barcode on the inside cover had caused a 'blip.' In the end we did clear security and were able to proceed toward the gate. To show their good will and regret for unnecessary delay, we each – my wife and myself – left with a Kit Kat bar. Kosher chocolate!

I am not looking forward to my next trip to Israel. Why? Well, it isn't the country! It is the likely formalities at the airport. The problem is that I have acquired a rather striking and attractive but much more embarrassing visa in my passport. It was from a time about three years ago when I represented a charity. It's much worse than Egypt and it will guarantee even more questions: it is for entry into the *Islamic Republic of Iran*!

Once you have got over the security hurdles at the airport you will be the one asking the questions. The answers are not always so easily dealt with.

WHAT DO YOU EXPECT FROM YOUR TRIP?

If you are anything like me you may have grown up with a mental picture of what a visit to the Holy Land will be like. You may remember scenes from travel brochures photographed to bring in the tourist. They always show the best angle and the prettiest sight. In my case these mental images go back a long way. In my teens there was a memorable black-and-white television series on the beauties of the Holy Land. It looked so idyllic!

Then there are the modern films about the life of Jesus. The outdoor scenes were probably filmed in southern

Europe or north Africa which, as well as being cheaper, give a passable imitation of what first-century Jerusalem looked like or may have looked like. These ideas are of course open to the opinion of the producer who may often be guided by an accountant rather than an expert on the life and times of Jesus and his history.

Naturally, twentieth- and twenty-first-century developments have also taken their toll. However, once into Galilee the tourist/pilgrim should not find so many of these. In Jerusalem it may not be quite so easy.

THE PILGRIMS' JERUSALEM: ESSENTIAL VIEWING!

At this point in the book may I ask the reader's pardon if I seem to be repeating some earlier material. It may be that, if you have read fairly rapidly, you will have a grasp of the facts. Other readers may be glad to take another look at the facts as we visit Jerusalem.

1. The Church of the Holy Sepulchre

Finding this should be no problem. Located in the centre of the Christian Quarter of the Old City, all the local shopkeepers know where it is. There are also some signs but not always at eye level. The present church is the fourth to be built on the site. The Emperor Constantine the Great, a new Christian, built it with the active encouragement of his mother, in the fourth century. This information has been preserved for us in the writings of the Bordeaux Pilgrim (333). Bishop Eusebius the Church historian was present at the

245

dedication ceremony and reported the event in 335. The invading Persians destroyed this original building in 614.

Prior to its dedication as a Christian shrine, this site had a rather chequered history. Before the death of Jesus, the site seems to have been used as a quarry. This fact seems to be borne out by the model of first-century Jerusalem, which can be seen at the Israel Museum[97] and by walking a short distance within the Holy Sepulchre itself. Turn right by the modern mural opposite the entrance and continue on. Through the stonework you will be aware of the underlying rock face. Finally, a steep flight of stairs will lead many feet below street level. This lower level is man-made and not natural.

About a century after the Crucifixion, a pagan Temple was constructed on the site and used for the worship of Aphrodite. This was ordered by the Emperor Hadrian (AD 117–138) and followed the Bar Kochbar revolt[98] against Rome, which showed, at least for a time, that the mighty Roman legions could be outmanoeuvred and shamed. The conflict caused them heavy casualties.

---

[97] This Museum in West Jerusalem contains a scale model of ancient Jerusalem in the year AD 66. It was built from archaeological finds, historical records and comparison with similar cities. Therefore, there is a degree of guesswork although I believe that overall the model is accurate and very well researched.

[98] This was a full-scale revolt against Rome over broken promises that Jerusalem's Temple could be rebuilt. Simeon Bar Kochbar became its leader and many Jews hoped that he was the Messiah. The revolt was a long and hard one and it nearly succeeded.

In the end, in the year 135, the Romans had turned the tide and slaughtered many Jewish troops and civilians. Hadrian's revenge was to put a statue of his horse on the Jewish Temple mount, the most holy place for all Jews. He also targeted Christians and desecrated the Christian site of Jesus's death by building the Temple of Aphrodite.[99]

Years later, partly through the growth of Christian faith and the decline of Roman religion, this building fell into disuse and when Constantine and Bishop Macarius, who did the legwork, began an investigation they found this likely site. Their search was helped when Constantine's mother, Helena, received divine help from a vision. At least, that is the tradition. The site had to be excavated and the Roman Temple demolished before a thorough examination could begin. In this area, Constantine built the Church of Anastasis (the Greek word for 'resurrection') and then the Church of Golgotha. Both of these earlier buildings are now covered by the massive Holy Sepulchre.

The present church was rebuilt in AD 1149, which was during the Crusader period but has undergone many changes as a result of fire, earthquake and necessary repairs and modifications. Some guidebooks say that you should allow three hours for a visit to take in the various crypts and tombs. The Rotunda is the only part

---

[99] Aphrodite was the Greek name for the goddess of love, beauty and fertility. The Romans worshipped her under the name of Venus.

of the church that is thought to bear any resemblance to the original building. At the very centre of the Rotunda (*Aedicule*) is the Holy Sepulchre itself. The only problem with it is that it is no longer possible to see what the original tomb looked like. A square canopy designed in the nineteenth century by a Greek Orthodox Christian covers it.

Before the Sepulchre there is something else to see of equal importance. On entering the church, visitors will see a set of stairs to the right leading to a balcony with altars. This is cut out of a rock face although that is not immediately obvious, as the rock face has been tiled. Pilgrims wishing to climb the stairs are advised that they are steep and the handrail closest to the entrance is not within easy reach. Further along, on the right there is another set of stairs going up to this level that seem a little easier. Those who ascend will be rewarded with beautiful places to stop, pray and photograph. But this is not the main reason for going.

This is believed by many to be the place of crucifixion. It is Golgotha, to give it its Aramaic name, and is also known as Calvary. This is derived from the Latin word *calvaria*, which appears in the Vulgate, a fourth-century Latin version of the Bible.

Constantine was happy to accept this was Golgotha and enclosed it with a courtyard. A very short distance away, a few dozen paces in fact, to the west beyond a hollow he built the Church of Anastasis (Resurrection) on a site believed to be the tomb. Visitors will have to be prepared to stand in line and wait while others enter what may be, for Christians, the holiest site in the world. I took my place at the end of the queue and waited.

As I ducked under the low decorated entrance I felt that I was following Peter and John and the women on the first Easter day. To my right was a raised platform slightly above ground level, which was about six feet long. Three people could kneel in comfort. Certainly the fact that it was on the right fitted the description of the women who *saw a young man dressed in a white robe sitting on the right side* (*Mark 16:5*). It was a deeply enriching experience. In a place of worship and devotion it would be difficult even for an unbeliever to remain unmoved.

As you enter the church, ahead of you is the Stone of Unction a slab of red limestone said, by tradition, to have been the place where the body of Jesus remained after he had been taken down from the cross. The unction was the anointing of his body prior to the sealing of his body in the tomb. Again this seems to be the correct distance from the tomb of Jesus to make this site of the Church of the Holy Sepulchre credible.

As to the exact location of Golgotha, all that can be said with certainty is that it would have been outside the city walls (refer *John 19:20 'near the city'*) while the letter to the *Hebrews 13:12* says that the execution occurred *'outside the city gate'*.

Matthew's Gospel mentions the fact that Joseph of Arimathea had excavated his own tomb himself. *Matthew 27:59–60* tells us that '*Joseph took the body, wrapped it in a clean linen cloth and placed it in his own new tomb that he had cut out of the rock.*'

The Synoptic Gospels are silent on the location. It is only John's Gospel that gives us details about the whereabouts: '*At the place where Jesus was crucified, there was a garden, and in the garden a new tomb, in which no one had ever been laid*' (*John 19:41*). John also mentions that it was the '*Day of Preparation*' (*v.42*) indicating that the arrangements made by Joseph and Nicodemus were temporary. It is possible that their thinking was that later, once the shame of crucifixion had passed, the body of Jesus could then be taken discretely to a family tomb.

I left the Church of the Holy Sepulchre with a good feeling. I had experienced a sense of worship as I had examined the building and its contents but there was something else to look at and that was the alternative site of the crucifixion and burial of Jesus.

After a brief stop for a necessary drink, I made my way to this second place. I wanted to know which was the more likely place for the burial of Jesus.

2.   The Garden Tomb

The Garden Tomb is found a short distance north of the Damascus Gate; west of Gordon's Calvary, this is the well-known site of the rock face with holes. If you have the Damascus Gate behind you, there are two roads on the other side of the street going away from you in a northerly direction. Take the narrower one to your right. This is the Nablus Road. The address to look for is in Conrad Schick Street. Look for a signpost on the right and then turn right. One travel guide is enraptured likening it to an English country garden and speaking of its being tranquil. There is no doubt it is a very beautiful spot.

The history of the Garden Tomb can be traced back to General Charles Gordon of Khartoum, who spent some months based in Jerusalem during the year 1883. Gordon was a devout Christian and as he looked out from his lodging he noticed a compelling-looking rock face. It had a skull-like appearance and the General became convinced that this was the real *'place of the skull'*. His further investigation in that area brought him to an ancient garden tomb. Gordon was totally convinced that this was *the place* and was able to convince others. After Gordon's death at Khartoum, the garden was purchased. This occurred in 1893. Excavations on this site disclosed a wine press and a water cistern.

This, then, is another contender for the burial place of Jesus! Unfortunately, although the site is popular with many Christians its credentials are really no stronger than Holy Sepulchre. The Garden Tomb is one of many similar burial places in the area, some of which would fit the New Testament's description well.

Archaeological work conducted during the 1960s by Kathleen Kenyon would seem, fairly conclusively, to place it outside the city's walls of the first century and so, by reason of location, it seems right. However, trying to find likely sites around the present walled city is complicated by the fact that first-century Jerusalem was approximately double the area of the present Old City.

Another point of contention is when exactly this tomb was hewn from the soft rock. Archaeologists vary in dating it and estimates range between 200 BC–AD 200. There is one suggestion that the tomb was part of a Byzantine cemetery. This would mean that it was excavated during the fourth century.

There are huge variations in the style of the tombs of this period, many have antechambers and with many there are recesses cut into the walls. The style and size would of course depend on the wealth of the owner and the size of the family.

From its description we know that the tomb of Joseph of Arimathea would have been fairly roomy because two angels of human size were seen on either side of where the body of Jesus had been placed, one at the head and another at the end where his feet had been. The body might have been at floor level or on a raised platform.

The entrance to tombs was, during this period, low and would mean stooping to look in. This agrees with the report of *John's Gospel* (*John 20:5*): '*He'* (the first of Jesus's disciples to reach the tomb after Mary Magdalene's report, *v.2*) '*bent over and looked in at the strips of linen lying there but did not go in.*' It is obvious that the place, within the tomb, where Jesus had been laid could not be seen from directly in front; you would have needed to stoop and look in. Mary Magdalene and her companions arrived, looked in and '*they saw a young man ... dressed in white sitting on the right side'* (*Mark 16:5*). This followed another angel's invitation to the women to: ' "*Come and see the place where he lay"* ' (*Matthew 28:6*).

This description helps us to better understand the events of Good Friday and Easter Day. To begin with it explains why Mary Magdalene and her companion knew so well what they had to do to give the body of Jesus the last rites. They knew exactly what they needed to bring on the following Sunday morning after the Sabbath had ended. How could they be so sure?

The answer is, as we have seen (see Chapter 5), that Joseph and Nicodemus, probably with help from others, wrapped the body outside for observers to see. There was not enough room inside. Once they had completed their temporary dressing of the body they would have, probably with some difficulty, manoeuvred it into the tomb.

This also helps us to make sense of the women's question as they travelled to the tomb. ' "*Who will roll the stone away from the entrance of the tomb?"* ' (*Mark*

16:3). It would seem that they knew that the stone was of the common 'cork' type and not the less common groove variety. With this type they would have needed several very able-bodied men to move it.

It also makes the fear of the chief priests more reasonable. That ' *"his disciples may come and steal the body and tell the people that he has been raised from the dead. This last deception will be worse than the first"* ' (*Matthew 27:64*).

IMPRESSIONS AND EVALUATION

My first impressions of the Garden Tomb were delightful. There had been no hype – the guidebook description was accurate, there are trees and plants everywhere. Even better, the site is well geared for pilgrims. It has toilets and there is a shop. It is a location where there are places for group or individuals to worship. It is also, at the time of writing, open every day apart from Sunday. There are also guides giving talks to help the visitor appreciate the Easter event.

The tomb itself lies in a hollow. This is likely to have been the result of earlier quarrying. With the positive experience of the Holy Sepulchre I realised that I had to keep an open mind and review the facts. So, does it measure up to the New Testament?

That is not a simple answer. What appeals is that this tomb is certainly closer in condition to the first century! The trappings of the Holy Sepulchre are absent. You do not have to use so much imagination. Inside this tomb are places for two bodies to be lain. As with the Holy Sepulchre site you have to look to your right. So far so good!

Let's now think about the differences. We have noted that the type of stone described in the Gospels appears to be of the 'cork' type, which could be handled by one able-bodied man. At the Garden Tomb there is an obvious groove although the sealing stone[100] that had to be rolled down the ramp cannot be seen. Does this rule out the site? Well, on the surface we have difficulties. But there is no serious obstacle to believing in the Garden Tomb. To begin with we have seen that Joseph did not think of this internment as being a permanent event. So, it is possible that this was a family tomb and may have been altered at a later stage by Joseph or later family members. In its present state the Garden Tomb seems to be too large to fit the New Testament's description.

From the eastern side of the garden we look out at the skull-like rock face where many Christians believe Jesus died.

3.   Gordon's Calvary

As we have just mentioned this lies next to the Garden Tomb. It is literally a stone's throw. Charles Gordon's imagination was fired by the holes in this hillock but in

---

[100] Readers may find it useful to look again at the section *The Stone That Sealed the Tomb* in Chapter 6.

point of fact there is some dispute as to how ancient they really are. These 'eyeholes' may be due to excavations carried out in relatively recent centuries. During New Testament times the shape is likely to have been rather different. It may not have had the skull-like appearance. On the top of the cliff is a Muslim cemetery. At the bottom there is a bus station.

We still have to deal with the name '*skull*' and each of the four Gospel writers mention it as something an inhabitant, or a visitor to Jerusalem would know or soon learn about. Matthew, Mark and John also give the Aramaic name Golgotha. Only Luke, believed to be a Gentile, does not bother with this.

We know it is said that the skull of Adam was found buried there but the origin of this is uncertain. Another idea is that a skull, or skulls, of executed criminals could be seen there. Romans crucifying prisoners might not have been concerned about this but Jews would not allow human remains to lie about unburied. In fact, any Jew facing crucifixion would be considered doubly cursed if his body was not quickly removed before sunset, having suffered the curse of being '*hung from a tree*' (*Deuteronomy 21:22–23*). God's law stated that this was a defilement of the land.

There are, of course, several other sites or areas that have been suggested for the crucifixion. One of these is worth mentioning. Bishop Eusebius, the historian who attended the dedication of the original churches had his own ideas about the place of Jesus's death and rising. He placed the site north of Mount Zion. This would mean that it would have been close to the present Old City walls in the area near where the Dormition Abbey now stands. So, did Eusebius have a change of mind or did he consider that to challenge his Emperor's project was a lost cause? In his favour is the fact that he lived at a time closer to the event we call the Passion of Christ.

4.   The Temple Mount

This is an area that is sacred to Jew, Christian and Muslim. In Hebrew it is called **Har Habayit** – 'the mountain of the house'. In Arabic **Haram esh Sharif** – 'the noble sanctuary'.[101] For the pilgrim or tourist there will be no problem in locating it as it dominates the Old City of Jerusalem's skyline.

For Jews and Christians its original importance is the fact that it was the site of Abraham's supreme test of faith when he thought that God was really asking him to sacrifice his son.[102] Mount Moriah, the place of this test, has an importance that pre-dates the formation of the Hebrew nation that Moses helped to form. Jerusalem seems to have had several names before King David conquered it during his reign (1000–962 BC). At that time it was called Jebus. It is likely that this city was the Salem of which Melchizedek was king (see *Genesis 14:18–20*). There

---

[101] Jerusalem is the third of Islam's holy cities, following Mecca and then Medina.
[102] See *Genesis 22*.

are references to Jerusalem in Egyptian literature from about 1800 BC.

Solomon, whose reign followed his father, David, began building the first Temple about 957 and finished it some seven years later. The last Temple, also built on the Mount, was begun by King Herod the Great (Herod the First) in 20–19 BC and the main building was complete ten years later and became the centre of Jewish worship. Some minor work continued until AD 64. The building was destroyed by the Romans six years later in AD 70.

THE DOME OF THE ROCK with its golden dome is most prominent and is built on the Most Holy Place (Holy of Holies) of the Jewish Temple. Caliph Abd-el-Malik built the Dome in AD 691. It is claimed, by Muslims, that the rock over which the shrine is built was the place where Prophet Mohammed ascended to paradise. This ought never to be thought of as a mosque; it is what is called a *mashhad*, a centre for pilgrims.

When the Crusaders took over the city, the building was converted for Christian worship about AD 1100. In 1187, the Crusaders were defeated by Salah-a-Din and the building was once again used for Islamic worship. So sacred is this site that non-Muslims are precluded from entering the building.

The area of the Temple Mount is important for Christians because of the events leading up to the Passion, most particularly, when Jesus entered to expel the traders who had turned the holy place into a commercial centre. The Temple was also a place where the very early Christian Church used to gather *'in the temple courts and from house to house, they never stopped teaching and proclaiming the good news that Jesus is the Christ'* (*Acts* 5:42).

THE EL AQSA MOSQUE is the main centre for Islamic worship in Jerusalem and lies south of the Dome of the Rock. It was built in the eighth century, then was used for secular purposes by the Crusaders (eleventh century) before being rededicated by Salah-a-Din. The mosque saw the murder of King Abdullah of Jordan in 1951 and was the victim of an arson attack by an Australian tourist in 1969.

Many Orthodox Jews and others less orthodox but hostile to Arab influence wish to see the Temple Mount back in Israeli hands.

The easiest way of entering the Temple Mount, at the present time,[103] is to find the Dung Gate and with the El Aqsa Mosque on your right continue on towards the security barriers for those wishing to visit the Western (Wailing) Wall. Do not join the long queue of people! They are going to see the Wailing Wall.

Go to the right of this and there is a passageway, which will lead into another security point. Once you are clear

---

[103] I can take no responsibility for any changes although at the moment I think them unlikely. Please remember that this is a political hotspot!

of this you will ascend a walkway that has marvellous views of the worshippers at the Wall and will bring you onto the Temple Mount.

5.   The Western (Wailing) Wall

This is located in the Jewish Quarter of the city. In the absence of the Temple itself it is the holiest place in Jerusalem. Jews come here in the belief that their prayers will be 'hotlined' to God. In the crevices between the stones countless petitions are placed. Boys ready for *bar mitzvah* are brought here, from overseas, for this very Jewish rite of passage. So important is the site that it is almost impossible to be alone here whatever the time of day. It is likely that you will see newly wedded couples here. If you wish to avoid crowds stay away on Fridays and Jewish festivals!

Visitors will have their belongings scanned electronically by Israeli security before being allowed close to the wall. Bareheaded males will be given a *kippur* (Jewish skull cap) to wear.

Before you go through security you may meet someone who asks you for money. It might be for a donation to a cause. Officially, begging is forbidden in the area but 'unofficially' be prepared to meet a forest of outstretched hands and imploring looks on your way to the security barrier. It is also likely to be a fruitful place for that scourge of tourists and pilgrims – the pickpocket!

6. Gethsemane and the Church of All Nations

This is located at the foot of the Mount of Olives and would have been on the road to Bethany that was about two miles east from the centre of Old Jerusalem. The village of Bethany was the place where Lazarus and his sisters Mary and Martha lived. It was here that Jesus and his disciples spent most of their evenings during the last few days prior to his arrest.

The Garden of Gethsemane forms part of the grounds of the Church of All Nations. This is also called the Basilica of the Agony. Today this area is surrounded by a stone wall and that may have been the case in Jesus's day because John's Gospel mentions the fact that Jesus and *'his disciples went into it'* (*John 18:1*). Later Jesus, seeing the arresting party approaching, *'went out and asked them. "Who is it you want?"'* (*18:40*). Only John describes it as a 'garden'. It has been suggested that this was a plot privately owned by one of the group of other disciples or by someone sympathetic to his teaching. Luke's Gospel is less specific but he tells us that here was a regular meeting place: *'Jesus went out as usual to the Mount of Olives ... the place'* (*Luke 22:39–40*). Clearly this was well known so that Judas knew where to bring the Temple police.

Luke also records the anguish of the place as Jesus struggled in prayer and perspired at the fearful thought of what was so soon to happen to him (*Luke 22:41–44*).

In this area there is also the Grotto of the Agony, a site, which is maintained by the Franciscans and should be looked at by any serious student of the life and Passion of Jesus as it does stake a claim to be the garden where the arrest of Jesus occurred.

'That tree is 2,500 years old,' the guide to Gethsemane and the Church of All Nations told me, pointing to a gnarled old olive next to the church. He could possibly be correct but historic records and botanists are not convinced. At best these are the descendents of the trees under which Jesus anguished before his arrest.

When planning to visit you could go to the viewing area of the Mount of Olives and if the weather is not too hot walk down the hill. This is not very steep and the traffic should not be a great problem. On the way down you pass the ornate Russian Orthodox Church of Mary Magdalene. Male visitors should avoid wearing shorts and ladies, wishing to enter, are best advised to cover their shoulders. This minor road will bring you down behind All Nations and Gethsemane.

To help visitors there is a Mount of Olives information centre near by. With All Nations in front of you turn right and it is about two minutes walk on the opposite side to the church.

Let me end with a warning. If you are, as you read this, planning a pilgrimage or visit you may have a glossy brochure to look at. This may show the eight olive trees heavy with foliage. This is a sight that you will almost certainly not see again. To keep these ancient trees in good health experts come every year from Italy to lovingly tend them and to prune the branches.

7. Bethlehem (Beit Lahm)

This town lies six miles south of Jerusalem and is served by frequent buses from near the Damascus or Jaffa Gates or the main bus station. It sounds like an easy excursion. It isn't straightforward!

IMPORTANT: before beginning a visit a few vital preparations must be made. Get out your passport and take it with you. The reason for this is that you will have to pass through the newly built security wall. Once there they will probably take little interest in your passport. I had mine in my hand but for all they knew it may have belonged to another person. My great advantage was my Western European appearance. Had I been dark-skinned, then it may have been different.

I took a number 124 bus from the Bus Station close to the Damascus Gate. This is immediately in front of Gordon's Calvary. I sat back and awaited events. After a few minutes travel, at approximately halfway the bus came to a stop with the Wall in front. Getting through was not a problem once I had worked out the rather ambiguous signs. On the other side it was necessary to take a taxi for the last five kilometres (three miles) to Bethlehem.

Bethlehem is a town that is changing. Its citizens were once mainly Christian Arabs. This has changed during the last few years with many moving away. The majority of the population is now Muslim. They make their living from tourism and selling crafts to visitors.

The main attraction is the **Church of the Nativity**, which is just off Manger Square. In 336, Constantine had a basilica built over a cave, which was then on the outskirts of the village, to mark the site of where, by tradition Jesus was born. The original basilica was demolished about 200 years later and replaced by the present building that seems to have survived from this period without major alterations. This was built by Justinian (528–565) and intended to vie with anything that Jerusalem could produce.

The inside of the church is really quite modest having stone pillars and an oak ceiling. The Grotto of the Nativity is reached from either end of the Greek Orthodox High Altar. As usual pilgrims are directed to form an orderly line. The grotto is rather compact in size being some twelve metres in length. It is lit by fifty-three lamps and beneath the Altar is a silver star set into the floor with a Latin inscription declaring that it was here that Jesus was born of the Virgin Mary. Greek Orthodox, Latins and Armenians administer this church, as they do others of the Holy sites.

About a mile out of the town is **Beit Sahur**, the 'village of the shepherds,' this is where, by tradition, the angel of the Lord announced to the shepherds the birth of Jesus. They were soon joined by *'a great company of the heavenly host who appeared with the angel, praising God and saying, "Glory to God in the highest, and on earth peace to men on whom his favour rests" '* (*Luke 2:13–14*).

This traditional site is a few minutes drive downhill from Manger Square. The shepherds would have faced a steep walk uphill if the traditionalists are correct. And what would these men who were considered unclean, by the nature of their work, have felt? What would their reception be like? We are not told but their directions from the angel would have assured them of a welcome.

Going back well into Old Testament times, about 1,100 years before, this is the village where Boaz met Ruth. We can read their story in *Ruth Chapter 2*. They were the great grandparents of King David who is an ancestor of Jesus (*Ruth 4:22*).

IS THIS A GUIDEBOOK?

The answer to the question is a definite 'no'! I have put down the findings of my most recent[104] visit to the Holy Land knowing that it could be of help, especially if you are going out on your own. It is rather limited because time did not allow a long visit. A month would have meant a fuller report. But this could not happen. A warning – some of this information could be changed fairly quickly. Other facts will remain the same. So, please do feel free to check this data.

If you are with a party with an experienced guide, this will be of little help. However, while I'm on the subject of guides and guidebooks let me give a warning. Some printed guides that I have come across were seriously

---

[104] November 2007.

out of date! Unfortunately, this included one I received from the *Israeli Government Tourist Office*. Yes, it was free, but there were some factual errors caused by change of circumstances. Another guidebook I have looked at had some historic errors. The answer to this is to choose one from a reputable publisher that has been recently revised.

THE FINAL HURDLE!

Readers will have realised that I did not, in the event, have any problems getting through Passport Control at Tel Aviv's, Ben Gurion Airport. Perhaps the girl did not notice the Visa. Perhaps she was feeling sleepy at 6 a.m. and did not want any hassle. I certainly didn't! It was good that I did not have to produce my 'backup' – a letter from the Israeli Consulate in London that confirmed Iranian stamps in British Passports would be no problem.

Chapter 10

THE JESUS OF FAITH AND HUMANKIND

So far in this volume we have been considering the Jesus of history, more exactly the Jesus of the Gospels; now we will think about the 'Jesus of Faith'.[105] Many of the beliefs concerning the Jesus of Faith have to do with his role after his being seen to be taken up into heaven, the event Christians call the Ascension.

Many people know at least a little about the events beginning with the betrayal of Jesus until his Resurrection but what of later?

Following his Resurrection appearances he was accessible to the apostles. Then they saw him removed; taken away from them. This is called 'the Ascension.' What is its significance and what difference did it make for them? What is its importance for people in the twenty-first century? So, let's begin with the subject of the Ascension.

---

[105] What do I mean by this phrase? I mean the Jesus that Bible-believing Christians follow. There is the thought, among some, that 'faith' and fact are opposed to each other. No – faith is based on solid fact. I also include this footnote because Rudolph Bultmann has used this phrase in another way. He seems to have been less sure of the Bible. Please also refer to footnote 7 in Chapter 1.

THE ASCENSION

Many people, quite happy to call themselves Christians, would probably not be happy if asked to explain the meaning of Ascension Day. Yes, they might be able to tell you what happened and tell you that it is celebrated forty days after Easter but then the flow of information may start to dry up. The meaning behind the events could well be unknown. If this is the case with believers then what is the understanding of those who are not convinced Christians? It's unlikely to be very much unless they have made a deliberate study. Ascension Day is both neglected and not clearly understood.

As Ascension Day is forty days after Easter it has the misfortune to occur midweek. Other main Christian holy days happen on Sundays with the exception of Good Friday and Christmas Day. Easter and Pentecost happen on Sundays so there is an easy opportunity for the Christian faithful to come along to a service of worship.

What is this all about? If we only go by the importance that churchgoers usually give to the Ascension then we lose its significance. We celebrate Christmas and we remember Easter, we ought to rejoice at Pentecost when the Holy Spirit of God came down on the believers in Jesus. But what do we make of Ascension? It is a festival that doesn't fall on a Sunday and may be neglected partly because of that very fact.

It occurs on a Thursday, which is not such a good day for a church service. During the past, this was not the case and often people would be given time off to celebrate Ascension. But that was a long time ago. So, let me see if I can bring some more understanding on its meaning.

WHAT HAPPENED AT 'THE ASCENSION'?

After the first Easter Day, Jesus's eleven apostles and other disciples had a number of encounters with the risen Christ. He was, so the Apostle Paul tells us, seen by *'five hundred of the brothers at the same time'*.[106] Luke tells us that Jesus *'appeared to them over a period of forty days and spoke about the kingdom of God'* (*Acts 1:3*).

Then came the Ascension. On that actual day Jesus led his apostles out onto the Mount of Olives. We do not know from Luke's account who these people were. Nor do we know where they began their journey to the place from where Jesus was to leave them. It would appear to be in or near Jerusalem. It is possible that they met in the Garden of Gethsemane.

Luke tells us that they had received instruction to remain in Jerusalem until they received power from the Holy Spirit of God. Jesus then gave them his blessing (*Luke*

---

[106] Paul, in *1 Corinthians 15:6*, mentions six appearances but he is not concerned with the number of times, nor perhaps with the order of the appearances, but with the people that Jesus had appeared to. Although Paul uses the word *brothers*, it would be wrong to exclude 'sisters' from this gathering.

24:49–51) – at that *'moment, he left them and was taken up into heaven'*. However, Luke then gives us further information in ***Acts Chapter 1***, which was written later than the Gospel. In this account he reports that, '*...he* (Jesus) *was taken up before their very eyes, and a cloud hid him from their sight. They were looking intently up into the sky as he was going, when suddenly two men* (angels) *dressed in white stood beside them. "Men of Galilee," they said, "why do you stand here looking into the sky? This same Jesus, who has been taken from you into heaven, will come back in the same way you have seen him go into heaven"* ' (*Acts 1:9–11*).

Then there was another appearance that occurred earlier, which is important to our thinking about the subject of Ascension. This occurred in Galilee and is recorded for us at the end of ***Matthew's Gospel*** (*28:18– 20*). Jesus had arranged a mountain rendezvous. Some of his disciples who gathered there had doubts. ' *"All authority in heaven and on earth has been given to me,"* ' Jesus assured them. The group appears to be much larger than Eleven. How large a collection of people we are not told. This may well have been the *'five hundred'* that Paul mentioned. These people, about to become the Church, were given their mandate. In fact this event is known as *The Great Commission*.

'Therefore go and make disciples of all nations, baptising them in the name of the Father and of the Son and of the Holy Spirit, and teaching them to obey everything I have commanded you. And surely I am with you always, to the very end of the age.'

After the Ascension they then, joyfully and confidently, returned quietly to their homes and awaited the coming of the Holy Spirit who would fill them with power. The coming of God's Spirit happened at the Feast of Pentecost[107] (which is also called *Shavuot* in Hebrew) when Jerusalem was again filled with pilgrims. This was ten days after the Ascension.

Those readers who know their way around the New Testament will probably wish to ask some questions at this point. Some may ask: if this is such an important event, why is it that only two of the Gospel writers report it? Luke, as mentioned above, does so twice, firstly at the very end of his Gospel then more fully at the very start of the Book of Acts. But what of the other Gospel writers – why are two of them silent?

The answer to this is probably that the young Church would have been taught about it and knew that Jesus had physically risen from the earth. What they needed to understand was the consequences for Jesus himself and for his own people. This would have been necessary for this almost exclusively Jewish Church, who thought of God's *Messiah* reigning on earth and not from heaven. His earthly reign is yet to be.

Also the significance of the event, what it really meant for the Church, far surpasses what had occurred on the Mount of Olives on that Thursday. His disciples knew

---

[107] Pentecost means 'fiftieth' and was the Jewish Feast that followed Passover. It occurs fifty days after. The Church has taken the name 'Pentecost' but it does not now occur fifty days after Easter unless Passover and Easter fall together.

that Jesus's power and authority was absolute from their meeting with him in Galilee.

Let's take an earthly example and compare that. In the case of Queen Elizabeth II, upon the death of her father (February 1952) she became Queen but this was made formal and constitutional at her coronation (June 1953). On the death of her father all the power of the monarchy passed to her. To say that this was the same for Jesus as he went into heaven is to grossly understate the meaning. However, it is possible to see his return to heaven as something similar to a coronation. The Ascension, in some sense, confirmed his kingship. We remember his informing his apostles and others that: ' *"All authority in heaven and on earth has been given to me"* ' (*Matthew 28:18*).

Luke took this well-known teaching and wrote about it for the benefit of the future Church and especially for those of Gentile origin who were attracted to the teaching of Jesus. The other reference to the physical Ascension, it is in Mark's Gospel[108] *Chapter 16:19.*

---

[108] There are a very few passages of the New Testament that scholars are uncertain about, *Mark 16:9–20* does not appear in some manuscripts. It is for this reason that in some versions of the Bible there is what is called the 'Longer Ending' (*verses 9–20*). To be authentic a Gospel has to be written by a companion of Jesus or based on eyewitness reports of events during his earthly ministry. We are not totally certain about where this passage comes from, but a look at the 'Shorter Ending' seems to end abruptly, possibly as if something had been lost or awaited further details. It is a mystery! *The Jerusalem Bible* wisely states, '*this ending to the Gospel may not have been written by Mark, though it is old enough.*' Jerusalem Bible, Geoffrey Chapman, 1971.

THE MEANING OF THE ASCENSION

The first and most obvious meaning of the Ascension is that it marked a turning point for the followers of Jesus. They now knew that he had physically left them for good. His resurrected body would no more be available to them. In its place he gave them the promise of sending his Holy Spirit to empower them. There is another way of considering this. We ought to think of it not so much as an ending but as a new beginning as the Church moved into Mission mode; when, a few days later, it began proclaiming the transforming power of Jesus to those who would believe, trust and then follow him.

We in the twenty-first-century look at this event as historical. For Jesus the event was also eternal as he passed from the world of time and space into the heavenly realm where time no longer governs life. All of the apostles must have glimpsed the fact that Jesus's Ascension was the climax of his Resurrection, the highest point of his earthly life.

Normally, when a close friend leaves there is a period of sadness. If any who were present on that occasion felt this it was quickly replaced *'with great joy'* (*Luke 24:5*). Also, there was work to be done. As well as the Eleven there were other close followers of Jesus – well over a hundred people in all. They had a meeting shortly afterwards and Peter took charge, dealing with certain matters of administration (*Acts 1:12–26*). It all sounds rather humdrum until we read in the very last verse of Luke's Gospel that *'they stayed continually at the temple praising God.'*

What caused them to be so joyful? Firstly and most obviously, they had seen that Jesus was alive and not just alive but living in a human body that although able to be physically touched was unlimited by solid obstacles. Next was the fact that: *'All authority in heaven and on earth'* had *'been given to him'* (*Matthew 28:18*), this meant that he was no less than God. These followers of Jesus believed, as the Apostle Paul later wrote that Jesus is *'at the right hand of God'* (*Romans 8:34*). The meaning of this was totally clear particularly in the first century.

In both eastern and Roman culture the idea of being at the *'right hand'* of a king or emperor meant that power was shared. This right was given to the heir to a throne, normally the eldest son. With several of ancient Israel's ageing monarchs their son, the new king-in-waiting, would be equal to his father. He would have been known as a co-regent because he had the same authority as the king.

Just as with a king, Jesus is sharing the rule with God his Father. So, as they believed that God was with them, they also believed that Jesus was present in their lives by the Holy Spirit. It was true that, in some ways, they would have felt very much alone. After all, the general population had just before Passover, a few short weeks before, rejected Jesus as God's Christ and shouted, ' *"crucify"* '. Their task was to change some hostile minds[109] and proclaim the good news that Jesus had conquered death[110] and had brought freedom for humankind. There would have been times when they felt that for them it was an impossible task. In spite of this they knew that in the power of Jesus anything was achievable. Jesus had the means to provide his Church with everything they needed for his mission in the world. He had assured them that they would succeed in the work to which he was sending them.

Again let's look at the words of Paul from *Philippians 2:9–11*. '*Therefore God exalted him to the highest place and gave him the name that is above every name, that at the name of Jesus every knee should bow, in heaven and on earth and under the earth, and every tongue confess that Jesus Christ is Lord, to the glory of God the Father.*' This truly staggering fact was what gave the followers of Jesus the will to continue.

'THE MAN WHO IS GOD'

The words, immediately above, were used by Graham Kendrick, a modern hymn writer to explain the nature of Jesus Christ. Man – also God? Does it make sense? Well, it is true that many have struggled with this

---

[109] It is likely that few people were actively hostile to Jesus. Many may have had an uneasy conscience as they remembered his dignity and the compassion that he had shown on the Cross.

[110] This should be thought of mainly as the *death* of not being in communion with God. This, of course, influences physical death because if we have real faith that Jesus died but now lives, then death has been overcome. His promise given to those dedicated to him is that they can also defeat death because of his triumph.

meaning. I remember being a youth group leader many years ago and one of my younger teenagers suggesting that Jesus was *'half-and-half'*. Which half was Man and which part he thought was God I dread to think. This is totally wrong! However, to have given him teaching of the New Testament at the end of that lesson when this lad was ready to go home for Sunday lunch would, especially for someone of his age, have been a bit too much!

This boy's idea may have led him to the belief that Jesus was some kind of superman. The pages of the New Testament do not give us any reason to think in this way. We will think a little more about this below.

It will be helpful if we begin this section with a brief look at one of the statements of the Nicene[111] Creed. This is the faith, which Christians use as a measure of what they can and ought to believe about God the Father and Jesus Christ. There are also many more statements of faith in this creed, which we will not need to think about now.

I imagine that some readers let out a loud sigh at the mention of 'creed'. If you are from a Free Church background the words may not be very familiar. However, the teaching of your church will, or should

---

[111] The Nicene Creed was produced at a town called Nicea, which is now Iznik in Western Turkey. On the agenda of this conference was the nature of Jesus and how the Church should view him. The fully correct name of the Creed the Council produced is the Nicene-Constantinopolitan Creed (AD 381).

be, based on this creed. Yes, your tradition of worship will be founded on its teaching. If you have little or no church background it may sound a very uninteresting subject – even boring. Well, don't worry; I will try to make it interesting and relevant to our thinking. This is the bit that we should consider:

God from God, Light from Light. True God from true God, begotten, not made; of one being with the Father.

Let us look at each of these statements one by one[112] and see what we can learn from them. *God from God* means that Jesus shares God's essential nature.[113] John the beloved Apostle, in the Prologue (opening) of his Gospel, says this of Jesus. *'In the beginning was the Word, and the Word was with God, and the Word was God. He was with God in the beginning. Through him all things were made; without him nothing was made that has been made' (John 1:1–3)*. In Hebrew thinking, the *'Word'* of God and his action are the same. The *'Word'* reveals something of the mind of God and also begins to reveal the nature and purposes of God for humankind.

This was not just the idea of John, because Jesus also believed that he was divinely equal with God. On one occasion he seems to have become exasperated in a

---

[112] This subject is so vast that I will use only two or three quotations. There are many more available.

[113] In more technical books on this subject the word used is *homoousios;* this is a Greek word, *homo* meaning 'the same' and *ousios* meaning 'substance or essence'.

discussion and told his hearers, ' *"before Abraham was born, I am!"* ' (*John 8:58*). This claim that Jesus made was to answer a challenge from the Pharisees in the Temple about his authority. During this the name of Abraham had come up and the Pharisees had shown great confidence that Abraham was their forefather. This was a very reasonable claim because the Hebrew Scriptures (Old Testament)[114] told them so, but they were putting too much confidence in this fact.

Jesus's words, ' *"I am"* ', produced an enormous shock! The jaws of the Pharisees and others would have dropped open! What Jesus claimed in these two words can be traced back to Moses's first encounter with God. This had been when he had seen a bush from which flames roared. This was not an unknown sight except that the bush was not being destroyed. God had caused this phenomenon. Moses, when he had recovered from shock, asked God's name and was told by the heavenly voice, ' *"I AM WHO I AM"* ' (*Exodus 3:14*). Jesus was claiming to be God!

Light from Light – this phrase again refers to the character of God. '*God is light; in him there is no darkness at all*' (*1 John 1:5*). Jesus shares this light and reflects it. '*In him was life, and that life was the light of men*' (*John 1:4*).

---

114 In fact God tells Abraham that he will be *the father of many nations* (*Genesis 17:4*) and not just the father of what was to become the Jewish nation.

True God from true God.

This statement would appear to come from someone who felt that 'i's needed to be dotted and 't's crossed. I imagine that a legal mind, or minds, helped to frame this. If we look into the background of the debate we see this to have been necessary.

Begotten, not made.

Once again the scholars at Nicea were making sure that there could be no mistake about the divine nature of Christ. But here their use of the word 'begotten' was based directly on the New Testament. Let us use **John 3:16** as an example: '*For God so loved the world that <u>he gave his one and only Son</u>, that whoever believes in him shall not perish but have eternal life.*' Our modern English versions do not like the word 'begotten'. It is old-fashioned and is not used in present day English. The words underlined above '<u>**one and only Son**</u>' would have been the one word '<u>**begotten**</u>' in earlier versions of the Bible. For example the *Authorised Version*, sometimes called the *King James* (AD 1611), uses it. The meaning is that a father can only 'beget', or pass on his own nature when a child is conceived. At the time of the Conference at Nicea there was a false idea around that God had decided to 'make' Jesus a son by some kind of adoption. This would have been seen as a reward or recognition for all he had done on earth.

This was not good enough! The bishops and other delegates working out the creed would, had there been any doubts, looked into the Old Testament and would have discovered that God's *Messiah* was fully God. *'For to us a child is born, to us a son is given, and the government will be on his shoulders. And he will be called Wonderful Counsellor, Mighty God, Everlasting Father, Prince of Peace'* (*Isaiah 9:6*).

Further confirmation on the real nature of Jesus could be found in the Book of Psalms: *'Your throne, O God, will last for ever and ever; a sceptre of justice will be the sceptre of your kingdom. You love righteousness and hate wickedness; therefore God, your God, has set you above your companions by anointing you with the oil of joy'* (*45:6–7*). Anyone present at the Conference should have known that the reference to *'anointing'* could only mean Jesus. God's *Messiah* is, after all the anointed one.

Let us come back to my discussion with the young lad and his misunderstanding of the nature of Jesus. My answer to him would have been in this form but probably not using these words: the New Testament does not analyse this in the way we modern humans would like it to. This seems to be rather remiss of the New Testament writers not to tell us. The most probable answer is that they themselves did not fully understand. God had either not told them or said that we, the Church then and now, had had enough Holy mysteries to be going on with. Having said this, the teaching of the New Testament does give us some valuable clues.

So, how does the New Testament help us? Here are some key verses: *'For in Christ all the fullness of the Deity lives in bodily form' (Colossians 2:9)*. The human person of Jesus is full of the divine essence or, as the compilers of the Nicene Creed would state it, *God from God*.

As I mentioned earlier the New Testament does not always give us specific answers and this is an example. So my Bible class member may not have had his understanding broadened. All we can do is to develop a hypothesis, a workable idea that stands up to inspection. This process can be assisted by what is called Christian philosophy. This may not give us the totally correct answer but measured against Scripture it should not stray too far.

Had circumstances been different the conversation might have gone along these lines: ' *"David, if Jesus is both God and man how can this be? What part of him was God?"* '

My response: the idea that I find most helpful is the theory that Jesus had two natures, one human and one divine and that they were in balance. What is my evidence for saying this? Let me give some examples.

There had been at least one occasion during the ministry of Jesus when from sheer exhaustion he had fallen fast asleep in a boat on Lake Galilee during a storm. In fact, he had to be shaken into wakefulness and told that they were in grave danger. Here we see the humanity and divine nature at work together. Jesus, like us ordinary humans, did not have an inexhaustible supply of energy. He needed rest but was, during his ministry, often denied it. However, faced with a legitimate need he used the divine power that he shared with God. Jesus only used this sparingly and for a specific reason.

He got up and rebuked the wind and the raging waters; the storm subsided, and all was calm. 'Where is your faith?' he asked his disciples. In fear and amazement they asked one another, 'Who is this? He commands even the winds and the water, and they obey him' (Luke 8:23–25).

CAN WE REALLY CALL JESUS SON OF GOD?

This is a title that has led to some misunderstanding of the nature of Jesus. The Jehovah's Witnesses cult has problems with this title. *'How can a son be the same as a father?'* they ask. Their difficulty may be explained, in part, by the idea that for much of his young life a son is the inferior, at least in law, to his father. Also in life experience the father has more to offer than the son. But let's think of the son as a legal adult and the differences begin to disappear. Let's move on in time and think of the father nearing retirement and the son in his forties with a settled career and a great deal of life experience. Parity! They are equals and often each can contribute to the knowledge of the other. In using this example it should be understood that in no sense will God the Father be retiring or reducing his authority.

A state of parity is how we ought to think of Jesus and God his Father. His Father by nature and – ours by adoption! This is when we come to have faith in Jesus and begin to grasp all he did in life and death. Remember, as mentioned earlier, how some of the kings of Israel used to, as they grew older, have their son as a regent, having equal royal power.

What more can be said of this title? It was used in a lesser sense in the Old Testament of the God appointed kings of Israel. ' *"You are my Son; today I have become your Father"* ' (*Psalms 2:7*). This was temporary and transferable from one monarch to the next. The title when used of kings was to show their God appointed authority and work of guiding the nation, fighting its enemies and protecting the worship of God.

In the New Testament Son of God is used in a similar way of Jesus. We remember that he was of royal descent from the House of King David. The vital difference is that this title is neither temporary nor transferable. This is what the writer of the Letter to some Hebrew Christians wrote: '*The Son is the radiance of God's glory and the exact representation of his being, sustaining all things by his powerful word. After he had provided purification for sins*' [by his death on the Cross and rising again] '*he sat down at the right hand of the Majesty in heaven*' (*Hebrews 1:3*). The sitting down meant that the work of Jesus on earth was complete.[115]

---

[115] Let us be clear, even before his work on earth had been completed, Jesus enjoyed equal status with God the Father.

BEFORE CREATION

What of Jesus before his birth in Bethlehem, before the event called the Incarnation? How did he exist? What did he do? We remember his claim to those irritating Pharisees who were insulting him and trying to goad him into a verbal fight: ' *"before Abraham was born, I am!"* ' (*John 8:58*). But nowhere in the Gospels does Jesus more than hint at what form his pre-existent life took. In the prayer that he prayed on the evening before his arrest he was heard to speak of ' *"the glory I had with you before the world began"* ' (*John 17:5*).

It is left to John, the Beloved Apostle, to give more information but he does not reveal everything. '*In the beginning was the Word, and the Word was with God, and the Word was God. He was with God in the beginning. Through him all things were made; without him nothing was made that has been made*' (*John 1:1–3*).

There it is spelt out clearly! Before time, Jesus was working with his Father and the Holy Spirit of God in creating matter including the planet on which he was to live as a human. Is it any wonder that at the creation of the human species God said, ' *"Let us make man"* ' (*Genesis 1:26*)? One of the names of God in the Old Testament is *Elohim*, which is a plural form. It can, and often does, mean 'gods' as in the case of the gods of other nations. However, it is also used of the God[116] of

---

[116] God is usually referred to as Yahweh (YHWH); this name is based on *Exodus 3:13–14*. Here Moses had asked God's name and was told: 'I am who I am' (*Exodus 3:14*). This name is thought to come closest to the original name of God in Hebrew.

the Bible. This is the mystery. The God Christians worship is tri-personal.

THE DIVINE 'BRIDGE' AND THE HUMAN CONDITION[117]

It is because of his unique situation that Jesus can bridge the natural gulf between God and humanity. We have noticed that the rebellion found in human beings brings division. Some people call this the 'selfish gene'. As explained, the Bible calls it *'sin'* and it is at the heart of almost all our problems.

This is not to deny that there is good in human beings. They can be capable of great altruism. Occasionally, we learn of someone who will go to the most extreme lengths to rescue a total stranger who is in grave danger and not always because it is their job! This does not explain why a man or woman can imperil his or her own life for a stranger. This is something that is uncommon and because it is rare it excites our admiration. Jesus said: ' *"Greater love has no one than this that he lay down his life for his friends"* ' (*John 15:13*). That kind of devotion is quite exceptional.

So, what are we to make of it when the one in danger is unknown and no friendship exists? During the Great War (1914–18) a Turkish soldier was killed trying to rescue a British soldier he had just met during a brief

---

[117] Readers will find their understanding of this Chapter helped by also referring to articles in the *Short Dictionary* on **Sin**, **Blood** and **Sacrifice.**

ceasefire, which had been abruptly ended when someone, for an unknown reason, opened fire. This cannot be easily explained but it sets humans apart as being special.

In spite of this, very often humans are suspicious or hostile of each other. At this time, in the early years of the twenty-first century, to mention the name of the nation of Iran to some people and facial muscles will be seen to tighten. There is an inbuilt suspicion. We do not have to think internationally. This can happen at a local level. If we think that our neighbours are planning changes that may affect us we can become apprehensive, especially if relations are distant. Our fears may later prove well founded or groundless. This may have a good deal to do with the social conditions under which we live and the way we have been brought up but that is not the entire answer.

HUMANITY – GOD'S PLAN

The being that God created has an interesting and totally unique pedigree. As we have seen in the very first book of the Bible we are told that: '*God created man in his own image, in the image of God he created him; male and female he created them. "Let us make man*[118] *in our image, in our likeness, and let them rule over the fish of the sea and the birds of the air, over the livestock, over all the earth, and over all the creatures that move along the ground"* ' (*Genesis 1:26–7*).

---

[118] The Hebrew word for 'man' is *Adam* and is better translated 'mankind' or 'humankind'.

The human is seen as the crowning point of God's work. As the late professor Louis Berkhof said, 'man' was *'the king of creation'*,[119] having been given, under God who is the Emperor of the Universe, responsibility for the earth. Humankind's original function, it seems, was to act as God's representative on earth. In addition, God had chosen to create a being with whom he could have a relationship of trust. It is as a result of this that man was made able to share God's task of 'ruling' the earth. That was the original divine intention and a very high ideal. It was different to the rest of the animal creation.

With other creatures it is a matter of less importance for God. ' *"Let the land produce living creatures according to their kinds: livestock, creatures that move along the ground, and wild animals, each according to its kind." And it was so'* (*Genesis 1:24*). The other creatures of God's creation are allowed to develop naturally. This does not mean that the rest of the animals created are unimportant. It would be a mistake to think that this was a completely random process. God was in control but seems to have allowed other factors to influence the development of life on earth. Humanity is an exception to this lesser order. Note the conscious choice that God makes in the creation of the human being.

There may be a few mistaken ideas that we can develop from the teaching that '*God created man in his own image*'. Firstly, it could be an error to think that humans

---

[119] Louis Berkhof, *Systematic Theology*, p.182.

and God share a similar appearance. To say that I physically look like God may be very wrong. This is something we really do not know. The Apostle Paul explaining the nature of God to the Athenian philosophers (about the middle of the first century) said that ' *"we should not think that the divine being is like gold or silver or stone – an image made by man's design and skill"* ' (*Acts 17:29*). If it is wrong to make an image of *'the divine being'*, it is also a grave mistake to try to imagine what God is physically like. The children's idea of the old man with a beard can be dismissed. God has not and will never grow old.

No, human beings were originally 'made' to be rational and morally responsible creatures like the God who chose to make them. In no sense does this imply equality just similarity. Humans, even as originally 'made', are a very poor *likeness*. They are intended to live lives that because of their relationship with God are morally superior and also better in terms of life experience. God wishes them to be fully 'human'.[120] That was what God originally intended.

Another mistake is to imagine that it is humanity's mind that bears the divine likeness. Not so, it is the total human being. In past times it was fashionable to think of man as being in three distinct parts. Greek philosophers began this trend but it is not a Biblical

---

[120] All that that entails is not fully clear from Scripture but perhaps it is one of those many things that we only begin to discover in this life.

concept and would have been completely foreign to Jesus. The Greeks argued that human personality divided naturally into mind, soul and body (*nous, psyche, soma*). Even today there is a tendency to make this distinction although serious modern thinkers see that such are the close connections that to view the human being as a whole is a wiser course.

This idea that the human being was in three parts led a few individuals in the southern Greek city of Corinth, during New Testament times, into moral error. These so-called Christians argued that the *psyche* (what we call the 'soul') was the only really important part of a human and that was the only part that really mattered. It would last eternally. The body and what was done with it did not matter. As a consequence abuse of their bodies or the sexual misuse of other people's was thought excusable. The Apostle Paul stamped down heavily on this gross error. *'The body is not meant for sexual immorality, but for the Lord, and the Lord for the body'* (**1 Corinthians 6:13**). Paul did not explain why they were wrongheaded, perhaps he realised that these were immoral by nature and only looked for any excuse that could justify their behaviour. Had these individuals thought about this in the light of the teaching of Scripture they would have realised that this idea could not be defended. Paul had written to them *'not to associate with sexually immoral people'* (**1 Corinthians 5:9**).

HUMANITY – THE MARRED IMAGE

It does not take much thought to realise that with this God-given pedigree, human life ought to be wonderful for all. It might seem that way for some but for myriads living below the poverty level in what is called the 'Majority World' it is dire! So, why is this?

Let's recap briefly: humans have been given *'rule ... over all the earth'*. This authority has remained but what has been lost is the natural relationship that God and humankind ought to be enjoying. We, as the special creation of God, have lost much of our moral edge. Yes, we do have a morality but one that is flawed. Our *'rule ... over all the earth'* has not been one of good management. The fashionable word is 'stewardship' and it has been awful! We have often overexploited land and still do. We have driven some animal species to extinction or near extinction. On occasions this has been done for no good reason. We have caused pollution on a massive scale. God help us because we are in an abject state!

As we begin to look further into the matter this state of things gets worse. As we have mentioned above humans are often at enmity with one another. War can result and a few individuals have made obscene millions while the mass of ordinary people suffer poverty and hardship.

The worst effect of this flaw on humankind is that what should have been a warm relationship with God is removed. Humans are separated from the loving God who created them. This breakdown is at the root of our mismanagement of the earth and our failures in human interaction.

The explanation given in Scripture for how humankind moved from a position of favour, enjoying communication with God, is not an easy one. The explanation for the entrance of evil given in Scripture seems, for modern readers, quaint. It is found in the very first book of the Bible, *Genesis Chapter 3*. The reason is that this seems to go beyond our understanding of natural things. In learning so much of the physical and scientific world, we have lost an appreciation of the 'unseen world'. Some modern people may think that that *other world* is only believed in by the less developed societies. Not so, as Francis MacNutt points out, the Japanese have a well-developed sense of the power of evil spirits and will resort to exorcism quite freely.[121]

Firstly, it is easiest to see the Genesis account as using poetic language and as such the writer may be using allegorical images, word pictures to convey vital truths. Let us begin with *Adam*, this name in Hebrew means 'humankind'. So, to think of an individual may not be good thinking. (I have to admit that it can be trying to get into the mind and culture of the writer or writers of Genesis.)

---

[121] Francis MacNutt, *Deliverance from Evil Spirits*, p.55. This quotes a report in the *Japan Times* (30 July 1978).

If we read the account we see that humankind were tempted to take power to become like God. *'The symbol of this power is called the tree of the knowledge of good and evil'* (*Genesis 2:9*). God had forbidden them to eat the fruit of this tree. There was another creature in the garden where the first humans lived. That creature had pointed out the advantages of the tree. He arouses the humans' interest in improving their 'education'. The temptation is in becoming like God. He, the creature, is called the *'serpent'* (*3:1–6*) and appears again in *Revelation* (*12:9*), the final book of the Bible as the enemy of the plans and purposes of God. There he is called *'the devil, or Satan'*. In the early verses of *Chapter 3* of *Genesis* there is an interesting conversation about the penalty of eating the fruit. *'The woman'* says that the penalty is death. The serpent says, ' *"Surely you won't die."* ' The humans then picked and ate the fruit of this tree. They become aware that their situation had changed. Later they encountered God (*3:8–24*) who knew precisely what had happened and he pronounced the penalty. Oh yes, the penalty was death but not the extinction of physical life but the end of the special relationship that these humans enjoyed with their creator. It was a spiritual death.

Also a whole package of ills was pronounced on the humans as a result of their disobedience. Worse still, the penalty, and the 'package of ills', was passed on to their children and to the rest of the human race including those born in the twenty-first century.

In the *Short Dictionary*, at the back of this book, I have written further on Satan but for the moment I would like to move on.

RESTORING THE SPECIAL RELATIONSHIP

It is clear from God's dealings with humankind that he was deeply saddened by the breakdown of this precious relationship. Most of humanity remains unaware of what had been lost. But had they known they would have been powerless to do anything to set matters right.

Reading the pages of the Hebrew Scriptures (Old Testament) we find that God was able to have a special relationship with individuals such as Abraham (*Genesis Chapters 12–25*) but it was not the same as before because originally humans had been without flaw in God's sight. He wished to have a special relationship with the Hebrew people but God found that the relationship tended to be hot or cold. The Hebrews, like the human being we call *Adam*, wanted things on their own terms. Something entirely different was needed.

God, as we have seen at the start of his dealings with the human species, had acted in person. He had been happy to directly communicate on a personal level, to be available in the place Scripture calls 'the garden' before that first disobedience had occurred. He knew that he had to become directly involved again. God had to be personally involved and nothing less was required. A repeat of what he had done before would not work. But he needed a human with whom he could have that unique special relationship. The relationship that he had wanted to have with the human we call *Adam*. *A Second Adam*, vastly superior to the first was needed. That *Second Adam* would have to suffer the *package of ills* that had been the other penalty incurred by the original *Adam* because of his disobedience – this would include physical death.

But he would be free of the 'spiritual death' which was the main penalty that *Adam* had suffered and is now the lot of every human.

The divine action was to send Jesus to act as the 'bridge' between humanity and the heavenly person we call 'God'. Or, when we believe and start to follow Jesus: 'God our Father'. We have already thought about the unique nature of Jesus. Born in time and yet belonging to eternity. He showed and explained the love of God by allowing himself to die just like a criminal. His death was, at a stroke, to remove the necessity for animals being sacrificed for the human rebellion, which is called sin. Jesus was humanity's substitute and this was an eternal, not a temporary solution to wrongdoing.

But a dishonourable death, and that is what it was, needed to be 'exonerated'. Jesus was raised from the dead. Besides this, as we have seen, the first stage of his earthly work was not fully complete until the event called the Ascension had taken place.

A VERY REMARKABLE OFFER

In Mark's Gospel *Chapter 8:34–5,* Jesus made a very remarkable offer.

'If anyone would come after me, he must deny himself and take up his cross and follow me. For whoever wants to save his life will lose it, but whoever loses his life for me and for the gospel will save it' (Mark 8:34–35).

He made it to his first-century hearers and he makes it to us his twenty-first-century readers. The language and meaning do seem rather strange. Let's face it, we are used to seeing adverts for goods or services that offer the 'taker' nothing but good. There is, in advertising, nothing to suggest that, apart from purchasing and maintaining the car, gas boiler, life assurance policy or whatever it is, that there will be any cost. The *Ad man* fails if he gives the impression of any difficulty or downside.

However, the offer of Jesus is no 'product' in our modern sense of that word: ' *"whoever wants to save his life will lose it, but whoever loses his life for me and for the gospel will save it"* '. This does not seem worth thinking about until we consider our normal human condition. There is the teaching of Jesus that those who have not made peace with God are not fully alive. As Jesus once told a would-be disciple who wanted to negotiate his own particular deal: ' *"Let the dead bury their own dead"* ' *(Luke 9:60).* To our modern ears it sounds rather dismissive, even unkind. However, Jesus was not that kind of man and he valued people.

In the culture of those times the meaning was understood and the would-be disciple would not have been offended. In a well-known parable, sometimes called the *Prodigal Son* or the *Lost Son*, Jesus used this idea of being *'dead'* to speak of broken human relationships. In this parable the younger son, who had been a disgrace, returned home. With joy his father exclaims, ' *"This son of mine <u>was dead</u> and is alive again; he was lost and is found"* ' (*Luke 15:24*). Jesus is not merely speaking about family relationships, he is also explaining that the outcasts who turned from their past deeds and lived a changed life would be received and made 'alive' by God.

This is a 'new life for old' offer! Even those who feel that they have spoilt lives and for them there can be nothing there in the future; even for them this is a valid offer. It may take time, sometimes years, but for God nothing is wasted. Even the worst failures can be turned around. These people can be completely renewed. It has been well said that: *God is no man's debtor* (or woman's) but is always seeking to improve the image. This is usually a slow painstaking work. We often take a long time to be convinced that God is up to the job. We are often a major factor in not allowing God to restore the damage.

Having lived on earth and either experienced or observed all that life can throw at humanity, Jesus is uniquely placed to understand the human condition. The emotions that drive you and me are something he understands. The frustrations and disappointments that we experience are not a twenty-first-century thing. He felt or saw comparable problems in his day. He really does understand our situation. He wishes to help and to share our burdens.

Nowhere in the Bible, if it has been properly understood, does it offer you an automatic quick fix. In the board game called Monopoly there is a *'get out of jail free'* card. The Christian life does not guarantee such easy options. As mentioned earlier, life's problems can often be growth points. There will be times that, when you look back, and remember a certain situation there will be a revelation. You will discover how the problem did not appear from over the horizon but that as you got nearer to the dreaded day, the interview or the medical it had shrunk in size and importance and you were given strength to get through. However, there are times when the crisis that we feared just vanished and you did not have to fight that battle.

IN CONCLUSION

It is my hope that many readers have approached this book with a desire to know more about Jesus. They have been the 'beginners' for whom this book is written. It is my most sincere wish that you have not only begun to know about him but sense that his voice is within you wishing to move you on. If you feel this or are willing to allow the Spirit of God to influence you then there is one other step that must be considered. This is not new, we thought about these words earlier in this book. They were the challenge of Jesus to his first-century hearers; they are the challenge to everyone who seriously looks at the life of Jesus.

'If anyone would come after me, he must deny himself and take up his cross and follow me. For whoever wants to save his life will lose it, but whoever loses his life for me will find it' *(Matthew 16:24–25).*

Yes, it is costly but I finish with some words of comfort. The Apostle Paul writing to a Church, now in Western Turkey, told them from deep personal experience that God is *'able to do immeasurably more than all we ask or imagine, according to his power that is at work within us'* *(Ephesians 3:20).* This is a very reassuring thought and it means that you or I cannot lose when we trust God and begin to follow Jesus.

THE SUPPORTING CAST
THE FRIENDS AND FOES OF JESUS

ANNAS 301

The former High Priest, father-in-law to Caiaphas and the controller of matters religious, a Sadducee by tradition.

CAIAPHAS 303

High Priest and politician, he was able to keep his position longer than many earlier men.

HEROD ANTIPAS ('THE FOX') 306

He was a client king used and tolerated by Rome, son of evil Herod the Great, something of a moral lightweight, a playboy.

JOHN, THE APOSTLE 310

The beloved Disciple, who is known as the Apostle of love.

JUDAS ISCARIOT 317

The enigmatic treasurer to Jesus's disciples, an embezzler, and in the end the betrayer.

MARY MAGDALENE 324

A lady with an awful past but with a tremendous future.

MARY MOTHER OF JESUS 331

A unique lady given an amazing and daunting task.

PETER THE APOSTLE 341

A natural leader who grew to understand that he too needed to be led. First earthly head of the Church.

PONTIUS PILATE 354

He had the power and authority of Rome, but a series of errors of judgement meant that he could be manipulated.

ANNAS

Greedy, serpent-like, vindictive,[122] this is not the kind of character assessment for any priest let alone the man who had occupied the office of High Priest in Jerusalem. His natural talents would have been ideally suited to medieval diplomacy rather than the service of God.

Annas, whose name means *merciful* or *gracious*, had been appointed High Priest in about AD 6–7 by Quirinius the Governor of Syria but lost this appointment in AD 15. Joseph Caiaphas, his son-in-law, replaced him about three years later. Through shrewd efforts he managed to ensure that this office was kept in his family for much of his life.

Losing his official status and the authority of Rome did not, in reality, make very much difference to the High Priesthood because he seemed to run the show in Jerusalem. He used members of his family and others who were happy to do his bidding. This fact was not lost on the Gospel writers who refer to '*the High Priesthood of Annas and Caiaphas*' (*Luke 3:2*) as if there was a joint priesthood. It is not surprising that after his arrest Jesus was led to Annas, only after that, was Caiaphas involved. This hearing was, however, informal and intended to gather information that would be used at the trial.

---

[122] *New Testament Commentary of John*, Wm Hendriksen, p.395.

As to his situation we are told that he was a Sadducee and was inclined to be arrogant, ambitious, and was enormously wealthy. Much of his fortune came from the practice of selling the animals for sacrifice and other necessities to those who visited the Temple for its sacrificial service. As well as purchasers having to buy at high prices they could only trade in the specially minted silver 'coinage' of the Temple, which operated a closed shop. In effect they had their own bank.

This was why *'Jesus entered the temple area and drove out all who were buying and selling there. He over-turned the tables of the money changers and the benches of those selling doves. "It is written," he said to them. "My house will be called a house of prayer, but you are making it a 'den of robbers' " ' (Matthew 21:12* & *13*). Not unnaturally, Annas and the High Priesthood had the reputation for being greedy.

Some have stated that it was Annas above all others that brought about the death of Jesus. Caiaphas was the mouthpiece but his father-in-law thought that Jesus should be executed and used his evil influence to bring him before Pilate.

Annas had a long life but did not live long enough to see his fifth son Ananus (Annas II) made High Priest in the AD 60s.

CAIAPHAS

It is generally agreed that Joseph Caiaphas was created High Priest about AD 18. He survived until thirty-six or thirty-seven. This makes him the longest serving High Priest of that period. He was the son-in-law of Annas, who had been removed from the High Priesthood approximately three years before him. We first meet the name Caiaphas when John the Baptist, the cousin of Jesus, is mentioned as beginning his ministry.

In the fifteenth year of the reign of Tiberius Caesar – when Pontius Pilate was governor of Judea; Herod, tetrarch of Galilee; his brother Philip, tetrarch of Iturea and Traconitis, and Lysanias tetrarch of Abilene – during the High Priesthood of Annas and Caiaphas, the word of God came to John son of Zechariah in the desert (Luke 3:1–2).

Some scholars are intrigued by the expression *'during the High Priesthood of Annas and Caiaphas'* and wonder what is going on. It seems unlikely that there was a formal arrangement regarding the religious establishment. It seems more probable that Luke is merely hinting at where the real power lay (please refer to note on **Annas** above).

The appointment of Caiaphas, as with all appointments to the High Priesthood, was a political one and was carefully controlled by the Procurator. This involved the removal of the robes from the Temple and their storage under lock and key in the Antonia Palace, the official quarters of Pontius Pilate when he was in Jerusalem. They were released upon seven days notice of their being needed for official use during Feasts. Pilate also wished to know when the Sanhedrin was in session. It is thought unlikely that this was intended to interfere with the Jewish administration, rather it was a means by which Rome showed who was really in control of Judea. The High Priestly office-holder had to have wisdom, diplomacy as well as management skills to be successful.

Caiaphas was the ecclesiastical politician, appointed, like one of Hitler's bishops, by a heathen government, expressly that he might collaborate with the New Order and see that the Church toed the line drawn by the State.[123]

Most Jews of that period would have regarded Caiaphas not only as High Priest but, because he wore the ceremonial robe with the two stones for making predictions (Urim and Thummim), as a prophet. With such powers it was believed that nothing would be unknown to him.

It is of course, for his part in the trial of Jesus that Caiaphas will be remembered. Having failed to find two witnesses, whose testimony could condemn him,

---

[123] Dorothy L Sayers, *The Man Born to be King*, Victor Gollancz, 1943, p.23.

he resorted to a legally irregular (some say illegal) procedure of putting Jesus under oath.

'I charge you under oath by the living God: tell us if you are the Christ, the Son of God.' 'Yes, it is as you say,' Jesus replied. 'But I say to all of you: in the future you will see the Son of Man sitting at the right hand of the Mighty One and coming on the clouds of heaven' (Matthew 26:63–64).

As a political appointee under the control of Rome, Caiaphas had a limited shelf life. High Priests were often removed when the Roman administrator changed. When Pilate was recalled, his Legate (military superior) in Syria also removed Caiaphas.

HEROD ANTIPAS ('THE FOX')

Antipas, or to give him his name in full Antipatros, was the second son of the fourth of Herod the First's ten wives. His father was also known as Herod the Great. It may not come as a complete surprise to learn that Antipas was part of a very dysfunctional family who were given to power struggles and intermarriage among their own extended family. As you may have guessed, this resulted in much internecine strife. His father was the King Herod of *Matthew Chapter 2* who on learning through the visitors from Persia (the men we call Magi), that he had a rival, attempted to kill the infant Jesus but only succeeded in murdering some male infants in Bethlehem. Having a murderous parent was not any help for Antipatros.

We do not know his date of birth so it would not be easy to guess his age at the time of his interrogation of Jesus. Although of the same family mould, Antipas had lost some power upon the death of his father in 4 BC and was given a fourth part of his father's realm, hence his title of Tetrarch.

Our introduction to Antipas is due to his imprisonment of John the Baptist (*Matthew 14:1–12*), who had called the morality of his marriage into account. Antipas had married Herodias, his brother Philip's wife. As they were already blood relations this kept things in the family. This criticism did not endear John the Baptist in royal circles, even today one does not readily criticise the establishment (particularly for stealing someone else's wife) – then it could quickly prove fatal.

It is Mark's Gospel, which gives further details of Herod Antipas's dealing with John the Baptist that provides a fascinating picture of a strange and complex character and the mix of emotions that his infidelity produced in the people involved.

Herodias [Antipas's new wife] *nursed a grudge against John and wanted to kill him. But she was not able to, because Herod feared John and protected him, knowing him to be a righteous and holy man. When Herod heard John, he was greatly puzzled; yet he liked to listen to him (Mark 6:19–20).*

Clearly Antipas was in awe of John and held him in esteem. At least, he would have found an honest man and one who was not given to flattery. That would have been the norm for his courtiers and those seeking favours. John was different and Herod Antipas's conscience was uneasy. Perhaps it was not so much the anger of God that he feared as his brother's. Yet repentance was too high a price to pay. He would have had to return Herodias but almost as damaging would have been the loss of face.

Herodias had her way in the end because of Herod's boastfulness. On his birthday, Salome, his stepdaughter (also his niece), had danced for him and Herod offered her anything she wished. To show his earnestness he *'pledged with an oath. "Whatever you ask I will give you, up to half my kingdom" '* (*Mark 6:23*). The young Salome consulted her mother. Herodias knew what to ask for and gave her daughter this request: *' "I want you to give me right now the head of John the Baptist on a platter." The king was greatly distressed, but because of his oaths and his dinner guests, he did not want to refuse her. So he immediately sent an executioner with orders to bring John's head. The man went, beheaded John in the prison'* (*Mark 6:25–27*). This would not have helped the mental state of Herod who *'considered him a prophet'* (*Matthew 14:5*) and you ought not to execute prophets.

When Jesus began to be known as a worker of miracles Herod was worried and he became, at least for a while, superstitious. He feared that John had somehow cheated death and had come back as Jesus but these feelings did not last long. Clearly Herod Antipas was also wary of Jesus because we read: *'At that time some Pharisees came to Jesus and said to him, "Leave this place and go somewhere else. Herod wants to kill you." He replied, "Go tell that fox, 'I will drive out demons and heal people today and tomorrow, and on the third day I will reach my goal' " '* (*Luke 13:31–32*).

Herod met Jesus when Pilate tried to extricate himself from having to pass judgement on Jesus. The Procurator[124] had discovered that Jesus was from the

---

[124] Strictly speaking, Pilate was called the Prefect at that time. The title Procurator came later after his time in office. Luke is using the new title. When this change came into force is uncertain.

region of Galilee and, as such, could be passed to Herod. It is possible that Herod could have locked Jesus up and sought the guidance of Rome. His other option was to find Jesus guilty and then order his execution.

Herod found nothing against Jesus but it was certain that he quickly realised that this prophet was of *'the house and line of David'* (*Luke* 2:4). That very fact meant that he belonged to Bethlehem in Judea and that area was under Pilate's authority. So he sent Jesus back to Pilate for sentencing. It seems that neither the king nor Pilate was convinced that Jesus was guilty of a capital offence. Pilate reported to the Sanhedrin.

Neither has Herod, for he sent him back to us; as you can see, he has done nothing to deserve death (Luke 23:13–15).

Herod is a moral lightweight whose interest in Jesus is as a possible entertainer, *'he hoped to see him perform some miracle'* (*Luke* 23:8). In the event he was disappointed and treats Jesus in a despicable way, *'they* [his bodyguard] *ridiculed him and mocked him'* (23:11) before returning him to Pilate.

It seems that justice was served in that Herod Antipas fell from favour with Rome and was finally exiled to Lyon in France in AD 39 where he lived out the rest of his days.

JOHN, 'THE BELOVED' APOSTLE

'Dear friends, let us love one another, for love comes from God. Everyone who loves has been born of God and knows God' (1 John 4:7). This verse seems to sum up the reputation and much of the later teaching of the younger of the sons of Zebedee and Salome.

The writer of the Fourth Gospel was perhaps the youngest of the Twelve. These were the closest followers of Jesus who were later called apostles. He could also be called, and would have been known, during his lifetime, as 'John son of Zebedee' during his years in the Holy Land.

His father was a merchant or, to use modern English, a businessman who appeared to have been running a thriving fishing company on Lake Galilee. As Zebedee senior hired workers to man his boats he was clearly prospering. These facts we know from the Gospel readings that tell us about the call to follow Jesus. John and his elder brother James[125] were *'preparing their nets' (Matthew 4:19),* when Jesus, who had shortly before called Simon (also called Peter or Simon Peter) and his brother Andrew to become disciples, called John and James. They got up, *'they left their father, Zebedee, in the boat with the hired men and followed*

---

[125] It would be more accurate to called John's older brother 'Yacob'. John's name would have been Yohannes.

him' (*Mark 1:20*). Peter and his brother Andrew were also *'partners'* with Zebedee & Sons. This we know from *Luke's Gospel 5:1–11*, which tells us of the call of Peter and then James and John who had taken a great catch of fish. *'So they pulled their boats up on shore, left everything and followed him.'*

It was no small thing for John and James to become first-century disciples. Teachers, not merely Jesus, asked for a full-time commitment! Leaving home comforts, family and even wife.[126] Most disciples were, naturally, single and were prepared for a hard life of travel out in the cold as well as the heat. It called for dedication to learning *Tanakh* (the Scriptures that we call the Old Testament) and other writings; also it called for total commitment to the teacher.

It would probably be a mistake to think that the call of Jesus to John and the other disciples from Lake Galilee came out of the blue. They had, I am sure, had the opportunity of getting to know Jesus for sometime before he called them.

It is also possible that before he followed Jesus, John had been a disciple of John the Baptist because he is mentioned as an unnamed disciple who came to see Jesus with Andrew, the brother of Simon Peter. These two heard John the Baptist refer to Jesus as *'the Lamb of God'* (*John 1:36*). They got into conversation with

---

[126] For a man to be away from home for more than a month needed, even in male-dominated first-century Jewish society, the consent of the wife.

Jesus and spent time with him. It is possible that John might have brought his brother James to meet Jesus.

WHAT DO WE KNOW ABOUT JOHN?

Jesus had his own name for John and his older brother James. He called them *'Boanerges'*, in English *'Sons of Thunder'* (*Mark 3:17*) this may have been a joke, which the other members of the Twelve disciples shared. It could indicate that they were a pair of brothers, who often argued with others. When Jesus was refused entry into a Samaritan village it was James and John who asked whether Jesus wished them to ' *"call fire down from heaven"* '. Naturally, Jesus was upset with them (*Luke 9:51–55*) for making this suggestion.

John and his brother were not without ambition. On one occasion, egged on by their mother who spoke for them, Jesus was asked: ' *"that one of these two sons of mine may sit at your right and the other at your left in your kingdom. 'You don't know what you are asking,' was Jesus's reply"* ' (*Matthew 20:21–22*). Not unnaturally, the rest of the Twelve were not happy about this. In spite of their faults and weaknesses John and James, together with Peter were being trained for responsibility and leadership in the Church that Jesus was to leave behind to carry on his work. It was years later that the Apostle Paul, reporting on a visit to Jerusalem, wrote of Peter, James and John as *'pillars'* in the Jewish Church in Jerusalem (*Galatians 2:9*).

It is clear from reading the Gospels that these three were given special insights into who Jesus was. Let's take just one incident, which is reported by **Matthew 17:1-13**, in **Mark 9:2-13** and in **Luke 9:28-36**. This is the Transfiguration of Jesus when these three disciples were shown the splendour of Jesus. This took place on a mountain and Jesus's whole person was mysteriously 'transfigured' by light. John, James and Peter saw Moses and Elijah, the Old Testament prophet, speaking to Jesus. They also heard a voice from heaven speaking to them.

Although John the Apostle has this commercial background, it is clear that he is, or became, a man of education with a deep knowledge of how the Sanhedrin and the Temple worked. It is possible that he gained this understanding during his ministry in Jerusalem, which continued for some years after the Gospel narratives finished. However, it is clear that he had influence because it was John who on the night of Jesus's arrest was not only allowed inside the garden of Caiaphas, the High Priest, but also managed to get Peter admitted. It may have been through supplying fish to the High Priestly household but clearly John could get doors to open – quite literally.

FAMILY CONNECTIONS?

Although it is impossible to make a completely 'watertight case' it seems very likely that John Zebedee and Jesus were cousins, their mothers were sisters. Let's look at the evidence shall we? '*Near the Cross of Jesus stood his mother, his mother's sister, Mary the wife of Clopas, and Mary Magdalene' (John 19:25).* The Gospel of *Mark 15:40* gives us the name of *'Salome'* which would seem to be the sister of Mary, Jesus's aunt.

Our next piece of evidence, from Easter Sunday morning, needs a brief note of explanation before it begins to fully make sense. Only relatives of the dead would normally be involved with the last rites, or 'laying out'. Normally, this might have involved a mother or brothers, although Jesus's mother would have been too distraught to think about doing this task. Unfortunately, none of Jesus's brothers[127] were present to do this. As to why Mary Magdalene went to the tomb we cannot be sure, although it might have been to give support to the older women and to keep a watch for anyone who approached the tomb.

'When the Sabbath was over, Mary Magdalene, Mary the mother of James, and Salome bought spices so that they might go to anoint Jesus's body' (Mark 16:1). If my thinking is correct, then Salome, as near kin would have done the more personal parts of the anointing with the help of these other women. The final piece of evidence is from Matthew.

Many women were there. Among them were Mary Magdalene, Mary the mother of James and Joses, and the mother of Zebedee's sons (27:55–56).

---

[127] Please refer to *Mark 3:31–32* and *Matthew 13:54–56*, which gives the names of Jesus's brothers as James, Joseph, Simon and Judas. Mathew also mentions sisters without saying how many.

A very strong case can be made for the family connection between Jesus and John and would help to explain that from his Cross Jesus gives to John the task of being a *'son'* to Mary, his mother. It would also help to explain the fact that John and Jesus clearly had an especially warm relationship that is seen particularly during the Last Supper as reported in John's Gospel.

JOHN'S WRITING AND LATER MINISTRY

There are no strong reasons for not believing that John the Apostle is the author of the fourth Gospel, although there may have been a secretary to take down his words.[128] It is not so easy to make such a strong case for the **Book of Revelation**, nor for his being the author of the three **Letters of John**. Some scholars have wondered if John died at the same time as his brother James. This happened in AD 44 when Herod Agrippa, the brother of Herodias the wife of Herod Antipas, moved against the Jerusalem Church. Finding firm evidence from the New Testament for this idea is impossible!

Should this have happened then we would need to look for another writer of the fourth Gospel, which is generally thought to date from AD 85–90. Some other scholars have wondered whether a Galilean fisherman would have had the necessary knowledge of Greek thought to have written a Gospel, which clearly seems to have been compiled for the benefit of Jewish expatriates living around the Roman world. This does

---

[128] This may account for the strange expression **the disciple who Jesus loved** which seems to be used instead of John.

seem to belittle the apostle and is not a well-thought-out argument.

After his time as one of the *'pillars'* of the Jerusalem Church John seems to have moved elsewhere. Some have wondered whether he went to Alexandria. This is quite a sensible suggestion as there were many very large Jewish communities living in Egypt at that time. If he did go there it is likely that he later moved on again.

We cannot ignore the **Book of Revelation** where a man called John spent some time in a Roman penal colony, a kind of first-century Devils Island. The writer does not identify himself as the apostle but that is quite normal for John.

The colony is a short distance from Asia Minor on the small island of Patmos, now one of the Greek Islands. This book was written in a kind of code and contains messages for seven Christian congregations living in the Roman Province of Asia. Geographically this is now western Turkey.

There is evidence that John the Apostle spent some time in Ephesus, one of the churches mentioned in the **Book of Revelation** and that he lived and worshipped there. As well as these documents there was a church dedicated to him and it was at that time the custom to dedicate churches to saints who had actually lived, or more often had died there.

JUDAS ISCARIOT

'...the most enigmatic person in the gospel story.'[129]

What made him do it? What sort of man was he and where he came from are all questions that are unanswerable, given our present knowledge. That having been said, there are various theories some of which are of interest. Does the name Iscariot help us by giving some clue? (a) As the keeper of the common purse Judas would have 'carried a *sortea* or leather bag'. (b) Some have suggested that the name is linked to the word for '*assassin, false one, liar,* and *hypocrite.*' (c) The final theory is that he was descended from the ancient Jewish tribe of Issachar.

The most widely accepted explanation for his name is that it means '*man of Kerioth*' (*Iskariōtes*), an indication that he was a southerner possibly from the area of the Negev close to Edom or to give it its present name Jordan. How he came to be one of the Twelve is unclear. Many members of the apostolic band were given a specific call to follow Jesus. John's Gospel gives us a small snippet of information about him indicating that his family were known: ' *"Have I not chosen you, the Twelve? Yet one of you is a devil!"* ' (*John 6:70–71*).

---

[129] F W Gingrich, *Interpreters Dictionary of the Bible,* vol. 2, Abingdon Press, 1962, p.1006.

(He meant Judas, the son of Simon Iscariot, who, though one of the Twelve, was later to betray him.)

Judas just seems to have appeared, mentioned as the one who betrayed Jesus (*Matthew 10:1–4*). Some commentators have suggested that his name comes at the end because of his treachery but that as treasurer he enjoyed some prestige at least initially.

Only Matthew's Gospel deals with the suicide of Judas Iscariot, the rest of the Gospels are silent on the subject. That said, Luke mentions his death in the first chapter of *Acts* (*vv.15–22*) but merely as an explanation of why the apostolic band, now under the direction of Peter, had chosen Matthias as a new recruit. Acts says that: *'With the reward he got for his wickedness, Judas bought a field.'* This is interesting but Luke's explanation does not immediately help us to know what actually happened about the purchase of the field and the manner of death that Judas suffered.

It could well be that before the sheer size and result of his treachery had struck home; Judas had contracted to purchase the field but had not used the thirty pieces of silver. As we have noticed, Judas returned the money (*Matthew 27:3–5*). The chief priests used it to purchase the potters field. This may well have been the plot of land that Judas himself had been interested in. That is speculation on my part, although there may not have been very many plots for sale around Jerusalem at that time. Professor Blaiklock was of the opinion that the legal-minded priests may have purchased the plot in

Judas's name[130] and that it is one of the twists of irony that Judas used this same piece of land for his suicide.

Now to Luke's report of the death of Judas, let us review the facts. Luke reports that *'Judas'* bought *'a field; there he fell headlong, his body burst open and all his intestines spilled out'* (*Acts 1:18*). On the face of it the account does seem to be at variance with Matthew's Gospel but is this in fact the case? Here I have to admit to assumption but suppose that Judas climbed into a tree or something equally suitable and threw himself from this, falling *'headlong'* with the rope around his neck. In Britain before the abolition of the death penalty a straight fall through a trapdoor resulted in death from a twelve-foot drop (3.6 m). A suicide throwing himself forward would probably need less rope to cause the same result. As to his body being *'burst open'* this could be the result of exposure to the sun. It is not unlikely that it took some days before the death of Judas was discovered, during which the physical symptoms had taken place aided by warm weather.

'THE GOSPEL OF JUDAS'

As I began to write this profile (April 2006) the *National Geographic* caused a stir by reporting upon the work called *The Gospel of Judas*. This was not a new work but a new report on the rediscovery of an ancient document known to the early Church father Irenaeus who reported negatively upon it in the late second century. Some two centuries after Irenaeus's complaint,

---

[130] *Acts, Tyndale New Testament Commentaries*, 1959, p.53

Epiphanius of Salamis, bishop of Cyprus, criticised *The Gospel of Judas* for treating the one whom he saw as the betrayer of Jesus as commendable, one who 'performed a good work for our salvation' (Haeres, xxxviii).

This so-called '*Gospel*' would have us believe that Judas was really a favourite of Jesus and that Jesus offered him 'the mysteries of the kingdom'. This in fact gives us a major clue to the influence behind this work – the acquisition of secret knowledge (*gnosis*) and through it power.

Towards the end of the first century, groups of people claimed that in addition to belief in the good news of Jesus, secret knowledge was required. These people claimed to have passwords that they could reveal.

This publishing by *National Geographic* looks to be another attempt to sanitise Jesus's betrayer. This document claims that Judas acted as he did in order that mankind might be redeemed by the death of Jesus. For this reason they, the Cainites who seem to have inspired *The Gospel of Judas*, regarded Judas as worthy of gratitude and veneration.

In this theory, it is suggested that Judas, who in common with other disciples looked for an earthly kingdom of the *Messiah*, did not anticipate the death of Jesus. Judas, it is claimed, wished to help cause a political crisis and hasten the hour of triumph, thinking that the arrest of Jesus would provoke a rising of the people. This would bring forward the hour of triumph for a conquering *Messiah* who would help them get rid of Roman rule.

The answer to the argument that for the Atonement[131] to take place it was necessary to have a betrayer is not entirely unsatisfactory. It is clear that the Jewish High Priesthood were out to get Jesus.

Refer to *John's Gospel 11:49–51, 53*: *'Then one of them, named Caiaphas, who was High Priest that year, spoke up, "You know nothing at all! You do not realise that it is better for you that one man die for the people than that the whole nation perish." He did not say this on his own, but as High Priest that year he prophesied that Jesus would die for the Jewish nation. ... So from that day on they plotted to take his life.'*

Therefore, Jesus's life was in danger from a corrupt follower and from the jealousy of the Jewish authorities. Being in conflict with Caiaphas was certain to cause Jesus deep trouble. This is reinforced by John who informs us that the High Priesthood were furious. They were so enraged that Lazarus had shown Jesus's miraculous ability, by being raised from the dead, that they wished to silence him too because *'the chief priests made plans to kill Lazarus' (John 12:10).*

OTHER POSSIBLE REASONS FOR THE BETRAYAL

As one examines the events of the Gospels other events emerge that might well have influenced Iscariot's decision. The first possibility is that he, as an orthodox

---

[131] 'Atonement' is a word that means that God and man are at peace. Literally it is 'at one-ment'.

Jew, could not agree with Jesus's differences with the Scribes and Pharisees over the law. Perhaps he had mental conflict with the fact of Jesus's emphasis, which was often in opposition to the Temple. Then, what were his own ideas of the true priorities for the nation?

Another possible motive is that Judas changed his mind and began to doubt that Jesus was anything else than a false messiah, a corrupting prophet. The Old Testament makes it plain that any who lead the people astray from God must *'be put to death'* (*Deuteronomy 13:5*). Those who seriously take this as a possibility may wish to make Judas look more respectable.

Then there is the incident at Bethany where Jesus was anointed with *'very expensive perfume'* (*Matthew 26:6–13* and *Mark 14:3–11*). Both Matthew and John indicate that there was a great deal of outrage. ' *"Why this waste?"* ' (*26:8*). The question was asked by many present including some disciples. John identifies the woman as Mary sister of Lazarus. *John* also tells us Judas was among those who objected to this act of devotion. ' *"Why wasn't this perfume sold and the money given to the poor? It was worth a year's wages"* ' (*12:5*). Another side to this anointing was that it had a messianic implication. It seemed that Jesus was openly claiming *Messiah*ship by allowing Mary to pour the costly oil on his head. Iscariot may not have wished to challenge the anointing but nevertheless reacted strongly by insisting that this was waste.

We will, of course, never know what motivated Judas and as interesting as this speculation is, that is really all it can ever be.

Just to complicate matters, there are several others mentioned in the New Testament with this same name, including one of Jesus's brothers who is mentioned in *Matthew 13:55*. It was not an uncommon name but because of the infamy, the writer of the last but one book in the New Testament seems to have shortened his name to Jude.

MARY MAGDALENE

Mention the name 'Mary Magdalene' and the imaginations of some modern writers and musicians tend to overheat. They imagine that there was at least a budding romance. *Jesus Christ Superstar* began this trend. '*Should I speak of love let my feelings out,*' sings Mary who is portrayed as a lady with a rather wayward history and who had had a number of lovers and now wished for a complete break with the past.

It is, of course, Dan Brown who, in his book *The Da Vinci Code*, states that a marriage between Jesus and Mary Magdalene took place and that a family line was established. To be intellectually fair to him it seems that he knew in his heart of hearts that he was following some very far-fetched conclusions in order to sell his story. The other possibility was that he really had a belief in this fantasy history of Jesus. In the opinion of many the plot does seem to be the invention of a fertile but misguided imagination.

WHAT WE KNOW OF MARY[132]

Mary Magdalene's name would seem to suggest that she came from Magdala. Her village may also have

---

[132] Mary is a variation of the Greek form (Maria or Marium). The Hebrew name Miriam first appears in Scripture as the name of Moses's sister (***Exodus 15:20***). The meaning of the name implies a 'plump' lady.

been known as Magadan or Dalmanutha. As far as we can tell the village stood on the western shore of the Sea of Galilee and lay between Tiberias and Capernaum. It is believed that the modern site is now known as *Kirbet Mejdel*.

Magdala, at that time, was economically an important town, for fishing, curing fish and boat building, and its people enjoyed a good living. Having a pleasant lakeside location many Gentiles came to live there and Greek speakers called it *Tarichaea*. Josephus, the Jewish historian tells us that it even had a hippodrome for horse racing and other events.

The town developed a reputation for immorality and rabbis later wrung their hands over its evil practices. The fact that Mary Magdalene came from a place with a bad reputation could not have helped her own moral standing.

We first meet Mary in **Luke's Gospel Chapter 8:1 & 2** and we learn that: **'Jesus travelled about from one town and village to another, proclaiming the good news of the kingdom of God. The Twelve were with him, and also some women who had been cured of evil spirits and diseases: Mary (called Magdalene) from whom seven demons had come out.'**

Biblical scholars have wondered whether they could identify her as the woman *'who had lived a sinful life'*, who had *'stood behind him at his feet weeping, and had wet his feet with her tears. Then she wiped them with her hair, kissed them and poured perfume on them'* (*Luke 7:37–38*). This is of course not proven but does not seem to be too far-fetched as a theory.

Mary was part of a band of women who helped support Jesus and the Twelve. Among those named are Joanna and Susanna although *Luke 8:3* tells us that there were many more who travelled from place to place with Jesus and his disciples.

It is not until the Crucifixion that we hear of Mary again. She and other women had *'followed Jesus from Galilee to care for his needs and were there, watching from a distance'* (*Matthew 27:55–56*). It was Magdalene, who, in the company of another woman disciple, *'saw where he was laid'* (*Mark 15:47*) following his crucifixion.

Again on Easter day Mary Magdalene is there taking a lead, setting out for the tomb, in the early hours to help complete the last rites for the body of Jesus her rabbi, and friend.

It is obvious that all four of the Evangelists have used the testimony given by this key witness of the empty tomb. *Mark's Gospel* gives the fullest list: he mentions Mary Magdalene, Mary the mother of James, and Salome (*16:1–2*). *Matthew* mentions Magdalene and the other Mary (*28:1*). The only exception is *Luke's Gospel*, which does not mention Magdalene immediately; he says *'the women ... went to the tomb'* (*24:1*). In no way is Luke denying Magdalene's presence because he mentions her as the one who brought the news to the Eleven (*24:10*). As far as John's Gospel (*20:1*) is concerned Magdalene might have been on her own and it is not difficult to miss the little word *'we'* in *verse 2.* *' "They have taken the Lord out of the tomb, and we don't know where they have put him!" '*

JESUS AND MARY MAGDALENE

One characteristic of the life and ministry of Jesus is that he treated women with a far greater respect than most of his contemporaries. As has been said elsewhere in this volume, the status of women in Jewish first-century society was extremely poor. By contrast Jesus is prepared to give personal attention in teaching another lady by the name of Mary, the sister of Lazarus, and Martha, their sister, who lived in Bethany a couple of miles outside Jerusalem. Jesus had to deal with a family tension and smooth a sisterly dispute. *Luke 10:38–42* gives us the story. Mary is at the feet, the traditional position of any disciple of Jesus, learning and enjoying the moment. Martha is in the kitchen quietly fuming at being left with all the domestic chores of entertaining Jesus and the Twelve.

We can imagine her thinking, *'Huh, I suppose she thinks this meal will cook itself!'* In the end she can take no more and asks for Jesus to tell her sister to put on an apron and go into the kitchen. Graciously Jesus points out that Martha is getting rather worried and needlessly upset about things *' "but only one thing is needed. Mary has chosen what is better, and it will not be* *taken away from her" ' (**Luke 10:42**). We can find other examples but we see that Jesus's treatment of women is far superior to the average rabbi let alone the ordinary man in the Jerusalem street. This of course gives us an insight into the relationship of Magdalene and Jesus.

As we have already learnt Magdalene had been delivered from seven demons. This is reported twice in the New Testament in *Luke* (see above, *8:1–2*) and also *Mark* reports it *16:9*. Where and how this happened we are not told. A question that is worth asking but impossible to answer is to the age of Magdalene; we do not know whether she was of nubile age, perhaps hoping for a husband and family, or a lady of mature years. Naturally this would affect those people who would like to see her romantically although it might not have greatly affected Magdalene's own feelings.

Another factor to be considered was how Magdalene saw herself. Let's suppose that she had had some past experiences of which she now felt ashamed. How might that have affected the way she thought about Jesus? Here was a man who had the stamp of God on his personality and ministry to others. She might well have felt that such a man was totally beyond her reach, even that having such feelings were wrong. Jesus had shown that a man or woman's past did not matter as long as they showed signs of being open to God and having turned away from their old life.

Mary had been delivered from some kind of oppression or even possession and felt a deep gratitude to the man who had been her rescuer. This resulted in her wishing to help in the support of Jesus and his disciples. This she did in the company of other women who gave their time and money. Magdalene and the others would have seen the anxiety in Jesus as he journeyed to Jerusalem and may have felt fear but they were not deterred from going with him.

THE FIRST EASTER DAY

Mary was to have her own exclusive meeting with the risen Christ and it was among the first of the recorded appearances of which there were two that appear to have happened early in the morning of Easter Day. Now this is important! I cannot just make that statement but I also have to evaluate it.

Jesus's first appearances were to women (*Matthew 28:9–10* and *John 20:10–18*). In first-century Judea they would have been classed as lower down the social scale to any man. In terms of the evidence they could give they would have been thought of as totally unreliable witnesses. In the case of Mary there was the fact that she came from a town with a reputation for less than moral behaviour. On top of which, she had been possessed by not just one but seven evil spirits! This is strange and not the way a modern public relations consultant would handle it. However, we are not dealing with a public relations exercise but with history and divine history at that.

The report of the meeting of Mary with the risen Christ is dealt with in Chapter 6 so I need not comment in great detail. Jesus's dealing with Magdalene is different to his later dealings with the other women who were not stopped from touching him. He discourages Magdalene by saying, ' "*I have not yet returned to the Father*" ' (*John 20:17*). The answer might be that he did return to the Father in the time between his appearance to Magdalene and the second group of women. This is possible but I discount it. In the event, Jesus did allow Mary to touch him but not to cling.

The reason that many commentators give for Jesus not allowing Magdalene to '*hold onto him*' (other versions translate this verse as ' "*Stop clinging to Me*" ' (*John 20:17*)[133] is that he is telling her that she was to realise that the old ways had changed. This I would not, for one moment, argue against. There is the possibility that Jesus does not encourage physical contact to protect Mary Magdalene. To stop her confusing the love she had for him as a trusted friend with the romantic love a woman has for a man. In the Gospels we are dealing with real people. They had real emotional needs including human sexuality. And doesn't it make them more human, more relevant to people such as you and me today?

Jesus gives Magdalene a special task. He, for reasons of compassion, needed to reassure all those faithful followers and others he cared for, including James, a disbelieving brother. James seems to have been a son of Mary and Joseph born after Jesus.

---

[133] *New American Standard Version*, Peabody, Mass., Hendriksen Publishers, 1977.

MARY MOTHER OF JESUS

A unique lady!

EPHESUS OR JERUSALEM?

The minibus had stopped climbing and our scenic uphill drive past the fragrant fig trees ended in a shaded car park. On that hot August afternoon the place was delightfully cool up among the thousands of trees in the area known as *Bülbül Dağı* (Nightingale Mountain). We were a few miles inland from the Turkish town of Seljuk, which is next to ancient Ephesus. The tiny settlement of *Panayia Kapulu* was why we were visiting this fairly remote spot.

Here among the trees was a small chapel. This is, by one tradition, the final resting place on earth of Jesus's mother. This tradition goes back to Anna Catherina Emmerich (1774–1824) who was a German nun who had visions of the Virgin Mary and wrote a book about them. In 1891, people acting upon the visions came across a ruin in the place, which the vision had accurately described.

Firmer evidence that Mary the Mother of Jesus had lived in the area of Ephesus comes from the fact that there are the ruins of a church in Ephesus dedicated[134] to her. Then, is it a coincidence that in AD 431 a major church council met there with an important item on the agenda, which

---

[134] In ancient times a particular saint had to have had a definite association with a place to have a church named after them.

was to decide what the Church ought to believe about Mary? No, I imagine there was no coincidence.

The case for Ephesus is also strengthened by the fact that John Zebedee the beloved Apostle had associations with the city. He too has a church dedicated to him and we know that he was a political/religious prisoner on the Isle of Patmos, which lies a few miles to the west and had sent the church there a message (*Revelation 2:1–7*).

This tradition does not go down well in Jerusalem. On the Mount of Olives there is a site marking her burial. But does this stack up? Jerusalem would not have held happy memories for Mary. After all, the memories of the crucifixion would probably have meant that the city held unbearable recollections for her and – the body of Jesus was not there. He had risen!

Had she returned to Israel to die then it would seem more likely that she would have wished to be buried in Nazareth or somewhere in Galilee close to the final resting place of her husband, the beloved Joseph, and of her parents.

MARY'S EARLY LIFE

Piecing together the events of Mary's (or to give her likely Jewish name Miriam) early life is no easy task. The New Testament does not give us a great deal to go on. Again we have to look seriously at traditions. One tradition from the second century is worth consideration. This tells us that Mary's parents were Joachim and Anna. Other indications are that they lived at Sepphoris[135] a town close to Nazareth.

---

[135] See Chapter 1 for further details about Sepphoris.

What we can tell from the New Testament is that Mary was of the Tribe of Judah; as the angel Gabriel told Mary: ' *"The Lord God will give him,"* ' her son Jesus, ' *"the throne of his father* [forefather] *David"* ' (*Luke 1:32*). This fact is also confirmed by Paul who, after speaking about King David, a descendant of the tribe of Judah, says: ' *"From this man's descendants God has brought to Israel the Saviour Jesus, as he promised"* ' (*Acts 13:23*). Some scholars have wondered whether there could have been genes from the Tribe of Levi in Mary. However, with the emphasis of Jesus's lineage being from David, this does seem a remote possibility. The fact that this has been mentioned is the family connection with Elizabeth, her cousin (or kinswomen) and Zacharias.

Mary is called the kinswoman of Elizabeth (*Luke 1:36*) who was married to the priest Zacharias. It was the usual practice and encouraged by tradition that priests looked for wives among their own tribe and Zacharias had followed this practice. However, the word kinswoman does not tell us much. In fact it immediately raises two questions (a) were they related by blood or marriage; (b) what exactly was their relationship. Most modern versions such as *New International* use *'relative'*, some have speculated with 'cousin' and even 'aunt'. This might be from the fact that Elizabeth was reckoned to be well past childbearing age while Mary was young. In addition, Elizabeth was thought to be barren.

MARY AND HER EARLY MARRIED LIFE

In the time of Jesus, marriages would have occurred early, with men being thought of as being marriageable from eighteen years of age. Before the formal marriage there would have been a period of betrothal. Generally the father of the young man would take the major role and have a hand in selecting the bride. The young lady would not have been able to take an active part in this procedure. I imagine she would have been vocal had the suitor not pleased her. Once a betrothal had taken place the 'happy couple' were married in all but name. It was a legal contract and would only be ended by a *divorce*. Witnesses would have been present at the betrothal and would hear pledges made either by word or in writing. A dowry would have been given.

In spite of the binding and final character of the ceremony the couple would not have shared a bed until after the marriage ceremony. In fact this would have been considered a sin so that sexual abstinence had to be observed.

Joseph, on discovering Mary's pregnancy, would have feared the quite possible accusation that he had forced his attentions upon her and might have been accused of rape.[136] During this time of betrothal the man would have been exempt from military service as the preparations proceeded. In the unfortunate event of her future husband dying then the betrothed girl would have been classed as a widow. Although there is no warrant for believing it, Mary is considered to be a young teenager possibly around fifteen years of age. Joseph is, by tradition and we will think about that later, considered to be much older but making a good case for believing that is difficult.

---

[136] Further details about the regulations on betrothal can be found in **Deuteronomy 22**.

The Emperor Augustus in Rome had ordered a census of all his lands and as Joseph's family connections were in Bethlehem he had to take his new wife there. When the newly married couple arrived in Bethlehem we are told that they had to use the stable *'because there was no room for them in the inn'* (*Luke* 2:7). It is unlikely that a complete stranger owned this inn. Joseph may have known him. It cannot be proved but the inn in question was quite probably owned by a member of Joseph's extended family and other family members had bagged all the rooms in the house and felt they should hold onto them. Or was it a case that Mary was so near delivery that they could not spare the time to get a room ready.

Mary and Joseph did not appear to have had much money during their early married life. This is shown by the fact that in common with all Jewish women, after the birth of a child there would be a time for purification. Once this had been completed the parents would bring a lamb or, if not able to afford that, then two doves or pigeons would be presented for a sacrifice at the Temple (see *Leviticus Chapter 12*). Luke's Gospel mentions a pair of pigeons (2:24). Although Joseph's family lived around Bethlehem he was away from his home in Nazareth so finding paid work may not have been easy.

Now, there are two connected events that we will need to think about. About eighteen months after they arrived in Bethlehem, Mary and Joseph had visitors from a foreign country. *'Magi from the east came to Jerusalem'* (*Matthew* 2:1). They are sometimes called *'wise men'* but they ought not to be thought of as 'kings'. It is also a mistake to assume that there were only three. Certainly there were only three gifts presented so three gifts, in popular thought, equal three visitors – possible but not a foregone conclusion. Modern research would indicate that they came from Persia, or Iran as it is now called.

Who were they and what were they doing there? The answer is that they were astrologers, possibly Medes, the people we now call Kurds (although there is some discussion about this). They had seen a new star and realised that it was a portent of a powerful king being born and so they had travelled westwards.[137]

We do not know how long their search lasted but they made an error when they called upon King Herod the Great. Here was a monarch who was deeply paranoid

---

[137] On the 15 September 7 BC there was a conjunction of the planets Saturn and Jupiter and this occurred in the constellation of Pisces. Back in the 1980s, Dr Percy Seymour, using published data on the movements of planets 2,000 years ago and aided by work done by Dr David Hughes of Sheffield University (UK), fed this data into an advanced electronic programme. He was 'amazed' by the result. A huge star appeared and it was traced back to the night sky of the 15 August 7 BC. What was also astonishing was that Dr Hughes, an expert on the star of Bethlehem, was able to give an astrological meaning to the results. Jupiter is the planet for kings and Saturn is the planet for protecting the Jewish people while the constellation Pisces has associations with the Holy Land. During the Middle Ages there was a revision of the calendar and some mistakes were made in the calculations. Therefore, if the Magi saw the star at home in the middle of September, it would have taken them sometime to organise an expedition and travel to the Holy Land. During this time they seem to have lost sight of the star but were to see it again later, once they had arrived and were travelling to Bethlehem. This indicates that the birth of Jesus occurred six or seven years earlier than we have previously thought. Refer: *The Times*, 18 December 1984 and 18 December 1999.

and did not tolerate any rival. This was partly because he ruled with the help of Rome and had no claim to the title of King. When Herod heard the reason for the Magi's visit he called his advisers and learnt from them that the new '*King*' these Persians were talking about might well be the *Messiah*.

The Magi were sent to Bethlehem,[138] which was where the *Messiah* was going to be born. It is interesting that Herod probably did not take this totally seriously or else he would have sent attendants to go with these foreigners. On the other hand, he played safe, ' *"Go and make a careful search for the child. As soon as you find him, report to me, so that I too may go and worship him"* ' (*Matthew 2:8*).

The Magi made their visit and we learn that they found the Holy Family now living in a house (*Matthew 2:11*). This home could have belonged to one of Joseph's extended family.

Well, as just about everyone knows, the Magi didn't go back to Herod. They had a dream telling them not to (*Matthew 2:12*). Herod, no doubt through his informants, had heard rumours of strange things happening in Bethlehem and realised that these foreigners were not coming back. So, in order to preserve his throne,

---

[138] The prophecy that Herod's religious advisers looked at is in the Old Testament book of *Micah 5:2*: '*But you, Bethlehem Ephrathah, though you are small among the clans of Judah, out of you will come for me one who will be ruler over Israel, whose origins are from of old, from ancient times.*'

ordered that a few small infants ought to be sacrificed, so the *'boys in Bethlehem and its vicinity who were two years old and under died'* (*Matthew 2:16*). Fortunately a dream was to warn Joseph and he decided that a stay in Egypt would be good for their health. Just as well that the Magi had given them *'gold, incense and myrrh'* (*Matthew 2:11*), it would have funded that expedition.

Jesus, his mother and Joseph remained in the safety of Egypt until the death of Herod the Great. This occurred in 4 BC, which may have been about two years later.

THE MARRIED LIFE OF MARY AND JOSEPH

Some time ago I was part of a discussion group and one lady insisted that Mary and Joseph did not have any other children.

'Well,' I asked, *'what of the mention of other children in Matthew 13:55–56? "Isn't this the carpenter's son? Isn't his mother's name Mary, and aren't his brothers James, Joseph, Simon and Judas? Aren't all his sisters with us?"* '

'Ah,' she replied, *'they were the children of Joseph's earlier marriage!'*

The lady in question is relying on a document, which seems to have been written about the fourth century[139] that mentions that Joseph had had an earlier wife and

---

[139] The document is called the 'Protoevangelium of James'.

was now a widower. The style of this document is rather strange with the events being told in the first person, then the third person and with Joseph telling part of the story. It does, in the opinion of many scholars, seem like the work of several writers.

More than this the document insists that Mary was a virgin before the conception of Jesus. That the marriage with Joseph remained unconsummated until after the birth of Jesus. Then it says that Mary remained a virgin after the birth of Jesus and remained so to the end of her life. I seem to recall that there are a very few cases in medical records where a hymen had remained in place after a birth but they are so rare that we ought not to seriously consider the possibility.

With the first part of the argument, that Mary was a virgin before marriage the New Testament has no quarrel. Likewise, with the second part, for we are told that Joseph *'had no union with her until she gave birth to a son' (Matthew 1:25)*.

For me, and for most Christians, Luke's Gospel deals the trump card. Luke writes of Mary that *'she gave birth to her firstborn, a son' (Luke 2:7)*. Luke, a physician by profession, makes the point that this was the firstborn of Mary. In those times it would have been considered unusual or unnatural to have just one child.

I have included a profile of Mary, the Mother of Jesus, because of her unique position in the events of the life of Jesus. She is extremely prominent, some would say too prominent, in some Christian denominations with the result that others have tended not to give her the honour that she ought to have. I have tried to give her the recognition that she plainly deserves.

Elizabeth, her kinswoman, called Mary ' *"blessed"* ' (*Luke 1:42*). Elizabeth's words declare her to be worthy of praise and glory above all other humans, less of course than Jesus. '*Mary, among all women on earth you are the most blessed one.*'

PETER THE APOSTLE

I have developed an increasing respect for the man who was to become so vital in the life of the early Church. Like many I have, in the past, tended to remember his huge failures and have often passed over the many qualities that he possessed. Peter has, after all, the kind of history that would, if known only by a reading of the Gospels, not put him in the running for the leadership of a large secular organisation let alone the Church of God.

One of the most famous of Peter's failures is that he set out to join Jesus by walking on the water, began well and then started to sink when he looked around. The pity is, we remember the failure and forget his courage in starting out (*Matthew 14:28* and *John 6:19*). It is not recorded that any other disciple thought of getting out of the boat with him.

Another failure was that in the garden of Gethsemane as Jesus was being arrested Peter drew a sword and injured one of the guards sent to arrest Jesus. ' "*Put your sword away!*" ' (*John 18:11*). That had been Jesus's order to him. Worst of all each Gospel records Peter's cowardice in denying that he even knew Jesus.

However, he was to become the leader of the early Church, an organisation that grew enormously during its early centuries. Humanly speaking, much of its very early growth was thanks to the dedication and leadership of Peter.

If we are to get a truer, fuller picture of Peter's qualities as spokesman and leader we have to turn to the *Acts of the Apostles* and then towards the end of the New Testament we find two slim books, *The First Letter of Peter* and then the even slimmer *Second Letter of Peter*, from these we will get the corrective. We will see Peter the leader.

WHAT DO WE KNOW ABOUT PETER'S FAMILY?

Peter, like his brother Andrew, was a fisherman on Lake Galilee.

His given name, as a Jew, ought to have been Simeon but rather surprisingly it is Simon. This is a Greek form of the name and would indicate that he had a background both in Aramaic and in the Greek of the New Testament. This background is confirmed by the fact that Peter's brother has a Greek name: *Andreas* (Andrew). It would have been very useful for Peter as the leader of the Church to speak Greek. His father was named as *Jonah* or *John*. There are two references to Peter being married. One, in the Gospels, concerns the healing of his mother-in-law (e.g. *Mark 1:30*), there is also a reference to a *'believing wife'* whom he *'took along'* on his travels (*1 Corinthians 9:5*). Peter's brother Andrew was the one that brought Peter to Jesus and introduced them (*John 1:40*).

Peter lived on Lake Galilee. *Mark's Gospel* gives Capernaum as the place where the family had a house. Certainly Peter's mother-in-law lived there (*1:21–31*). *John's Gospel* names Bethsaida as '*the town where Andrew and Peter lived*'. This was a city with a great deal of Greek influence. At this time it was administered by Philip, the brother of Herod Antipas, as part of the region of Gaulanitis. The present name of this area is Golan.[140] Bethsaida and Capernaum are about five miles apart.

The only other piece of information that helps our understanding of Peter and his brother is that John the Baptist had influenced both men before they became Jesus's disciples.

PETER'S NAMES

Throughout the Gospels Peter is referred to as *Simon Peter* but in the *Book of Acts* he is more often called *Peter*. Later in the New Testament we find another name *Cephas*,[141] this is an Aramaic form of *Petros* a Greek word for 'rock'. The name Peter seemed to be Jesus's or possibly Matthew's pun. When Peter and the Twelve disciples are asked about who they thought Jesus was, it was Peter that used the words ' "*the Christ*" ' (*Matthew 16:16*).

---

[140] Much of the area of Golan is militarily sensitive as it is close to the Syrian border. The Golan Heights was taken by Israel from Syria during the Six-Day War (1967).

[141] Probably it is more accurate to say *Kep'has*.

Jesus tells him that he is correct and that he is a ' "*rock*" ' and that on the 'rock' of the statement of faith that Peter has just made, Jesus is going to build his Church. ' *"I tell you that you are Peter, and on this rock I will build my church"* ' (*v.18*).[142] Although Peter is called *Cephas* in the later books of the New Testament it was Jesus who first used this name in the New Testament (*John 1:40*).

Following Peter's statement of faith there had been a ceremony of Peter being given an appointment, we could call it a commissioning. As a symbol of this 'commissioning', Jesus told Peter: ' *"I will give you the keys of the kingdom of heaven; whatever you bind on earth will be bound in heaven, and whatever you loose on earth will be loosed in heaven."* ' (*Matthew 16:19*) (Not for one moment do I believe that a literal set of keys was given to Peter.) This authority Peter shared with the other men who became apostles and those authorised by them. Peter's position was first among equals.

Peter first used the '*keys*' some weeks after the Resurrection to open the Gospel to the Jews on the Day of Pentecost[143] when '*about three thousand*' new believers in Jesus '*were added to their number*' (*Acts 2:41*), later Peter was to use the '*keys*' to proclaim the

---

[142] The pun is '*Petros*' (rock) for Peter and '*petra*' for the statement of faith that Peter has just made.

[143] Pentecost was also known, among Jewish people, as the *Feast of Weeks* (Shavuot). It was an early harvest celebration and still marks the giving of the *Torah* or Law of Moses, even today.

Gospel to the Gentile household of a Roman centurion called Cornelius (*Acts Chapter 10*).

PETER THE LEADER

All leaders are made rather than born. Yes, men and women with leadership potential are often easy to spot but usually need much training and guidance to fit them for their roles. Peter was no exception to this; he was to take a great deal of training. He had been the first to grasp, or at least to state, that Jesus was *'the Christ'* – that had shown leadership. Leaders have to trust their own judgement. Jesus had commended him for this. However, this incisiveness then caused Peter to tell *'the Christ'* how he ought to behave. This is another example worth quoting that shows the 'downside' of Peter's leadership. In *Mark 1:37* after Jesus had left Peter's house early one morning to spend time in prayer in a quiet spot Peter and others went to find him. There seems almost a tone of disapproval in Peter's words: ' *"Everyone is looking for you!"* ' Certainly the future earthly leader of the Church had much to learn at this stage.

Peter had to come face-to-face with his weaknesses, in particular with what had happened in the courtyard of Caiaphas, the High Priest. Three times he had denied knowing Jesus. On the last occasion there had been a challenge that Peter could not ignore.

Surely you are one of them, for you are a Galilean.' He began to call down curses on himself, and he swore to

them, 'I don't know this man you're talking about'
(Mark 14:70–71).

Peter's language had got very strong but worse, there is a suspicion that Peter might have even 'cursed' Jesus! With this in his mind it is little wonder that Peter was in a state of severe depression on that first Easter Morning. He had seen the empty tomb and had not, at that stage, understood the reality. He had to realise that in his own strength he would fail totally. He, in common with the rest of Jesus's disciples, needed the Holy Spirit of God. This was to come, as we know, on the Jewish Feast of Pentecost.

A LEADER EMPOWERED

How did Peter escape from the depression that had overcome him when he realised the extent of his failure? Something out of the ordinary was needed. He had his own very personal appearance from the risen Christ. We have no details but Jesus visited him. Our informants are Luke and Paul.

' "It is true! The Lord has risen and has appeared to Simon" ' (24:34). The Apostle Paul confirms that Jesus *'appeared to Peter, and then to the Twelve'* (*1 Corinthians 15:3–5*). One can only imagine that there had to be a very large reconstruction on a very broken man. The assurance would have been given that Peter, now thoroughly repentant, had been forgiven. Peter had been too quick to trust in his own human abilities. He had to learn the lesson that his ability was in the strength of his Lord and God alone.

There was just one more stage of Peter's rehabilitation which we need to think about and that is found at the end of *John's Gospel*. Let me set the scene. Peter and several others of the Twelve (James and John are mentioned) were together by Lake Galilee. ' *"I'm going out to fish"* ', said Peter he was joined by others (they are named in *21:1*). While they are busy on the boat Jesus appeared but was not recognised. Later, on shore, there is a conversation between Peter and Jesus that is overheard by the rest of the apostles.

'Simon, son of John, do you truly love me more than these?' 'Yes, Lord,' he said, 'you know that I love you.' Jesus said, 'Feed my lambs.' Again Jesus said, 'Simon son of John, do you truly love me?' He answered, 'Yes, Lord, you know that I love you.' Jesus said, 'Take care of my sheep.' The third time he said to him, 'Simon son of John, do you love me?' Peter was hurt because Jesus asked him the third time, 'Do you love me?' He said, 'Lord, you know all things; you know that I love you.' Jesus said, 'Feed my sheep' (John 21:16–17).[144]

What are we to make of these verses? Some commentators have understood these three statements of devotion as Peter undoing the three denials that he made in Caiaphas's garden. Although there is much value in that argument I think that they were also for

---

[144] There is in these verses an interesting use of two Greek words both referring to love. Jesus used *agapas*, which is the strongest word for love. It is a word often used to describe the love of God. Peter offers *philo*, a word used for the love between friends. We find this used in English as a prefix in such words as *philanthropy*.

the benefit of those others with Jesus and Peter. They would see that Peter had been reinstated in Jesus's estimation. The past failures of Peter are over, as far as Jesus is concerned, but to set the record totally straight Jesus shows the other apostles that Peter is still his man. Peter is again shown as the first among equals.

PETER'S DEATH

At the beginning of *Chapter 8:1-2* of the *Acts of the Apostles* great persecution broke out against the Church in Jerusalem. This followed immediately after the death of the first Christian martyr Stephen (*Acts 7:54-59*). As a result much of the Church in Judea left the area and travelled to other parts of the Roman Empire. The most popular destination was Antioch in Syria, a journey that could be done on foot and would take only a few days.

For the first period of Peter's ministry he moved away from Jerusalem and had a ministry to both Greek and Aramaic Jews and Christians. This was for a period of about fifteen years and we find details in the first *twelve chapters* of the *Acts of the Apostles*, much of this seemed to have happened within a day or two's walk from Jerusalem. After this, the tracing of Peter's movements is rather less easy.

It is assumed that he travelled away from the area we call the Holy Land. The book *Acts of the Apostles* gives us a clue. In *Acts Chapter 12*, we learn of a fierce persecution against the fledgling Church. This perse-

349

cution was initiated by King Herod Agrippa I, the nephew and then later the brother-in-law of Herod Antipas, and occurred sometime before Agrippa died in AD 44. At some point during this period, James the Apostle and brother of John was murdered. This was during the early 40s of the Christian era (AD) now often referred to as the 'Common Era'. Peter was arrested but escaped from gaol with angelic help. In *verse 17* we are told that he *'left for another place'*. We cannot be sure where Peter and his wife went. Antioch in Syria is certainly a possibility for we are told that he visited the city where he and the Apostle Paul had had a lively discussion (refer to *Galatians 2:11*). Peter's journeys are now a matter of discussion and opinion but certain things can be said with a fair amount of confidence. He had contact with congregations in Asia Minor, the land now called Turkey, and his first letter is addressed to them (see the very first verse of this letter). It is almost certainly written from Rome, which Peter refers to as *'Babylon'*[145] (*1 Peter 5:13*). Peter addresses them as exiles so it is clear that they are Jewish believers. Using this would seem to suggest that Peter was either imprisoned or under something like house arrest.

That Peter died during the persecution of Nero is considered most likely. An enormous fire had

---

[145] The word 'Babylon' to Jews meant the years during the sixth century BC when they had been removed from Judah and forced to live as slaves in an Empire whom they had upset. The ancient City of Babylon is now part of modern Iraq.

destroyed much of Rome and the Emperor looked for someone to blame. The Christians, who were a very misunderstood group of people, looked to be good scapegoats. After all they were believed, by some, to be guilty of 'cannibalism'. This was a misunderstanding or a corruption of the words from the sacrament of Communion: *this is my body* and *this is my blood*. Naturally, Nero would claim that he was doing the citizens of Rome and the Empire a service in destroying them.

There is evidence that human remains found on the site of what is now St Peter's Square are those of Peter but this cannot be proved. What is not in doubt is that the apostle had influenced the life and work of the first-century Church in Rome.

The tradition about Peter's death by crucifixion, head down, comes from a rather strange document called the *Acts of Peter*.[146] This document was known to the early Church historian Eusebius who did not think that it was accurate. The story goes that Peter had been advised by the local Christians to leave Rome and did so with a heavy heart. On the road he met with Jesus walking into Rome. Peter asked him, 'Lord, *where are you going?*'[147] Jesus's reply made Peter change his mind

---

[146] This document contains some rather strange teaching, which does not agree with the teaching of the New Testament. It is believed that *Acts of Peter* was written about AD 200.

[147] Some readers will know this quote by the Latin words *Quo Vadis*.

about fleeing the city. *'To Rome to be crucified!'*[148] So, according to this tradition Peter returned and died choosing to follow Jesus's death by being crucified upside down, not the more 'dignified' position that Jesus had endured. As the origin of this tradition is so odd, I am not inclined to take it very seriously but I include it because it may well contain elements of truth regarding the death of Peter.

PETER'S ONGOING LEGACY

Peter's ongoing legacy for the Church throughout the ages has been and still is the ***Gospel of Mark***. This probably began life as the spoken teachings of Peter to those being prepared for the Christian rite of baptism.[149] These people were called Catechumens. It is likely that Peter made notes and these were in Aramaic, the first language of Peter and the Jewish people living in the Holy Land. At some stage Mark, or John Mark to give him his full name, must have had a discussion with Peter and it was decided that Peter's memoirs ought to be written down for future generations.

This may well have occurred in Rome where there was always the chance of the regime that had allowed

---

[148] The Crucifixion of Jesus was a *one-off* unique event never to be repeated. So the idea of a second crucifixion is quite unthinkable!

[149] Baptism is one of the sacraments of the Christian Church, during which adults are received into the membership of the Church universal, or in the case of infants there are promises made, which, when the child comes of age, they can confirm.

Judaism to exist might change its mind and become hostile. During its early years, Christians considered themselves, legitimately, as a developed form of Judaism. The Jews did not like this and quickly pointed out that *'that lot'* were nothing to do with them. The Romans began to investigate and this led during the reign of Nero to severe persecution.

In style the Gospel is a short and to the point account of the life of Jesus. It starts at the beginning of his ministry and ends at his Resurrection and Ascension. On the surface it looks to be arranged in a chronological sequence. Although many events must be in a time line this cannot be so in every case. We see this from a comparison with the same events as reported in Matthew and Luke.

Mark's reporting of the events in the life of Peter does not defend his mistakes and failures. It is very much 'a warts and all' approach. Both Luke and John in their report of this event do not report the 'curses' that Peter uttered (***Luke 23:54-62, John 18:15-18*** and ***18:25-27***). Only Matthew uses the same wording as ***Mark's Gospel*** (***26:72-74***) but then as he followed Mark's report he felt it was something that he ought to do. It is possible that John Mark completed the apostle's memoirs after his death but it is unlikely that this altered the contents of the report. The relationship between Peter and John Mark was obviously excellent as Peter referred to the younger man as *'my son Mark'* (*1 Peter 5:13*).[150]

I began this biography by listing Peter's failings and they were many. Peter, like many of us, developed and grew in strength of character. Can I use an analogy to show Peter's development? When first extracted, meerschaum, a clay-like substance used for ornaments or smokers pipes, is soft but it hardens on exposure to solar heat or when dried in a warm atmosphere. That is a picture of Peter who had enormous potential but had to realise his own limitations before he moved on to become the 'rock' that Jesus had predicted he would be.

---

[150] John Mark had a rather mixed career as a servant of God. He did not begin well but finished as a valued member of both Paul and Peter's teams. From his name we can infer that he was a Hellenised Jew (one who was from a Greek-speaking and educated background). John was a Jewish name while Mark is Roman. It is believed that he lived in Jerusalem with his mother who was probably a widow.

He became a companion of Paul on the Apostle's First Missionary Journey. How he served and what he did is unknown. At Perga, now in modern Turkey, Mark decided that he had had enough and returned to Jerusalem (*Acts 13:13*). We can only guess at the reasons for this. This did not make him popular with Paul who did not want him as a member of the team on the Second Missionary Expedition (*Acts 15: 36–39*). However, the disagreement did not last, as can be seen from *Colossians 4:10* and *Philemon 24*. Also Mark was a much-valued helper to Peter as *1 Peter 5:13* shows us.

PONTIUS PILATE

Governor of the Roman province of Judea, AD 26–37

He is neither knave nor fool; his trouble is that he is an ambitious government official, who has blotted his own record in the past by tactless dealing with the people he rules and despises.[151]

History has not been entirely sure of how to assess Pontius Pilate. Like any man in authority he had many detractors. The Jewish historian Josephus (AD 37–38 to c. AD 100) was one, and reported incidents that do not show skilful and sensitive control of his subjects. Josephus mentions two rather similar incidents, which involved displaying Roman symbols in the Holy City of Jerusalem much to the fury of the local people. It was the ancient equivalent of showing a cartoon of the Prophet Mohammed in the grounds of a Mosque. The use of Roman military symbols would have caused resentment enough. Add to this the fact that the Emperors were considered divine and one sees the scale of the problem. Josephus believed that, at least in one case, this action was a deliberate insult. It would only have weakened Pilate's standing that the Emperor Tiberius was forced to overrule Pilate on one of these cases.

---

[151] Dorothy L Sayers, p.264.

There was also an apparently well-meaning attempt to build an aqueduct to improve the water supply of Jerusalem but as Pilate intended to use the Temple's revenue for finance, protests followed as night follows day. Pilate's response was to punish the protesters with Roman batons. Some commentators wonder whether this relates to what Jesus was told about one of Pilate's actions. *'Now there were some present at that time who told Jesus about the Galileans whose blood Pilate had mixed with their sacrifices' (Luke 13:1).*

Another of Pilate's critics was Philo[152] who ascribes inhuman treatment, insult, rape and murder. Then, of course, there are the Gospel accounts that do not place Pilate in a favourable light.

It is strange and ironic that the one historical reference to Pilate in Roman documents mentions the fact that he was Procurator in Judea when *'Christus ... was executed ... in the reign of Tiberius' (Annals of Tacitus XV 44).*

In more recent times historians have been better disposed to Pilate. They point out that his tenure as Prefect lasted some ten years, whereas the usual office holder lasted three or four. Surely, he must have done some things right! Cynically I wonder whether Judea was considered as less than a plum job. Was it an appointment that many seeking high office dreaded being offered and feared refusing? After all, most of the

---

[152] Philo was an Alexandrian Jew who commented on the influence of Greek culture on the Jewish community. He is thought to have been born about 20 BC and to have lived after the Crucifixion.

citizens of the Roman Empire were fairly happy to go along with the Roman religious cult. The Jews were an exception to this and demanded special treatment for themselves and for the worship of their God.

One factor that could have greatly aided Pilate's career is that he made a very good marriage. The lady in question was Claudia Procula who was the grand-daughter of Augustus, Emperor of Rome between 29 BC and AD 14. Pilate was able to gain a rather unusual privilege; his wife was allowed to accompany him to his new appointment as Governor of Judea. Socially she was very well connected. This fact may have caused some of the complaints about Pilate's mismanagement to be overlooked or, at least, treated less harshly by Rome.

THE TRIAL OF JESUS

The fact that he was the presiding judge at the trial of Jesus is, historically speaking Pilate's only remaining claim to fame, or more accurately – notoriety. The trial raises an interesting question.

It does seem strange that Jesus seems to have been hauled up in front of Pilate before normal office hours. Granted that working days began much earlier in the east to avoid the heat and to make the best of daylight it is, by any standard, exceptionally early. Some have argued convincingly that Pilate had been briefed that an important Jewish trial is going to take place. The foremost proponent of this view is Frank Morison.

Further support for this idea is seen in the very political and evasive answer Pilate gave to the following question:

'Is that your own idea,' asked Jesus, 'or did others talk to you about me?
'Am I a Jew?' (John 18:34–5).

Pilate, as the representative of Rome, has the final say in whether the sentence can be carried out. He has no difficulties as long as the Pax Romana (the Law of Rome) was not overridden by local law.

Pilate was aware that the problem with this rabbi, Jesus of Nazareth, was that he was at odds with the Jewish religious hierarchy. That, if not dealt with carefully, could cause problems for Pilate's governorship. Therefore, if this rabbi was to be done away with, the matter had to be properly handled in accordance with Roman law. It would show the Sanhedrin that he was in control but if they could be kept happy with the outcome that would be the best result.

However, upon meeting with this itinerant preacher, we get the impression that from the onset Pilate felt Jesus was worthy of respect. Besides he is unhappy with the legal intricacies of Jewish law, and with the High Priest who is seeking a judgement under it for his own personal benefit.

As his interrogation proceeds, he feels unhappier that he is being asked to rubber-stamp a crude death warrant. Besides, he is, after all Roman and Law and Justice are important to Romans.

It was during this exchange that Pilate learnt that Jesus was a Galilean. This gave him, so he hoped, some 'breathing space', and as that part of the country was under Herod's jurisdiction he could pass the buck. Herod would be able to pass a death sentence and the matter would be dealt with. Perhaps, he would refer it to Rome or, more likely, as in the case of John the Baptist settle the matter in-house (refer to *Matthew 14:3–10* and *Mark 6:18–27*). Jesus was therefore taken to Herod. Herod interrogated Jesus and discovered that he had been born in Bethlehem, which was in Judea. That town was outside of Antipas's authority. It was under Pilate's jurisdiction. Jesus was returned to the Governor.

Pilate called together the chief priests, the rulers and the people, and said to them, 'You brought me this man as one who was inciting the people to rebellion. I have examined him in your presence and have found no basis for your charges against him. Neither has Herod, for he sent him back to us; as you can see, he has done nothing to deserve death' (Luke 23:13–15).

During some stage of his interrogation, Pilate had become disturbed. Firstly, there had been his wife's message about a *'dream'* concerning the accused that had greatly disturbed her (*Matthew 27:19*). Then the Jews told him that Jesus had ' "*claimed to be the Son of God*" '. This is enough to make Pilate really anxious. In

Roman religion, the idea of a 'son of the gods' appearing on earth is a distinct possibility. Pilate's reaction is a further interview with the prisoner. ' "*Where do you come from?*" ' (*John 19:7* & *9*). It would not be unreasonable to imagine that there is awe in the Governor's voice. There is something about this man that is beyond his earthly experience. Jesus's silence does not aid his state of mind. ' "*Don't you realise I have power either to free you or to crucify you?*" ' (*John 19:10*). Pilate tries to reassert a little of his authority but to no avail. Jesus answers, ' "*You would have no power over me if it were not given to you from above.*" ' The authority passes back to Jesus and Pilate's terror is confirmed.

From then on, Pilate tried to set Jesus free, but the Jews kept shouting, 'If you let this man go, you are no friend of Caesar. Anyone who claims to be a king opposes Caesar' (John 19:12–13).

There is another option open to Pilate. It had become a custom to release a prisoner at Jewish feasts. It helped to keep these difficult Jews happy or, at least, less unhappy. Mark's Gospel mentions the fact that some members of the crowd reminded Pilate of this concession (**Mark 15:8**). Pilate must have shuddered when he thought of who was in the cells. The thought of setting one prisoner at liberty must have been awful. Pilate is feeling that this matter is getting out of control. What would his Syrian-based superior say to this?

'*At that time they had a notorious prisoner, called Barabbas' (**Mark 27:15–16**). Mark adds that he 'was in* *prison with the insurrectionists who had committed murder in the uprising'* (*Mark* 15:7).

A reading of Matthew's Gospel (***Chapter* 27**) could be understood to indicate that Pilate may have received the message from his wife at this very moment. ' *"Don't have anything to do with that innocent man, for I have suffered a great deal today in a dream because of him" '* (*Matthew* 27:19). The crowd, given the choice, decide that they would like Barabbas released. When Pilate tried persuading the crowd it seemed that a riot would break out.

Pilate is caught in a trap; he wishes to free Jesus but his past history of mismanagement of this command has made his position insecure, even precarious. The Temple clergy watch him hesitating. The High Priestly retort about his loyalty to Caesar was, almost certainly, made in front of some of his soldiers; his position is thus further undermined. Pilate's loyalty to Rome must, in the eyes of his fellow Romans, be beyond question. Besides this, charges concerning *neglect of the security of the state* were frequent in Rome during this period.

Pilate has been outmanoeuvred by Caiaphas and Annas. His conscience is troubled and he will have to face the censure of his gods in the next life, and the terrors of his own wife in this one. '***Pilate brought Jesus out and sat down on the judge's seat at a place known as the Stone Pavement (which in Aramaic is Gabbatha)'*** (*John* 19:13).

Deeply unhappy about the course of events Pilate has one more try but he must have realised that he had lost. Pontius Pilate's position is a very delicate one. Another complaint to the Emperor is something he cannot risk. It would not merely mean the end of his career, it could well jeopardise his life.

' "Here is your king," Pilate said to the Jews. "We have no king but Caesar," the chief priests answered' (John 19:14 & 15). The crowd had made up its mind and demands the death penalty. *' "Take him away! Take him away! Crucify him!" '*

Pilate had clearly hoped that he could have got out of this situation by giving the crowd the chance of choosing Jesus and giving him a free pardon but they had decided on Barabbas. It is likely that the people were suspicious of Pilate's motives and had thought that his trying to persuade them to choose Jesus had been for his own benefit.

It was then that Pilate *'...took water and washed his hands, "I am innocent of this man's blood," he said. "It is your responsibility!" All the people answered, "Let his blood be on us and on our children!" Then he released Barabbas to them. But he had Jesus flogged, and handed him over to be crucified' (Matthew 27:24–26).*

THE 'SUPERSCRIPTION'

As we know Pontius Pilate capitulates but he makes one small stand for justice and it is over the 'superscription' or charge that told passers-by the crime for which a condemned man was being crucified. In the case of Jesus there seems to be a slight departure from the norm. This placard, which was smeared with white gypsum, was then written on in black. It would normally be placed around the condemned man's neck as he carried his own cross to the place of execution. It seems that Jesus began by bearing his own cross until it became obvious that he was not physically able to carry it the whole distance.

The wording on the 'superscription' that had been attached to the Cross remained unaltered, in spite of the protests of the High Priests. They seethed at the words above the head of Jesus, *THE KING OF THE JEWS*, and wanted the charge to state that Jesus had merely *'claimed to be King of the Jews'*. It is easy to imagine the contempt in Pilate's voice as he replies, ' *"What I have written, I have written"* ' (*19*:21 & 22). John tells us that it was in three languages: Latin, the official language of Rome, Greek, the language of commerce, widely known around the Mediterranean, and finally in Aramaic, the first language of Jews. Clearly, Pilate wants everyone to know what he thinks of the deceit of Caiaphas and Annas. There is also another thought in the wording of the *'superscription'*; Pilate is guarding his own position. He is astute enough to wonder whether this trial may come back to haunt him. He will not want any Roman official challenging him as to why the charge of 'King of the Jews' was not taken seriously.

THE FALL AND DEATH OF PONTIUS PILATE

In his tenth year Pilate's heavy-handed treatment of the local populace brought him into conflict with first, his immediate superior, Vitellius, Legate of Syria, then with the Emperor Tiberius. The cause of his recall was yet another blunder.

A group of Samaritans seeking the recovery of holy vessels, supposedly buried on Mt Gerizim during the time of Moses, aroused the suspicions of the Governor.[153] They were gathered in rather large numbers, so Pilate sent in his troops to disperse them. There were later executions of prominent Samaritans. Complaints were made and Pilate was recalled to Rome. Unfortunately for Pilate, a new Emperor, Caligula banished him to France following a trial. It was here that Pilate committed suicide.

****

Although there is nothing in Scripture giving information there is an interesting and creditable belief that Pilate's wife became a Christian, and was known as Procula or Procla. Pilate's wife was created a saint by the Eastern Church and is commemorated on the 27 October.

---

[153] Pilate, the Governor, is often referred to as the 'Procurator' but he himself was a Roman Prefect. The title of Procurator was given to Pilate's successors some years later. When this change of title happened is not entirely certain.

A SHORT DICTIONARY

****

Words, phrases, customs, ceremonies that occur or are mentioned in this book.

APOSTLES

THE ORIGIN AND USE OF THE NAME

This word 'apostles' appears a few times in the pages of this book and it is not totally necessary to completely understand its meaning to get benefit from reading *Jesus – A Serious Beginner's Guide*. However, it is a word that is often used by readers of the Bible and clergy. So, I think a fairly brief note will be helpful.

As in the case of most of the New Testament we have to look back to the Greek language, not just the *Koine* (common) Greek of the New Testament but to the use of classical Greek. The word *apostello* – 'one sent' – had both diplomatic and naval meanings. It could mean someone representing the government, not unlike a modern ambassador. It could also refer to the fleet and its commander.

Flavius Josephus, the ancient Jewish historian, who was born about two years after Jesus, knew of this word and he suggests that it was used by Greek speaking Jews (sometimes called Hellenistic Jews) at that time. Some have suggested that it was used in the synagogue for agents sent out with authority to act in matters legal, financial or pastoral. There has been much discussion and the question remains unproven.

IN THE NEW TESTAMENT

In the New Testament the word is used supremely of Jesus *'the apostle'* [*apostolos*] *'and High Priest whom we'* confess (*Hebrews 3:1*) as the one sent from God with a particular purpose: to rescue humankind from the power of evil and the moral effects that this brings.

Then, it is used of the Eleven remaining disciples, plus Matthias, who had been chosen by prayer and the drawing of a lot as a replacement for Judas Iscariot (*Acts 1:23–26*). Then there is the Apostle Paul, converted after having a vision of the risen Christ on his journey to Damascus (*Acts of the Apostles Chapter 9*).

It seems that there were others who might have a claim to be called apostles. At the end of his Letter to the Romans, in the good wishes he sends to friends and supporters (*Chapter 16:7*), Paul writes, *'Greet Andronicus and Junias, my relatives who have been in prison with me.'* He goes on to say that *'they are outstanding among the apostles'*. Of course, Paul could be saying that these two people were 'known to the rest of the apostles' not that they themselves could be thought of as being apostles.

The name Junias has led to much discussion. The reason is that it could be Junia not Junias, one of my commentators, F F Bruce, was unable to decide. Junia is the female form of the name, which makes for some very interesting speculation. This verse does not make the matter thoroughly clear although in the male-dominated society of the first century any apostle, other than a man, would be unique! So, I am of the opinion that Paul meant *known to the rest of the apostles* not that they were apostles themselves.

THE QUALIFICATIONS FOR BEING AN 'APOSTLE'

Naturally, it was necessary for apostles to believe in the fact that Jesus was the *Messiah*. But more was required! Peter and the rest of the remaining disciples, now called apostles, made a decision. The *Acts of the Apostles 1:22* tells us of their thinking. Any new apostle *'must become a witness with us of his Resurrection'*. With the choice of Matthias there was no problem, he had been around long enough to know when Jesus began his ministry and what had happened on the first Easter Day. With the Apostle Paul, it was some time later when he was able to believe that Jesus was alive. It was then, after having a personal meeting, that he became a witness to the Resurrection and a powerful apostle and teacher.

BIBLE

The Bible contains the holy writings for both Jewish worshippers and for Christians. It is divided into two parts. The first and by far the largest, called the Old Testament, is particularly sacred to the devout Jew.

Christians also believe it to be authoritative and an important source for belief and action.

It is worth spending a few moments thinking about the word 'testament'. As we know this is a legal term that today usually refers to the disposal of the goods, money and property of someone who is deceased. It has an alternative meaning and refers to a legally binding agreement between people. Another word used often nowadays, which is rather more accurate, is 'covenant'. What about 'contract', is this an alternative word for covenant? No! It is a mistake to think of our modern idea of a contract because this is usually between parties who are, more or less, equal. Naturally, equality is out of the question when God and men are concerned. (See **Covenant** below.)

THE OLD TESTAMENT

The first thing to say is that the word 'old' should not make us think that this section of the Bible is obsolete. It is <u>very far</u> from this! It should be remembered that for the early Church in the first century these were their Scriptures. Yes, it is true that they were a largely Jewish organisation. However, even Paul the Apostle, who was very much an innovative thinker, was happy to allow himself to be placed under Old Testament vows.[154] The first century, even without the New

---

[154] Refer to *Acts 18:18* and to *Numbers 6:1–3*. This was probably done as an offering to God and to show his devotion to the Law of Moses during his time in Jerusalem. Then again, Paul, in *Acts 21: 21–24* accepted a vow. It would be wrong just to see this as a compromise just to keep non-Christian Jews happy.

Testament being set down in writing, was a time of extraordinary growth for the Church.

The 'Old' Testament is to be thought of as the foundation for the New. Unfortunately, there are quite a number of Christians who have not realised this vital fact. The New Testament is really a commentary on the Old.

The Old Testament (OT) begins with an account of creation but deals with the 'why' rather than the 'how' that modern science is concerned with. The account uses much poetic language, which is rather strange to Westerners. It then gives a history of God's dealing with the people who he called to worship and to discover themselves, their full humanity, and the creator who had brought them into being. These people came to be known firstly as Hebrews, later Israelites and finally Jews.

Much of the OT is in the form of regulations for living and formal worship. This is more formally known as *The Law of Moses*. There are also books of sacred poetry, wisdom and prophecy. When we hear the word 'prophecy' we automatically think of predictions about future events and although this is correct many of the OT prophets spoke about contemporary issues in the nation such as injustice, which did not please God and often had a bad effect on the poor and powerless.

Prophecy is sometimes difficult because readers in the twenty-first century cannot always be sure whether the prophet is speaking about events that were occurring then or that would happen in the future. However, reading them often gives guidance on situations that can occur nowadays in our daily lives because many principles regarding justice are still issues today and unfortunately are unlikely to ever go away. Sometimes a prophecy about the future was conditional. If the nation or its king did not mend their ways then certain dire consequences would follow. Clearly, warnings on these situations were heeded but often not immediately. The prophets spoke in the name of God and we have written accounts of their words. This was due to the fact that in the Holy Land people had learnt the art of writing early in their history and so the prophets themselves or their helpers and followers had written down their messages.

There are thirty-nine books in the OT, beginning with Genesis and ending with the prophet Malachi who lived about 450 years before the birth of Christ. The Hebrew name for these Jewish Scriptures is the *Tanach*.

THE NEW TESTAMENT

The New Testament (NT) has twenty-seven books. It is the Scriptures of Christians and for them takes precedence over the OT. It deals with the life of Jesus and the lifestyle, worship and devotion of those who believed and had begun to follow his teaching.

THE GOSPELS

The NT begins with the four Gospels. St Matthew wrote quite soon after the Gospel of St Mark, this (reckoned as the earliest) was written during the early or mid-60s of the Christian era. St Luke, can probably be dated a few years later about the end of that decade. These three Gospel writers, also known as Evangelists, are known as the *synoptic* writers as they tended to see things in the same manner. Matthew and Luke start with the events leading up to and following the birth of Jesus then continue until he left the earth. Mark also uses a time line but begins with the time Jesus became a preacher. The first three Gospels write about the life of Jesus as a biography. Each of them usually reports the same events but often give us additional details, which can provide a fuller narrative. This said, Luke and Matthew give us details that Mark excludes which concern the birth and infancy of Jesus.

John, in his Gospel, does things differently, giving us a series of events; often he calls them '*signs*' to prove to his readers that Jesus was the *Messiah*, the One promised by God. Jesus was God's special messenger who would bring blessing to all humanity. John is quite open about his motives '*that you may believe that Jesus is the Christ, the Son of God, and that by believing you may have life in his name*' (*John 20:31*).

John's Gospel is usually considered as the latest Gospel to be written and is thought to have been compiled around AD 85–90. This would have meant that St John had had a rather long life, which, for the leaders of the early Church, was quite an achievement.

THE LETTERS

The letters of the NT, sometimes known as the Epistles, were written by different people and deal with correct Christian conduct, beliefs and practical matters. John, Peter and Paul are the main Letter writers and began during the 40s and 50s of the first century. This pre-dates the Gospels often by many years but in spite of their earliness they appear well back in the order of the books of the NT.

THE ACTS

In between the four Gospels and the Letters is an interesting book known as *Acts* or to give it its full title: the *Acts of the Apostles*. This book does exactly what its title says. It is an early history of the Church and of the events that occurred to its leaders.

The Christian movement's growth is told, errors in some of its members are not hidden and the learning that had to occur is explained. One of the most impor-tant tasks of this book is to tell us about St Paul. (Please refer to **Apostles, in this section** for more details on this great man.)

The author of *Acts* is Luke who wrote this book after the Gospel that bears his name. There are twenty-eight chapters in the book and there would probably been many more had the persecution of the Emperor Nero not occurred. In AD 64, a great fire destroyed much of Rome and Nero, to divert attention from rumours that he had started the fire himself, blamed Rome's Christians. Paul and Peter are strongly believed to have died during the persecution that resulted.

THE REVELATION

At the very end of the NT is a very curious book called *The Revelation* and when I say 'curious' I am speaking about its contents, which is full of symbols. Christians down the years have not been fully sure of how to take them. The book uses imagery that has led some people into rather strange conclusions. In 1976, the horror movie *The Omen* hit the big screen. So successful was it that it was remade in 2006. The plot involves a live baby substituted for a stillborn child who grows up to be the Antichrist, a being who is mentioned in later letters of the NT[155] but not in *Revelation* itself. But what was taken from the book is the number of the beast *666*. Before we look at the contents of the book, a brief look at the author and his background may help to partly explain the writing.

The writer John, probably John Zebedee who was the Apostle John and writer of the Gospel of that name, although this is not proven, was in trouble. He had been banished to the Isle of Patmos, which was a long-established Roman penal colony. If the Empire thought that you and your views did not quite fit in with the politics of the time you would be shipped off for a spot of 're-education'. It is believed, and this is well

---

[155] There are four references to *antichrist* in the *first* and *second letters of John* near the end of the NT. The *antichrist denies the Father and the Son* (*1 John 2:22*).

founded, John was banished there in AD 95 during the reign of Emperor Domitian, an ill-tempered egomaniac who thought he was a god and who persecuted Christians. Domitian was at the end of his reign and died the next year. Fortunately for John, Nerva, the next Emperor, was more tolerant and released him soon after his reign began.

By tradition, John spent about a year on the island during which time he compiled the text of what we call *Revelation*. It is unlikely that John was the only Christian on Patmos but it is likely that there were many more dissidents with whom Christians had to be cautious as to what was said and written in their presence. Informing on another prisoner could be very helpful in reducing your own sentence. Some of them may have been planted.

John, at the very beginning, introduces his main theme as a warning *'of what must soon take place'*. This warning had come by a very special angelic messenger – Jesus himself. His readers are urged to *'hear it and take to heart what is written in it, because the time is near'* (*v.3*). There then follows seven messages to seven churches in the Roman province of Asia (now western Turkey). Refer to *Chapters 2 and 3* of *Revelation* for the list and the messages.

There is only limited space that can be given to the subject of the images and code words that are widely used in the book. The name *'the beast'* (*13:11*) was a codename used to describe the Emperor. The name

'*Babylon*', once the capital of Persia, is used six times in the book, and is used in reference to the city of Rome. The '*enormous red dragon with seven heads and ten horns and seven crowns on his heads*' (*Revelation 12:3*) refers to the seven Roman Emperors who had thought themselves gods and encouraged people to worship them. Naturally, this was soon to cause grave problems to Christians, especially in Rome, who reckoned that '*Jesus is Lord*' (*First Letter to the Corinthians 12:3*) rather than Caesar.

BREAKING THE CODE

Now, what about 666, what does it mean? Did the movie *The Omen* get it right? '*This calls for wisdom. If anyone has insight, let him calculate the number of the beast, for it is man's number. His number is 666*'(*Revelation 13:18*). How do we do our sums on this one? Well, let's forget multiplication or division for the moment. At the end of this quotation we are given a helpful clue, '*it is man's* (humanity's) *number*', this gives us the breakthrough! But we need to go back to the very beginning of the OT to the poetic account of creation in *Genesis 1:26–27* where we learn that human-kind was created on the <u>sixth</u> day. We are now on the way to a solution.

Before we draw any conclusions we need a quick lesson in the ancient belief that numbers have a meaning. It is known as numerology. The number 'seven' is a number of perfection and seven was also a sacred number among several peoples during ancient times. To go back to the picture language of *Genesis 1*, we see that God finished creating on the seventh day.

Before we get to our answer we must think about another number: the number is 'three'. The number three is a number that signifies completeness. Christians believe that God exists as three. He has been called the tri-personal God. In the book of the prophet *Isaiah Chapter 6*, God's servant Isaiah had a vision of God while in the Temple at Jerusalem. He saw angels who called to each other, ' "*Holy, holy, holy is the LORD Almighty*" ' (*v.3*). To have called '*holy*' just once makes the point about the nature of God. To have used the word a second time gives it much more emphasis but to use it three times means that God is totally '*holy*', so completely and utterly that you cannot get any holier.

Jesus was in the tomb but rose from death on the 'third day'. The fact of this being on the third day means that it was a completed act.

So, we can now get back to thinking about the number *666*. Six, as any child, who can count will tell you is less than seven. It fails to be the number of perfection. Now, let's think back about the number three or three times (1 x 3). Therefore, *666*, is a number of total failure. I was interested to notice that some commentators would say that this number could be used of a human or an animal. We could say a 'beast'! That is a significant word in *Revelation*.

The Revelation is a demanding book, and because it is there are few people who wish to tackle it. It is a rewarding book but if you wish to look at the Bible start elsewhere.

READING THE BIBLE: A FEW SUGGESTIONS

Firstly, if you wish to read the Bible, do make sure that the version you get hold of is a modern one. Do not rely on using great-grandmother's, you will probably find it hard going. I have used, for the most part, the *New International Version* in these studies. There are several other versions that are modern and relevant. When I first became a Christian I struggled to understand the Shakespearian English of the *King James Bible/Authorised Version*. Fortunately, I quickly discovered that there were modern English versions available.

Versions of the Bible come in two types. The first has used the original Hebrew of the OT and Greek of the NT and has tried to keep as close to the meaning of these languages as possible. The second type of Bible is called a 'paraphrase'. This concentrates not so much on keeping to the original languages as producing a text that comes across in vivid English. Often this works very well. However, with this type of Bible some, usually small, liberties were sometimes taken in translation. Ideally the best thing is to have one of each type, remembering that the first type will be closer to the true meaning of the original languages than the paraphrase.

Finally, it may not be a good idea to begin at the very beginning and try to read to the end. Try a Gospel – John's is an invitation to consider the person of Jesus. On the other hand Mark's Gospel may suit you better as it is the shortest of the four. Also, it is possible to buy some of the Gospels as a booklet. Certainly, St John's Gospel can be purchased for very little. Then you will find organisations such as the *Gideon's International* who may be happy to give you a whole Bible or New Testament at no cost to you.

BLOOD

Blood was in ancient times and remains today a symbol of life. When certain kinds of wrongdoing occurred in ancient Israel such as murder, the lifeblood of the murderer was demanded. However, there were other acts, which although committed against a person, also were an offence against God. *Deuteronomy 22:25* gives an example: *'if out in the country a man happens to meet a girl pledged to be married and rapes her, only the man who has done this shall die.'* Not only did God wish to see the protection of the weak, he wanted to have a close relation with humanity, his creature.

Although this punishment was severe, the people were left in no doubt as to the penalty. Also, to safeguard those who might be unjustly accused of murder, rape or other capital offences, there were safeguards built into the Law of Moses. In practice, the full penalty did not happen in every case. There were also cities of refuge to where a man could flee until all his accusers had had time to look at the whole matter.

What did happen fairly often was that the people of God chose to get involved with the practices of other religions. These people knew the penalty. The Law of Moses had spelt it out very clearly. When they returned to their God an animal's lifeblood was needed as a substitute for their lifeblood. Therefore, at some personal cost, the wrongdoer was allowed to remain alive. The animal sacrifice took the penalty. As the writer of the letter to the Hebrews explained, *'without the shedding of blood there is no forgiveness'* (9:22). The Priest would present the animal's blood for the life of the sinner at the altar making peace between the wrongdoer and God.

It was the Apostle Paul who explained the OT ideas of blood in the light of the coming of Jesus Christ. There is still the idea of a substitute. Now, since the death of Christ, it is the lifeblood of Jesus, who at Calvary was *'making peace through his blood, shed on the cross'* (*Colossians 1:20*). Please also refer to **Sacrifice** (below) for more details.

CHRISTIANS

It is a strange fact that the word 'Christian' was originally a name that non-Christians gave to believers in Jesus. *'The disciples were called Christians first at Antioch'* (*Acts 11:26*). This was a city in Syria[156] to which Christians travelled to avoid persecution from Jerusalem's religious hierarchy.

OTHER NAMES USED FOR CHRISTIANS

These original believers in Jesus called, or thought of themselves as belonging to *The Way* (*Acts 19:9*). Paul the Apostle, who did much to help Gentiles understand the Gospel and also his fellow Jews to better understand their own Jewish faith in the light of the *Messiah*'s coming, had his own phrase for being a Christian. A dedicated believer in Jesus was in Paul's words *'in Christ'*. This was because he thought of the Church as being like a human body. Paul's Letter to Rome explains his thinking: *'in Christ we who are many form one body, and each member belongs to all the others'* (*12:5*). Paul used this same analogy in another letter to a different church. In the thinking of Paul every part of this *'body'*, however modest, has a part to play. *'The*

---

[156] Bible students may be slightly confused to learn that there is another Antioch several hundred miles west. This is called Pisidian Antioch; it lies north of Antalya in modern Turkey.

eye cannot say to the hand, "I don't need you!" And the head cannot say to the feet, "I don't need you!" ' (*1 Corinthians 12:21*).

In yet another of Paul's letters he changed the analogy a little and makes Christ 'the Head'. *'God placed all things under his feet and appointed him to be "head" over everything for the Church, which is his body, the fullness of him who fills everything in every way'* (*Ephesians 1:22–23*).

BEING OR BECOMING A CHRISTIAN

What exactly is a Christian? The answer can only be found in the teaching of Jesus and his apostles.[157] First, it could be easier to say what does not automatically make a person a Christian.

Having devout parents who give instruction in the faith does not make a person a Christian. However, let me say that having such parents is an advantage. We will look at these, below because there are definite benefits.

Neither does the Sacrament of Baptism performed for us as infants make us fully Christian. This is, with infants, intended to be a *pro tem*[158] which means that it allows a child to receive the membership of the Church (the universal Church not just your local congregation)

---

[157] See note on **Apostles** in this section.

[158] *Pro tem*, or to use the phrase in full *pro tempore*, is Latin and often used as a legal expression. Its easiest translation is 'for the time being'.

but with the understanding that the child, upon reaching an age of understanding, will make his or her own personal commitment to Christ. The person then makes this clear in the ceremony, called Confirmation, or in some similar ceremony to mark an entry into the Church and, as long as this is a fully sincere and informed free choice, the person then is a Christian in the complete sense. Again, let me say that I am writing about the universal and not the local church.

In many churches, the act of baptism is only performed when the person has reached an age of understanding of what it is to be a Christian and feels able and willing to make his or her own individual commitment.

As a teenager, at lessons in school, I was greatly attracted to the person of Jesus by the kind of teaching that is found in the Sermon on the Mount (*Matthew* 5–7). I rather thought that I had arrived. I somehow imagined that I had discovered that, by following the rules, I was being a Christian. It was true that following and obeying the rules was a hard task but, as an immature teenager, this did not seem to be a great burden. I was very wrong. I had not even begun to understand!

Martin Luther, the German Reformer of the sixteenth century, had also believed during his early years that it was the rules themselves that made a person a true Christian. He became a monk and found that the rules were too frightening and uncertain. How could he be sure that he had, by his life, pleased God? He had a burden of failure and guilt.

It was later, while he was teaching that he discovered *'faith'* and that Christians lived by it. This discovery changed Christian history and it utterly changed Luther himself. This is what he reported: *'I felt myself to be reborn and to have gone through open doors into paradise'* (Ronald Bainton, *Here I Stand*, p.49).

Many others, even some who have been clergy, have had to have this experience of God starting a new thing in their lives. Charles and his better-known brother John Wesley, who had been clergy for some years, experienced what they called a *'heart-warming experience'* in the eighteenth century. This was to result in the Christian movement now called Methodism.

I, although I would not put myself in the same league as Luther and Wesley, had that 'new thing' happen to me in the twentieth century. I had seen that all my failures and rebellion could be dealt with by the life but more especially by the death of Christ and I took his words seriously. ' *"Follow me"* ' was not just an invitation to obey his rules of what he called the ' *"Kingdom of Heaven"* ' (*Matthew 5:3*) but to make a personal commitment to him. Obeying the rules, which is never easy, was just a response to Jesus and a sign of my commitment to him. I came to make a discovery; I stopped knowing about Jesus and began to know him personally. That was many years ago and I am still learning.

Jesus said to his disciples and some would-be followers, ' *"If anyone would come after me, he must deny himself and take up his cross and follow me. For whoever wants to save his life will lose it, but whoever loses his life for me will find it" ' (Matthew 16:24–25).*

I can imagine that for many readers this seems totally unappealing but I can assure you it is worth a second look. This is a 'new lives for old lives' offer. You may protest, 'I don't think there's much wrong with my present one.' Let's face facts, we are all resistant to change even to such things as the brand of instant coffee we drink at breakfast.

Readers may have been discouraged by the word *'loses'*, in the above quotation. There are bad losses, such as your wallet or purse, and there are good losses, such as losing the fear you had of a certain illness or a certain situation developing.

Can we concentrate on what is often a much more positive word? Let's have a couple of examples, shall we? We might say, *'We find that living here has not been as expensive as we thought.'* I have *'found my missing keys'*. Yes, there are 'finds' that we would rather not make but mostly the word is used for positive outcomes.

It is quite possible that someone will argue against this. They will say, 'I'm not convinced I need this.' They could and often say, 'Why should I become a Christian?' The answer is that within the nature of all human beings there is an inbuilt rebellion. This is seen in our dealings with one another and at its most extreme level it results in crime and wars between nations and similar evils. I am writing this on the 200th anniversary of the ending of the awful trafficking of slaves from Africa to the New World. This was a heinous crime against humanity. God was deeply offended! It stemmed from the natural selfishness that we all have. This gives us all a tendency to rebellion against each other and, more importantly, against God.

There is a very misunderstood word that the Bible uses for our natural rebellion and that is *sin*. People used to speak of 'living in sin' and they meant marriages that were informal, without benefit of clergy, unlicensed. No, sin is far worse than that because it causes the breakdown of human relationships, which cause so much sadness and deep hurt to so many individuals.

God, who so deeply cares for his creature the human being, is grieved more than can be explained. God is also offended that he sent Jesus to rescue us from our rebellion and we say, 'Why should I become a Christian?' Is it any wonder that God is offended by us?

THE BENEFITS OF A CHRISTIAN UPBRINGING

I must now make good my promise to look at the benefits of being brought up in a Christian home and having devout parents or other close relatives. Well, does it make a difference or not? The answer is that it most certainly can. Take Eric, for example, who, when I met him a number of years ago was a newly retired headmaster. He was just aglow with God but as he later confessed there had never been a moment when he had decided to become a Christian and make a definite commitment. He had had the loving support of devout parents. Eric did say that he regretted that there was, in his life, no sudden moment of realisation; what is sometimes called a *Damascus Road* experience[159] but this was not necessary. Another example of something a little different is Diane. For her, coming to faith occurred after a period of learning at the local church that she was attending. Again there was no moment of decision, or great decision but she was able to look back and to discover that God had done a new thing in her life. There may well have been a series of small decisions along the way but no particular moment, no crossroads where she could have gone one way or another. So, we can say with confidence, that God uses different means, which may depend on the kind of people we are in life experience or personality.

Jesus promised to those who followed him a discovery of a richer, fuller, happier and more meaningful life. As he promised, ' *"I have come that they may have life, and have it to the full"* ' (*John 10:10*). This does not mean that life will be carefree and without difficulties and that once a person becomes a Christian they will automatically and quickly leave their problems behind.

On too many occasions the good news about Jesus is presented as a kind of delivery; a complete cure from

---

[159] For further details read *Acts 9:1–31* the story of Saul, later called Paul or St Paul.

the problems of your past life. What you do get is a completely new start with help from the very highest authority of all – God. Let the final words on this subject come from a man who became a Christian and paid dearly for it. Paul the Apostle endured persecutions, hardships, shipwrecks and many other troubles. In spite of this he wrote: ' "*I consider everything a loss compared to the surpassing greatness of knowing Christ Jesus my Lord, for whose sake I have lost all things. I consider them rubbish, that I may gain Christ" ' (Letter to the Philippians 3:8*).

Over the years and down to the present day there are many people from various traditions who call themselves 'Christians' and whether they are Coptic, Catholic, Orthodox, Protestant reformed or even liberal, if they are truly believers, they have this in common, a devotion to Jesus Christ as Lord.

CHURCH

When Peter, the future leader of the Church that Jesus was to establish, told his leader, ' "*You are the Christ, the Son of the living God*" ', Jesus's response was to confirm that Peter's life work was to be the '*rock*' of the Church. Peter must have felt thoroughly challenged by what Jesus then told him, ' "*on this ... I will build my Church*" ' (*Matthew 16:16–18*). Please also refer to the profile on **Peter** in the section *Supporting Cast.*

Being Jewish, Peter and those with him who heard these words of Jesus might, immediately, have thought that Jesus was going to set up a building in competition to the Jerusalem Temple. No, that was not to be the case. They used the Greek[160] word *ecclesia*, meaning 'a congregation' or 'an assembly', before it came to mean, since New Testament times, 'church'. The idea could be summed up by the idea of a community.

During its very early stages the community or 'Church' grew enormously quickly with several thousands giving allegiance to Jesus. Many of these were converted during the Festival of Pentecost held a few weeks after the Passover, in the same year that Jesus died. They were Jews and many would, soon after, have to return to the countries around the Eastern Mediterranean and further away, to the places where they had settled. They took their newfound faith with them.

Many local Jewish converts used the Jerusalem Temple precincts for their main meetings with smaller groups gathering in homes.

Naturally, during cold weather, even in the Mediterranean there is the need for shelter and so Jewish Christian believers met in synagogues. This soon proved impossible especially when Gentiles became followers of Jesus and naturally wished to meet with them. In the course of time, Christians needed their

---

[160] Please see article on **Languages** below.

own buildings to gather in but as already explained this idea was not in the mind of Jesus. (Please also refer to **Christians** in the section above.)

COVENANT

The word covenant is a legal term which most of us will have come across especially if we own real estate, either land or houses. It *'is an agreement between two or more persons, entered into in writing and under seal'*; usually this is a promise to do or to refrain from doing a certain action.

THE MOSAIC COVENANT

The earliest covenant between God and all his people was the covenant that God made with Israel after he had brought them out of the slavery of Egypt, probably during the thirteenth century BC. The covenant was that the nation of Israel would live as God's people. For their part the people would accept and seek to live by the standards that God set them. This is set out in the Law of Moses but a look at the Ten Commandments in *Exodus Chapter 20* or in *Deuteronomy Chapter 5* will give a summary of the morality expected. The Mosaic Covenant is also called the Law of Moses.

This covenant gave the people a new national identity, but, at its highest level, it is an unobtainable standard: *' "I am the LORD your God; consecrate yourselves and be holy, because I am holy" '* (*Leviticus 11:44*). This covenant was celebrated each year at Passover and, indeed, this still continues today.

INDIVIDUAL COVENANTS

As well as the Mosaic Covenant there were also covenants made between God and individuals, one of which has a particular interest and relevance for Christians. About 1800 BC we learn of Abraham (Abram) who found favour with God.

I will make you into a great nation and I will bless you; I will make your name great, and you will be a blessing. I will bless those who bless you, and whoever curses you I will curse; and all peoples on earth will be blessed through you (Genesis 12:2–3).

Abraham is singled out as an example of a man who took God at his word. This called Abraham to be obedient and that was costly.

It was because of his trusting commitment to God that the writers of the New Testament use him as an example: *'Abraham believed God, and it was credited to him as righteousness, and he was called God's friend'* (*James 2:23*).

We must never think that Abraham in any sense persuaded or 'negotiated' with God to be in a 'covenant' situation. God made the covenant and Abraham kept it. This is a golden rule for any type of covenant with God.

COVENANT IN THE NEW TESTAMENT

'The time is coming,' declares the LORD, 'when I will make a new covenant with the house of Israel and with the house of Judah. 'This is the covenant that I will make with the house of Israel after that time,' declares the LORD. 'I will put my law in their minds and write it on their hearts ... they will all know me, I will forgive their wickedness and will remember their sins no more' (Jeremiah 31:31–34).

Clearly, God is going to do a new thing. There would not be the need for priests. Teachers like Moses who personally communed with God would not be required. People would know and be personally taught by God.

THE WORK OF GOD ALONE

The writers of the New Testament soon realised that a new situation had developed. With earlier covenants there had been the idea of God and human beings cooperating. Now there was the need for a new word because *it was all the work of God*. They realised that God had given a bequest – a free gift. The *gift* had come through the death of Christ on the Cross and they looked for another word for this inheritance. The word they chose was *grace*[161] and in the New Testament this

---

[161] In Greek the word is *'charis'* and is pronounced with a 'k' sound like the word chemistry. We can use this word for a pleasant and attractive attitude, for example the beaten finalist showed 'good grace' when he was beaten. This use is also found in the New Testament. In the NT it also has the idea of 'thanks'.

often takes the meaning of 'approval' and 'favour'. Certainly the word covenant is acceptable and is used in the NT, but the meaning needs to be developed and explained.

There has always been some kind of covenant between God and his people. All of them, from start to finish, have needed a relationship but it is only with the final New Covenant that we see the fullest development. As Jeremiah says in the quotation above, ' "*they will all know me*" '; the meaning being of commitment and a deep relationship touching the minds and emotions of God and his own people. And, it means, that the past misdeeds of God's people have been forgiven. In this relationship those in the covenant union are free to experience and to enjoy God.

It was during his last night, at supper with his closest followers, that Jesus told them that the New Covenant had finally come and used the symbols of bread and wine.

CRUCIFIXION AND THE CROSS

'*A crucial or decisive point*' is the meaning of the innocent sounding Latin word '*crux*' but this is the word from which we get our word cross. Although the Romans gave us the name for this symbol of slow, agonising death and although they frequently used crucifixion for slaves, robbers and foreigners, it was very rarely used for citizens. In fact, it was too barbaric for Roman rulers to even consider for members of upper class Roman society. And Emperors were a group not usually over-squeamish!

THE ORIGINS OF CRUCIFIXION

It is believed that the Persians were the first to use this as a means of execution, although the ancient Assyrians practised something not too dissimilar. Phoenicians are also credited with using this form of execution. The Greeks learnt of its use after conquering Persia and the Romans used it from about the third century BC. It was even used during the first century BC by a Jewish king as a punishment for those he considered traitors and some 800 died as a result.

Putting dead bodies, or heads, impaled on spikes has long been a means of supplying a warning to people who might consider doing evil, antisocial or politically incorrect deeds. In fact, there are regulations in the Old Testament to prevent bodies being left hanging from trees overnight. *'They are to be buried the same day, for a hanged man is offensive in the sight of God. You shall not pollute the land'* (*Deuteronomy 21:23*). The victims of this practice were called 'God's accursed'. However, in these cases the victims would probably have died from stoning and only after death had their remains roped onto trees. It was because a crucifixion was to serve as an example to others that it was usually carried out in a public place. The exact site for the death of Jesus is not known for certain but one thing is clear: it occurred in a public place such as an important road into Jerusalem. A place where some gathered to mock but also to be reminded of Roman control.

A cross was not necessarily in the traditional '✝' shape that we have grown used to. There are variations such as the 'T' or even 'X' but we can assume that the Cross of Jesus was likely to have been the traditional shape. This is because of the 'superscription' or charge, which Matthew tells us, was placed above Jesus's head: '*THIS IS JESUS, THE KING OF THE JEWS*' (*Matthew 27:37*).

DEATH BY CRUCIFIXION

Modern discoveries have increased our knowledge of the process of death by crucifixion and it seems that quite a number of variations were practised. It has been questioned whether the hands of a victim, nailed to a cross, would have been able to support the weight of his body without some other form of support. We may have seen pictures of the empty Cross of Jesus with cloths to support the weight of the arms but these may only be an artist's impression intended to make crucifixion less awful. We do know that ropes were sometimes used to attach the arms or torso to the cross. Often a narrow piece of wood, called a *sedicula*, was added to support both or just one of the buttocks. Was this intended as a kindness to the victim? No, it was to prevent the collapse of the body, which would have shortened his agony.

Victims unable to move had to cope with flies, heat or cold, the insults of the crowd and the shame of being stripped naked. Yes, crucifixion was intended to be thoroughly degrading. Death would have come slowly, sometimes taking days. Muscles racked with cramp tormented the condemned man. Hunger, thirst and fatigue just made death seem like a wonderful relief. Before this happened the crucified would usually lapse into unconsciousness. If his executioners felt like it they would have offered him wine vinegar with a narcotic substance to deaden the pain. Local women anxious that the condemned man had his torment lessened would have supplied these.

THE DEATH OF JESUS

Jesus was spared the long-term effect of death by crucifixion. He died quickly. There were the two thieves who were either side of him. It was not so easy for them because having Jesus there, sharing their execution, would have brought more people to stand and stare. It was decided by the fact that the Jewish Sabbath was due to begin in a few hours (with sunset) that the three men's lives should be brought to an end and their bodies taken from their crosses so that the Law's demands about bodies be respected (see <u>Origins</u> above). To bring about death was a simple enough process, all that was necessary was to break the legs of the condemned men. Death from pain and shock may have resulted within minutes following the blow from a large hammer.

Worse still was the fact that the victim became unable to breath and in fact suffered a form of suffocation. The

Romans had a name for this bone-breaking procedure, *crurifragium*, and because the Jewish Religious Authorities had insisted on not leaving the bodies hanging overnight, Pilate gave permission for its use.

The soldiers therefore came and broke the legs of the first man who had been crucified with Jesus, and then those of the other. But when they came to Jesus and found that he was already dead, they did not break his legs (John 19:32–33).

There have been some interesting theories on why, medically speaking, Jesus died so soon. One theory is that he died of a broken heart but again, (medically speaking) it is more probable that the scourging by Roman soldiers hastened the end of his life. After all men were known to die from that number of lashes.

John, the Beloved Disciple, gives us the authentic answer as to why Jesus died and it is simply *'that he gave up his spirit'* (*19:29*).

THE SYMBOLISM OF THE CROSS

Nowadays the Cross is seen in almost romantic terms as a symbol of self-sacrifice and quiet heroism but then, in the first century, it was viewed as highly discreditable. The apostles had to deal with this offensive mode of death. It was an obstacle to the preaching of the Gospel for the Church of the first century. *'Cursed is everyone who is hanged on a tree,'* says *Galatians 3:13*. To Jewish listeners, hearing the preaching of the apostles, victims of crucifixion were God's accursed. It was scarcely any better for Gentile listeners because the victims of this vile form of death were socially inferior persons such as slaves and robbers and were, at best, considered as 'losers' in this life. For the more compassionate they were objects of pity, for the less compassionate merely objects of shame.

Having such an unattractive symbol was yet another burden in the spreading of the Gospel. A modern public relations company would have despaired at having such an image. It is all the more remarkable that the Church's message of the love of God for all men should succeed – but succeed it did and mightily!

THE END OF CRUCIFIXION

Although many in Rome, from pre-Christian times, thought of crucifixion as a barbarism fit only for villains of the worst kind, it took nearly three hundred years, following the death of Jesus, for it to be officially banned. This was due to the coming to power of Constantine the Great, Emperor from AD 312–337. He was to make Christianity the religion of the Empire.

Since the death of Jesus there has been a complete turn around. Today many women, even in secular Protestant Europe and men and women in Catholic Europe wear a cross as jewellery and a sign of their Christian tradition. Many wear it as jewellery that is always fashionable.

DEMONS

The mention of demons in the twenty-first century may raise a few eyebrows. And let's face it some people will prefer to think that what those people in the first century that Jesus helped, were cured of, was some form of mental illness or epilepsy. It's just not cool to talk of evil spirits being at work in modern times. However, our western scepticism with demons is not shared by other societies. The Japanese believe in the power of these spirits and the benefit of exorcism. When I asked friends to share experiences on the subject I got some very positive reactions from overseas.

However, the emergence of the *Harry Potter* books and films show that it is a subject that has a certain attraction for modern man. Worse still there are some individuals who actively seek the power of evil spirits when they gather in covens for the performance of magic rituals – yes Satanists do exist. Some of them would deny that they are anything but 'good people', some are completely and utterly unscrupulous. They are without exaggeration shamelessly evil!

There are many cases particularly in the New Testament of people being *'oppressed'* and *'possessed'* by demons. One of the most notable is Mary Magdalene.

In her case I admit that we have to do some guesswork. We can only speculate as to how Magdalene acquired her seven evil spirits. We know that Jesus freed her but other details regarding her gaining her freedom are unknown. On the surface her case does seem to have been very severe as no less than seven demons were *'driven out' (Mark 16:9)*. 'Driven' is a very strong word.[162] There is, in Magdalene's case, the likelihood that they were occult spirits and these strongly resist the exorcist.

KEEP THE DOOR CLOSED!

Without wanting to be over dramatic there are some people who play with fire and get burned. They are, in some instances, wilfully prepared to take risks. Others stumble into the occult without knowing the dangers. One of the easiest routes is when people use the *ouija* board in the hope of trying to discern the future. Spirits can oppress people who use this. I remember speaking to a friend who had recently spoken to a victim who felt that she was haunted by a presence which was frightening, especially at night when she was alone in her bedroom. She was, not surprisingly, in a fearful state of nerves, feeling that she was being spied upon. Fortunately, this girl lost her demon for the simple reason that it had decided to go home with my friend after the conversation had ended! Fortunately, for my spiritualist friend it left voluntarily after a few days.

---

[162] The New Testament Greek word confirms that Jesus had to use more than just persuasion. It can be translated 'throw out' or 'eject by force'.

However, using Spiritualists as well as being dangerous is condemned in the Bible along with other things.

Let no one be found among you who practises divination or sorcery, interprets omens, engages in witchcraft, or casts spells, or who is a medium or spiritist or who consults the dead (Deuteronomy 18:10–11).

As the Bible is an honest book it tells what happened when Saul, the first king of Israel, tried to find a medium. During an earlier more devout period of his life, he had banned the practice of spiritualism. Now he had entered an arid period in his relationship with God. Now God was not with him, so he looked for help from other means. He did manage to get through to the deceased prophet Samuel. Israel's enemies the Philistines were about to attack. He needed some advice before the battle and remembered how much he had trusted and relied upon Samuel during the prophet's lifetime.

The medium managed to dredge up the spirit of Samuel and the witch, very much alarmed, realised that it was Saul who was using her services. Samuel told Saul that God had forsaken him and that he and his sons would die in the battle. This incident can be read in full in *1 Samuel 28*.

If the story of Saul seems rather remote let's take a more recent case. At the end of the First World War there was a renewal of interest in Spiritualism. This is the experience of one lady who had lost her only son and like Saul did have a message from beyond the grave. But please note that this was a message of warning!

She had spent a great deal of time and money at séances and elsewhere, but had entirely failed to get any message from her son or to establish communication with him. But the mediums whom she consulted assured her that she herself had considerable psychic gifts, and for a time she was willing to be sent into trances and to give communications to others. However, one day in prayer she became vividly conscious of her son's presence and even his voice. He bade her give up her association with Spiritualists, because nothing but evil came in this way from the unseen world. He told her that she could and did have communication with him in Christ, and that when she prayed, he was conscious of her fellowship with him. The greatness of her joy can easily be imagined, and she at once renounced any dealings with mediums. But there followed six months of agony, during which time she was tormented by evil spirits using the most revolting and blasphemous language, and even, it would seem, resorting to physical violence. Finally the assaults ceased, and the peace of God once more ruled in her heart.[163]

The only other comment that I need to make on this quotation is that this lady was allowed to communicate with her son not through a séance but in prayer.

Dealing with others who have the gift of second sight also carries grave risks. Palmists, crystal ball gazers,

---

[163] K N Ross, *Spiritualism*, SPCK, 1965, p.13f.

tarot card readers, may often appear to be harmless, though some are charlatans. But these people, by dabbling with the occult, are taking severe risks for themselves and others who consult them. Then there are others who do have a spirit at work in them and they are to be avoided at all costs.

DEVIL

Please see article on **Satan**, below.

THE PEOPLE CALLED 'HEBREWS'

No one has found a completely convincing answer to the origin of the word 'Hebrew' (*'ibri*) but it is certainly old having been used of Abraham who is described as being a *Hebrew* (*Genesis 14:13*) and Abraham lived approximately 1,800 years before the Christian era. It is a name that is often used of God's people by foreigners although Jewish people sometimes used it in recent times when speaking of themselves.

The word 'Hebrew' continued to be used in the Old Testament but after they had received the *Law of God*[164]

---

[164] *The Law of God* is also called the Law of Moses.

they preferred to be called 'The People of Israel'. The word is also found in the New Testament. Paul the Apostle is not ashamed to use it about himself: ' *"Are they Hebrews? So am I"* ' (*2 Corinthians 11:22*). In using this form, Paul is defending himself against some of his critics by saying that he was of 'pure blooded' Jewish stock and also of having had a rabbinic education.

The other sense in which the word 'Hebrew' is used in the New Testament is to distinguish Jews, often from outside Israel, with a Greek speaking education, and Jews brought up with a more traditional Jewish education who were more likely to be living in Israel.

HOLY LAND

IN JESUS'S TIME

When King Herod 'the Great' died, he decided that he ought to divide his realm among his children rather than leave them to kill each other in battling for the whole kingdom.

The largest part of the realm would go to Archelaus. This would include, from north to south Samaria, Judea and Idumea. Idumea was the territory from where Herod and his forebears had originated and it had once been part of the land of the Edomites, a people related to the Jews but often in conflict with them. Idumea is now part of the Kingdom of Jordan.

Antipas, or to give him his full name Antipatros, the younger brother of Archelaus, was given Galilee, a region to the north of Samaria. He was also given a separate region called Perea to the east. No doubt Antipas would have preferred two adjoining provinces but it was not to be.

Then there were the other children of Herod the Great (I) who had had a different mother. Philip was given the region to the northeast, most of which was much further away from Jerusalem although it had a border with Galilee and with the lake of the same name. His sister, Salome, was given the revenue of three wealthy cities: Jamnia, close to the Mediterranean Sea, and Azotus, which had been Ashdod one of the cities of the Philistines. She was also given Phaselis, a town in the Jordan Valley founded by her father in honour of his brother Phasael. Then, as a bonus, she had been bequeathed Herod's palace at Ascalon. This palace was also in part of the ancient Philistine lands and was known as Ashkelon. This being on the Mediterranean coast ought to have pleased her.

That was how Herod the Great divided his realm. Herod had made a will so the whole matter was straightforward. Well no, it wasn't! The Emperor Augustus had to approve this legacy. Rome was in control of this difficult country and although they usually took great care to keep the inhabitants content, nothing could be guaranteed. Herod's will was really unenforceable – a complete legal fiction! The country did not consist of these regions owned by Herod's children, it was one unit ruled by Rome. This was the Holy Land that Jesus knew and he had no difficulty moving from area to area.

THE HOLY LAND, IN ANCIENT TIMES

(a) CANAAN
Sometime, probably in the thirteen century BC, the people of God who at this stage would have been called Hebrews escaped from the slavery of Egypt. At their head was Moses, a man who had lived in Egypt during his early life and knew about how the Egyptians thought. Further details of what led up to their leaving can be found in *Exodus Chapter 3–12*.

After a long time in the Sinai Desert the Hebrews got to Canaan. The land was divided among twelve of Israel's sons, while the tribe of Levi were given the role of being priests so there is no area on the maps at the back of Bibles showing a patch of land given to the Levites. They owned land among the territories of the other twelve tribes.

(b) ISRAEL
Once the Tribes of Hebrews had settled the land they had no problem in what to call their new country. They named it after Abraham's grandson, Israel (formerly called Jacob). At this time each tribe was more or less self-governing and if a foreign invader threatened it could not be guaranteed that all the tribes would turn out to fight. On, at least one occasion, there was conflict

between them, as the book of *Judges Chapter 12* will show.

The administration would prove to be more of a problem. Firstly, they had judges, men who God had chosen. They combined roles: religious and legal – usually the same thing – and military. In theory, the job of *Judge* could be passed from father to son, but often the sons were a disappointment to both the people and their fathers.

It was partly due to this situation, but also Israel's peoples seeing how other nations were governed, that made them ask for a king. Samuel, Israel's judge at the time, was consulted. Samuel in turn consulted God who told him that if that was really what they wanted they could have it. This was clearly not God's choice for the people and Samuel was told to spell out the consequences.

This was the deal:

1.   If you are male expect to do military service;
2.   If you are a woman you could be ordered into domestic service;
3.   You will all have to give a *tithe* (a tenth) of grain, wine, sheep and cattle to his majesty;
4.   Kings always reward their favourites so be prepared to lose land as the king wishes.

'With me,' said Samuel, 'and the other *Judges* you could appeal but with a king there will be no appeal.

Remember that *"you yourselves will become his slaves"* ' (*1 Samuel 8:10–17*). Samuel tried again, *'Are you really sure that you want a king?'* In fact, the people had made up their minds and told Samuel, ' *"We want a king over us"* ' (*1 Samuel 8:19*).

The people got a king called Saul who began well but then started to show paranoia becoming jealous of one of his generals who he attempted to kill. This highly successful general, a man called David succeeded Saul and began a God-given dynasty, which is still valid today. Jesus, who is a direct descendent of David, is his heir.

Under David[165] the Kingdom of Israel prospered. He was the writer of some of the *Psalms*, which continue to inspire people and teach them about God's faithfulness. David certainly had his faults but handed the kingdom over in very good order to his son Solomon, a very bright boy. It was he who ordered the building of the first Temple, because the people, until that time, had gathered in a decorative tent, which was called *The Tabernacle*. Certainly this did not disgrace God but the king who lived in a beautifully built palace thought that the LORD God of Israel deserved something better. The Temple was a no-expenses-spared venture and cost the country dearly. It took thirteen years to complete.

---

[165] King David reigned about 1000 BC. One of David's best-known exploits was killing Goliath, the giant Philistine, but this deed is also credited to Elhanan (*2 Samuel 21:19*). From this it seems that 'David' may have been a nickname. It is also possible that there was a change of name. For instance we know that Jacob became Israel. The name *David* seems to mean 'beloved' of God.

Unfortunately, Solomon for all his intelligence, made some mistakes. They were shockers! First, he made an alliance with Egypt by marrying Pharaoh's daughter. Then later he married foreigners in defiance of God's commandments. These women, worshippers of alien gods, turned Solomon's heart away from devotion to the God of Israel. Having more than one wife, even legally, is a mistake for modern man, but then Solomon was a king in a man's world.

The mistake that caused much upset with the populace was the massive building scheme that impoverished the common people. During his lifetime Solomon got away with this because he was a popular monarch. When he died and the rule passed to his son, Rehoboam, things did not improve.

The new king received a very large deputation, a man called Jeroboam plus the whole assembly. They politely pointed out the hardship being experienced by the population. Rehoboam asked for three days to consider their request and, I imagine, the deputation went away hopeful of some improvement. The king took counsel from the elders who said, *'Yes, they've got a good case.'* He then went to the younger men; they gave the opposite advice, in effect they said, *'Look you're King, they are the people; tell 'em to get lost!'* Perhaps readers think that I am exaggerating. This is what Reboboam told the people:

'My father made your yoke heavy; I will make it even heavier. My father scourged you with whips; I will scourge you with scorpions' (1 Kings 12:14).

You will not be surprised that this was to lead to a division of the country (*1 Kings 12*). Jeroboam took ten of the twelve tribes and took the northern territory. The Tribes of Judah and Benjamin remained faithful to Rehoboam. There is probably rather more to this argument than we know but this statement from the king was clearly the final straw.

(c) JUDAH AND THE NORTHERN KINGDOM

During his lifetime King Solomon had found Jeroboam a man of great ability but he was also a man with a great deal of ambition. We are not given details but Jeroboam, who was in charge of the forced labourers building Solomon's palaces and architectural show-pieces, rebelled and went to live in Egypt. On Solomon's death he returned and became the spokes-man for the ten northern tribes in their negotiations with Rehoboam.

Rehoboam tried to get his forced labourers back on the building sites. Their knowledge of history told them that a few hundred years before they had been slaves of Pharaoh but now they had their own country and freedom. They were not going to be Rehoboam's slaves. Therefore, the prophecy of Samuel, the last judge of all Israel, had come true. The man sent to get them back to work was stoned to death. Rehobaom decided that he could be next and rather wisely made a bolt for Jerusa-lem. He thought of going to war against the ten tribes but a prophet warned him against this. For once the new king took sound advice. Later there was continual conflict and Jeroboam and the north tended to be the losers. The division of the land into the two kingdoms of Israel and Judah took place about 950 BC.

Jeroboam was not a faithful follower of the God of Israel and as well as promoting the worship of pagan deities, such as Baal, on hilltops, set up two national shrines one at Dan in the north of his realm and the other at Bethel in the south. Bethel had long religious associations with Jacob, later called Israel, who had had a vision of God when he was travelling (***Genesis 28:11–19***). This was a clever piece of thinking on King Jeroboam's part. Jeroboam's thinking was partly political. He did not want to encourage the faithful worshippers of the LORD to keep going to Jerusalem for the festivals. They might decide to move there permanently. It is likely that many, during the early days of the Northern Kingdom, did not like the changes being brought in and did go to live in the Southern Kingdom.

In some ways it is strange that the ten tribes continued to use the name Israel. It is strange because the two tribes in the south had a king who was a descendent of King David and as such was the only authentic monarch who was a true descendent of the patriarch named Israel. The two remaining tribes, Judah, and the smaller Tribe of Benjamin took the official name Judah; although sometimes the later prophets referred to Judah as '*Israel*', this was usually after the collapse of the Northern Kingdom. This was because the people of God had for several centuries been called 'Israel' so it was natural.

The Northern Kingdom, Israel continued under a succession of kings who mostly did not seem to be concerned with the worship of God and his rule. One of the worst of these was Ahab whose wife Jezebel's name has become a byword for a *shameless* woman. Many evil things happened during Ahab and Jezebel's lifetime in spite of the ministry of the prophet Elijah.

Around the year 880 BC Omri the King, built Samaria, a hilltop city that would last until the end of the kingdom of Israel. The choice was a good one because the name Samaria means something like *'watching place'*. However, the politics of the region were working against both Israel and Judah. The power in the region was Assyria and you had to keep them happy. The official name is *Tribute* – you pay them money and they stayed out of your country. It was an international 'protection racket'.

The other major power in the region was Egypt. They resented the growth of Assyria and encouraged little Israel to rebel. In 735 BC, Hoshea, their king, and several other neighbouring countries attempted to force Assyria to let them live in peace. It was a brave attempt but in spite of its good defensive position the city of Samaria fell in 722 BC after a three-year siege. The population of Israel was taken en masse into the Assyrian empire. The ten tribes of Israel were assimilated into an area to the north and east. Some of this area is now the present state of Iraq.

The southern state of Judah was troubled by Assyria but escaped being conquered. For them it must have seemed strange not having their troublesome northern neighbour with whom they had shared a common language and much history.

(d) PALESTINE

This name for the Holy Land is still in use today although it is ancient. Jesus would not have used this name. The Romans introduced it only after the Bar Cochba rising in AD 132–135. It is a corruption of the name 'Philistine.' It was intended as an insulting reference to the old enemy of Israel.

The Philistines, who occupied land on the Mediterranean coast, due west of Jerusalem, were a threat to Israel from about 1188–586. They seemed to disappear during the period when the Babylonians destroyed Israel's first Temple, 587–586 BC. Unfortunately for them they chose to side with Egypt, the enemy of Babylonia.

LANGUAGES OF THE BIBLE

ARAMAIC

The main point of interest for people like you and me is that Jesus, and many people in Judea, Galilee and other parts of the Holy Land spoke this language before, during and after his lifetime.

415

About the time when Abraham moved west, during the period 2000–1500 BC, there was a people called the Arameans. To be more accurate they were a group of peoples, related by race and language that lived as semi-nomads.

Arameans were also related to the Hebrews, the people we now call Jews. In fact, Hebrews were taught to acknowledge it: *'you shall declare before the LORD your God: "My father was a wandering Aramean"'* (*Deuteronomy 26:5*).

They lived in Syria and Assyria, modern northern Iraq. In the course of time they were conquered by the Assyrian nation and because their language was so widely known it became the language of traders and rulers. Some writers have stated that it was the language of 'diplomacy' but not as we understand the use of that word today – especially with the very brutal Assyrian kings!

The Assyrian Empire, which was at its most powerful between the ninth until late seventh century BC, lost power and was superseded by another Empire the Babylonian.

The people of Judah were taken over by the Babylonians, another Aramaic-speaking people,[166] who transported many thousands of them to Nineveh,

---

[166] This occurred after the capture and destruction of Jerusalem by the Aramaic-speaking Babylonians in 586–7 BC. In fact, the transportation of people had begun a few years earlier.

Babylon and other areas, where they discovered that to exist it was necessary to learn Aramaic. Other Aramaic-speaking people were sent to live in Israel. This was in the region that had once been the northern kingdom and occurred during Assyrian rule. After Assyria, Babylonia was the power in the region and conquered Judah but they fared less well than the Assyrians. Cyrus, a Persian captured Babylon the capital, which is about fifty miles south of present-day Baghdad, in 539 BC. One of his early policies was to allow the people of Judah to return to rebuild their Temple and Jerusalem.

When these Jews returned from their exile in 538 BC, they continued to speak Aramaic. In fact, parts of the Old Testament are written in Aramaic. This use of the language was to continue into New Testament times. Jesus was an Aramaic speaker, as were most Jewish people living within the Roman province of Judea.

I imagine that some of my readers will be asking about the Hebrew language. The answer is that it was the language of the Jewish Scriptures and was used in prayers and was very much the official language of the Temple. However, recent research shows that the Hebrew language was more common than had previously been thought and was also being used and kept alive by people in more ordinary occupations. When Jesus was crucified, the charge attached to the cross was written in Latin, Greek and Aramaic.

Aramaic still exists today as a spoken language and is mostly found in the Middle East. Worldwide there are some 445,000 speakers of this long-lived tongue.

THE GREEK of the New Testament

The New Testament is written in Greek. This said, the language is not quite the same as the classical Greek that university students learn. There are also many differences between both classical and the Greek of the New Testament and modern Greek.

The Greek of the New Testament developed during the time of Alexander the Great (356–323 BC) and became the language of his army which successfully spread it around the Eastern Mediterranean and even further as they conquered. So successful were they that their Greek became the language of diplomacy and commerce and was to replace Aramaic (see note above). This version of Greek is also known as *Koine*.

When the translators of the early versions of the Bible came to translate the New Testament they discovered that certain words did not appear in classical Greek. This was not a major problem but needed some guess work. For instance what did the word *arrabon* mean? Such riddles were not solved until the later years of the nineteenth century when archaeologists dug up documents in Egypt, which contained this and other words missing from classical Greek. By the way, *arrabon* means a 'guarantee,' or 'pledge'.

I would not like readers to think that I feel that these early versions of the New Testament were spoilt by not having these extra words. No, in spite of not having this knowledge, the scholars did a fine work translating the New Testament in such versions as the *King James Bible*, also known as the *Authorised Version*. Modern versions do have some advantages in an understanding of this important language.

HEBREW

Hebrew today is the official language of the State of Israel. It is also spoken by other Jewish Communities around the world, in all some 7 million people. Jews, not unnaturally, call it *The Holy Tongue*. It is a Semitic language, which is related to Arabic and Aramaic. It has an alphabet of twenty-six letters.

The first written form of Hebrew dates from the eleventh century BC and is an adaptation of Phoenician script. Over the years, there have been adaptations in the script; one of the most important was forced upon the rabbis after the Jewish *Bar Cochba* uprising of AD 135 when the writing of Hebrew was in danger of dying out. This was due to the fact that the Romans expelled Jews from the Holy Land and caused problems with their education.

Although Hebrew continued in written forms, it declined as a spoken language, being replaced by either the language of the country where the Jewish community lived, or in central Europe by *Yiddish* a mixture of Hebrew and German.

In the nineteenth century Hebrew was revived as a spoken language. This was the result of the growth of

Zionism and the desire for Jews to have their own country.

LATIN

Although the Roman Empire took over from the Greek Empire, Latin, which was their language, did not enjoy the same success as Greek. That said many Latin words have had an influence on English and other European languages. Then again so has Greek, although it is classical Greek, not the *Koine*, (common) Greek of the New Testament, which, as mentioned above, was a dialect spread by the army of Alexander the Great.

PASSOVER MEAL

Almost from its very beginning *Passover* (*Pesach* in Hebrew) was a sacred drama, a play that had to be re-enacted every year as an everlasting memorial to what God had done in freeing his chosen people from their slavery in Egypt.

At the first Passover the whole Hebrew community was to eat in a state of dress ready to leave. *Where were they going?* They were going on EXODUS. Exodus literally means 'way out'. A specially prepared meal was before them.

*This is how you are to eat it: with your cloak tucked
into your belt ... sandals on your feet (12:11).*

Scholars debate the date of the original Exodus from
Egypt. Remember, the Jewish nation had originally been
received as honoured guests in the land. They were now
leaving, having forced Pharaoh's hand. Moses, their
leader, had failed to persuade Pharaoh to let them return
to their original homeland peacefully. According to
Paul's calculation the people of God had lived for 430
years in Egypt (refer **Letter to Galatians 3:17**), now it
was time to leave. The history of what led up to Passover
is dealt with in the early part of Chapter 3.

What do we know about the meal that is recorded in
Exodus Chapter 12? We have a number of pieces of
information. We learn that the animal was a lamb,
although the Hebrew word indicates that a young goat
could have been used instead. Also, that it would have
been a male, a year old, without blemish. The whole
animal was to be roasted with bitter herbs.

Smaller families would pool resources because the
whole animal was to be eaten at one go. The bones
would be put on the fire after the meal was finished.

What about the blood of the slaughtered animal? This
was spread around the doorframes. As we know, when
God saw the blood, he would spare or *PASS OVER* the
household. From this reading let's remember the
importance of the blood and the fact that God spared
the Hebrews because of it.

Now, when we get to New Testament times, we find that this ritual is still being faithfully carried out. And what better place to celebrate Passover than in Jerusalem? This is assuming that you could manage to get there. Tens of thousands of Jews often thronged to Jerusalem for this festival. The population of Jerusalem was perhaps 30,000 with, and estimates vary, from 100,000 to 500,000 pilgrims. That meant big business! The ancient equivalent of the Jerusalem Hilton and all other inns were packed and many would have stayed in Jerusalem and nearby villages under canvas! Only the feast of Tabernacles, which was a harvest festival, could draw greater crowds to Jerusalem.

What do we know about the celebration in Jesus's time? The head of the family would arrange for a lamb, and a place where his family, or party, would eat. The minimum number to sit down together would have been ten. A priest would have slaughtered the lamb at the Jerusalem Temple and even Jesus and his disciples would have had to pay the inflated prices for this service. The lamb would then have been spit-roasted with its legs and its head attached.

Our picture of the Last Supper with the thirteen seated at an upright table is wrong. They would have reclined on cushions and eaten off of low tables. Normally, they would have been dressed in white. During the evening someone in the family, the youngest son, would ask: 'why is this night different from all other nights?' Then the story of Passover would be retold.

PHARISEES

The Pharisees were a group of Jews who followed a particular religious code within the life of Judah. During the time of Jesus there were four schools of religious practice. These were Pharisees, Sadducees, Zealots and the Essenes. The last named is not mentioned in the New Testament; in fact, we have only really had good information since the discovery of the *Dead Sea Scrolls*, which began in 1946. The name Zealot has come, in popular usage, to mean the murderous *Sicarii* who were zealous in their hatred of all things Roman. It is a mistake to confuse these two groups.

The Pharisee movement seems to have begun after the return of the Jews from their exile in Babylon in 538 BC. Many of the leading Jews had been taken away from their land in order to control what had become a part of the Empire of Babylonia. With the fall of that Empire, they returned and found that the land was in a pretty poor state.

It was during this time that the movement seems to have come into being. The name is believed to mean (or imply) a separation. The historian Josephus, who was born soon after the Crucifixion reports: *'the Pharisees on the basis of tradition teach the people many precepts that are not recorded in the Law of Moses'* (Antiquities).

One precept that the Pharisees taught was Resurrection. This was different to the Sadducees with whom they often strongly disagreed. They also looked to a future age of reward for the righteous and eternal punishment for the wrongdoer. They believed in angels, peace, disapproved of violence and had a commitment to the Law of Moses.

Some of the Pharisees managed to become members of the Sanhedrin, the Jewish Council, and I am sure that this made for some very lively debates, because the differences between them and the Sadducees were very marked.

In spite of their rejection of evil, they did plot against Jesus and intended to kill him if possible (***Matthew 12:14***). In ***Chapter 23***, Jesus denounced them six times for hypocritical behaviour.

Although, Jesus called them hypocrites it would be wrong if the whole sect were dismissed as being corrupt. There were undoubtedly some noble Pharisees. Paul the Apostle of Jesus had been taught by Gamaliel a teacher of the law who was prepared to allow the very early Church some leeway: '***if it is from God, you will not be able to stop these men; you will only find yourselves fighting against God***' (***Acts 5:39***).

SACRIFICE – an offering for sin

In a special place in Jerusalem, outside the Sanctuary of the Temple, was an altar where animals were sacrificed. Part of the flesh of the animal became the property of the priests, given to them as their keep while they were on duty away from their homes and their normal work. This could have been on the other side of the land. The rest of the animal would usually have been burnt.

Human beings, then as now, fell short of the high standards that God set them. Acts of self-will that can cause us to commit murder, theft, violence against the person etc, etc, are also an offence against God; we usually call such acts as these sin. This would have included insult and cruelty by word of mouth. God's punishment for the worst offences was death to the 'sinner' but instead he accepted the death of an animal as a substitute. That animal would only be acceptable if it had no injury or illness – it had to be costly to the giver. The 'sinner' had to bring the animal to the priests who would kill it. No part of the animal's carcass would be returned to the one who presented it to the priests.

The punishment would fall upon the animal instead of the person who had done wrong. The blood of the animal was put upon the altar. Blood was a symbol of life in the ancient world, and without understanding the physiology, they had got it right. Jews believed that *'the life of every creature is its blood'* (*Leviticus 17:14*). Today we have a fuller understanding of how blood supports life and have no difficulties in agreeing with this ancient wisdom.

This section on **Sacrifice** will become more relevant if read in conjunction with the article on **Sin** and also **Blood**.

SANHEDRIN

The Great Sanhedrin, to give it its full title was the Jewish Court, which sat in Jerusalem. It began, in its New Testament form, during the Persian Empire and it continued into the Roman period. Although there was a precedent from the time of Moses, because in the Old Testament book of *Numbers 11:16*, we are told that there was a council of seventy elders.

The exact time that the Sanhedrin began is doubtful but there appears to have been some form of Council from the time when the Jews were allowed back from Exile. This happened during the sixth century BC after Cyrus, the King of Persia, issued his Edict of Restoration in 538. Certainly it was there to give support to Jews returning to their homeland.

It enjoyed a good degree of self-governance from the foreign powers that controlled it. In matters religious all Jews came under the influence of the Sanhedrin. In matters civil its authority was, during NT times, confined to Judea and supervised by the Roman Governor or his superior, the Legate in Syria.

Those eligible to serve were High Priests and members of the ruling families. At the time of the trial of Jesus and beyond, these would have been Sadducees. Also there were tribal elders, heads of families, and legal experts (scribes). The scribes would have been drawn from the Pharisees.

Its President was the High Priest, who had formerly been given the role on a hereditary basis, but the Romans, realising the importance of the Sanhedrin, turned High Priests into political appointments. The Sanhedrin's task was to direct the religious affairs of Judea according to the Law of Moses. During the time of Jesus it had a majority of Pharisees.

Their remit was not just religious affairs but some civil matters including the running of the lower courts; the Sanhedrin handled matters of Jewish law. They had their own police force that had the power to make arrests. The Sanhedrin should, by its own rules, have met during daylight hours. The fact that the hearing concerning Jesus took place at night and in the High Priest's house makes it sound rather irregular.

It seems possible, looking back, that the Jewish Legal Authorities felt badly about the trial of Jesus. In later years, they brought in a large number of regulations about when and how accused persons should be treated. These rules would have hopefully ensured that Jesus had a fair trial.

Much of the power of the Great Sanhedrin ended with the Jewish Wars (AD 66–70).

SATAN

What are we to make of this strange being that the Bible calls Satan? I shall refer to him as male but should I say 'it'? Certainly there are some strange ideas around.

We can immediately forget the popular image of the half-man half-goat figure of cartoons. This seems to have more in common with ideas of the Greek god *Pan* who has horns and cloven hoofs. I am unsure of where the idea that he carries a trident comes from. It all seems a little far-fetched and fanciful.

Certainly, many modern people will smile at the very notion of a devil. Unfortunately, evil itself is all too common and obvious for anyone but the most light-hearted optimist to dismiss. However, the idea that the instigator of evil is a personal being seems almost surreal – evil itself is far too real. After viewing Auschwitz, one sceptical observer said that he found belief in Satan easier than believing in God.

This idea of impersonal evil has gained some support among church people. They have clearly forgotten or not absorbed the fact that Jesus himself had no doubts about the reality of a personal devil that he called, on one occasion, *'the strong man'*.[167] In the case of Simon Peter, Jesus told him that ' *"Satan has asked to sift you as wheat. But I have prayed for you, Simon, that your faith may not fail"* ' (*Luke 22:31–32*). At a more personal level Satan in the desert tested Jesus, after his baptism.[168]

So, what do we know about this being? To begin with his name 'śāṭan' comes from a Hebrew verb which means 'enemy'. He is also known as 'accuser', such as one who brings complaints against another person to the legal authorities. He is chief among a group of angels who wanted to share God's glory and power instead of being content with the purpose for which he was created, namely the service of God. In the poetic language of *Genesis 3*, he appears as one who is called the '*Serpent*'.

Satan and the spirits, some good some bad, were thought in ancient societies to live in the area between earth and heaven. Paul the Apostle, writing to the *Ephesians*, refers to Satan and his evil messengers as the *'powers of this dark world ... the spiritual forces of evil in the heavenly realms'* (*6:12*). The idea here is of a country where alien

---

[167] Both *Matthew 12:29* and *Mark 3:27* record Jesus, after he had been accused of using evil spirits, giving a picture of a *strong man* who had to be bound before his house could be robbed. The one who tied up the strong man had to have superior strength. Jesus was that one!

[168] Refer to *Matthew 4:1–11*.

groups can operate against the legitimate ruler. At times God's people are hard-pressed. However, the forces of righteousness are poised at the right moment to completely restore God's sovereignty.

It is an error for human beings to hold Satan entirely responsible for all their misdeeds. As *James*, the writer of the letter found towards the back of the NT, writes, *'each one is tempted when, by his own evil desire, he is dragged away and enticed'* (*1:13–15*). However, the enticements of Satan can be resisted: *'be wise about what is good, and innocent about what is evil and then The God of peace will soon crush Satan under your feet'* (*Romans 16:19–20*).

The fate of Satan and his disreputable band of angels is grim as the little letter of *Jude verse 6* reveals: *'the angels who did not keep their positions of authority but abandoned their own home – these he has kept in darkness, bound with everlasting chains for judgment on the great Day.'* The judgement that has been passed will take effect when God's purposes have been served. In the meantime, it is as if a length of chain has limited Satan and his minions. In his own good time God will reel him in. Those who have suffered will have justice. The writer of the final book of the Bible had a vision and saw that *'the devil, who deceived them'* (God's people) *'was thrown into the lake of burning sulphur'* (*Revelation 20:10*).

The question that you may wish to ask is why a righteous God can tolerate an evil being. There is, unfortunately, no clear-cut answer. To say that it suits God's purposes is accurate but does not give us the solution.

SIN

The idea of 'sin' is not just an Old Testament teaching. It is very prominent in the New Testament and has the same idea of rebellion against God. The notion of wanting to do one's own thing without due thought to doing God's will or obedience to moral standards or how my actions may affect others is at the root. There are several words used in the Greek of the New Testament to express what sin is. We will concentrate on three of them.

The first is translated as 'missing the mark'. The Greek word is *hamartia*. Imagine an archery contest with the target set at a considerable distance. There are three rings on the target. Each archer is, of course, aiming for a centre spot on the target that is the only one that counts. The first archer takes direct aim for the centre but his arrow fails to reach the target and ends a few centimetres in front, sticking out of the ground. Another archer aims higher into the air but his arrow falls short by two meters. The last contestant takes aim and it looks good. Yet when the target is approached he has only hit the outer circle. He too has missed the target. Each one has underachieved. This is a picture of the normal human condition that puts us at odds with

God and we are forever underachieving. In fact, we have totally failed

<u>The second</u> word is *trespass*, which translates the Greek *paraptoma*. This is not a continual ongoing act but a single one. Here is an example: a strong young man sees an older person putting away a well-filled wallet and decides that it could be his without much trouble. Perhaps a bit of violence but what of it – no problem! He acts and takes the money leaving the victim shocked and bruised. Yes, it is an extreme example, many 'trespasses' are much less violent but each has the idea of a definite act.

<u>The third</u> word *paranomia* carries much the same meaning as 'the last': 'the single act'. The word transgression means 'a going beyond'. (The Greek word *parabasis* is also translated 'transgression'.)

In most cases 'missing the mark' and 'trespass/transgression' go together. Our young mugger will be most likely a selfish individual. He is this all the time but only an opportunist thief on occasions. These two 'sins' may seem different. The first kind seems less severe than the second but the first usually leads to the second.

A REMEDY FOR SIN

It would be helpful to those looking at this topic to also read **Sacrifice**, above. It is because of the death of Christ that God's justice has been satisfied.

When we have understood the process of an animal sacrifice being a substitute for wrongdoing then we are on our way to understanding the death of Jesus Christ as a remedy for sin. Unlike the animals presented to the priests at the Temple he was willing to take the place of all sinners. In a sense his life and blood, the symbol of that perfect life, was presented as a once-for-all sacrifice for sin. *Sin is my self-will working to cause me to do acts of wrongdoing against others and offending the character of God.* These acts as we have been discussing are called 'sins'.

THE TEMPLE

The last Jerusalem Temple was a magnificent building. Herod the Great began it in 20–19 BC although he did not live to see it completely finished. He built it not so much for reasons of religious piety as an attempt to gain status with the people with whom he was not popular. In its construction he accepted the advice of the priesthood. The main building was complete by about 9 BC although work continued until AD 64. It replaced earlier ones with the first being constructed by King Solomon who lived about 1000 BC. Before this God's people had had a large mobile tent. This was called the *Tabernacle* and served the same purpose.

Visitors coming to Jerusalem today will see nothing more than a section of the original structure of Herod's Temple. This is known as the *Western* or *Wailing Wall* and formed the outer wall of Herod's Temple.[169] This is now a gathering place for Jews, especially the *Hasidic*.[170] From the air it is possible to have a true idea of the scale of the complex, which measured some 500 x 325 yards. In all the Temple Mount covered an area of about thirty-five acres or about fourteen hectares.

Aerial photographs of the site also show the Dome of the Rock and the Al-Aqsa Mosque, the third holiest to Islam, both of which date from the seventh century AD.

The Temple was of course the centre for the worship of Israel's God and Jews, during and before New Testament times, would wish to go to the Temple as often as possible for the Festivals. Many would travel from around the Mediterranean, although some would have longer distances to journey.

I have mentioned the size of the Temple complex but at the centre of this was the sanctuary, a special building which was divided into two sections: the Holy Place and the Most Holy Place, also known as the Holy of

---

[169] Today's visitors to Jerusalem can view a scale model of ancient Jerusalem, including the Temple, at the Israel Museum in West Jerusalem.

[170] The Hasidic movement began in Eastern Europe in the eighteenth century. It was founded by rabbi Israel ben Eliezer who relied on a mystic approach to worship. Long curled ringlets of hair under wide-brimmed hats and black coats can identify Hasidic Jews.

Holies. Only priests were allowed to enter the Holy Place but the High Priest could only enter the Most Holy Place once a year.

We tend to think of religious buildings as being for the benefit of worshippers but the sanctuary was for the presence of *Yahweh*, the God of Jews. Only on certain festivals would worshippers gather in the courts outside. There were courts for the priests, Jewish men and Jewish women, but the most interesting is the Court of the Gentiles where the animals for sacrifice were kept and where Jesus made a stand against this misuse of this place of God's presence. It was in the Most Holy Place, unlit by lamp or candle, that God's glory could be seen as a *shekinah*, a kind of illumination that showed his glory. This was how Jews thought of how Yahweh, their God, existed.

'Heaven is my throne, and the earth is my footstool.'
Isaiah 66:1

Heaven was the main place where God was but he also was present upon earth and, although he could choose to be anywhere he liked, the main place that he desired was his Temple in Jerusalem.

In AD 70, at the end of the Jewish War,[171] the Temple was destroyed and the sacrificial system ended with its destruction by the Roman Tenth Legion. Today the

---

[171] To be accurate, this conflict continued but only on one site. The fortress of Masada overlooking the Dead Sea held out against the Romans until AD 73.

ritual of sacrifices is no longer carried out. But then it no longer needs to be.

TESTAMENT

The Bible is divided into Old and New Testaments. For further information about this word refer **Bible** and **Covenant**, above.

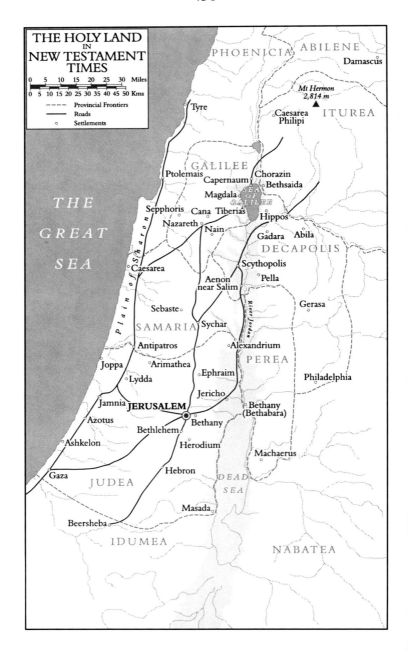

BIBLIOGRAPHY

A Commentary on the Epistle to the Romans **C K Barrett** A & C Black 1962 LONDON

Acts **E M Blaiklock** The Tynedale Press 1959 LONDON

A Dictionary of Christian Theology **Alan Richardson, Ed.** SCM Press Ltd 1969 LONDON

A History of Christianity **Tim Dowley, Org. Ed.** Lion Publishing 1977 BERKHAMSTEAD

A History of Israel (Revised edition) **John Bright** SCM Press Ltd. 1972 LONDON

Atlas of the Bible **Joseph L Gardener, Ed.** Readers Digest 1981 NEW YORK

Christianity: The Witness of History **J N D Anderson** Tynedale Press 1969 LONDON

Deliverance from Evil Spirits **Francis MacNutt** Chosen Books 1995 GRAND RAPIDS

Dictionary of New Testament Theology **Colin Brown, Ed.** Zondervan 1967 GRAND RAPIDS

Documents of the Christian Church (2nd Ed.) **Henry Bettenson** Oxford University Press 1963 OXFORD

Easter Enigma **John Wenham** Paternoster Press 1984 EXETER

Encyclopaedia of the Bible **Pat Alexander, Ed.** Lion Publishing 1978 BERKHAMSTEAD

From Christ to Constantine **M A Smith** Inter-Varsity Press 1971 LEICESTER

Genesis **Derek Kidner** Inter-Varsity Press 1967 LEICESTER

Genesis (3rd Revised Ed.) **Gerhard Von Rad** SCM Press Ltd. 1972 LONDON

Handbook of Christian Belief **Robin Keeley** Lion Publishing 1982 BERKHAMSTEAD

438

Handbook to the Bible **David Field, Donald Guthrie, Gerald Hughes, Howard Marshall & Alan Millard** Lion Publishing 1973 BERKHAMSTEAD

Happiness That Lasts **Martin Israel** Cassell 1999 LONDON

Here I Stand – A Life of Martin Luther **Roland H Bainton** Mentor Books 1950 NASHVILLE

I Believe in the Creator **James M Houston** Hodder & Stoughton 1979 LONDON

Islam **Alfred Guillaume** Pelican 1954 HARMONSWORTH

Israel and the Nations **F F Bruce** Paternoster Press 1963 EXETER

Israel, Land of God's Promise **Murray Dixon** Sovereign World 2006 LANCASTER

Jesus the Jew **Geza Vermes** SCM Press Ltd. 1973 LONDON

Jesus, the Man of Many Names **Steve Maltz** Authentic 2007 MILTON KEYNES

Jesus Who He Is – And How We Know Him **E L Mascall** Darton Longman and Todd 1985 LONDON

John – Tyndale New Testament Commentaries **R V G Tasker** Inter-Varsity Press 1960 LONDON

Leading Lawyers Look at The Resurrection **Ross Clifford** Albatross Books 1991 SUTHERLAND, NSW

Mere Christianity **C S Lewis** Fontana Books 1952 GLASGOW

Messianic Jews **John Fieldsend** Olive Press/MARC 1993 TUNBRIDGE WELLS

Near-death Experience **Marisa St Clair** Barnes & Noble 1997 NEW YORK

New Testament Commentary **William Hendriksen** Banner of Truth EDINBURGH

    Matthew   1973

    Mark   1975

    Luke   1978

    John   1954

New Testament Foundations **Ralph P Martin** Paternoster Press 1975 EXETER

439

New Testament Introduction **Donald Guthrie** Inter-Varsity Press 1970 LEICESTER

Occultism in North Africa **Bernard Collinson** AWM 1977 LOUGHBOROUGH

Pearls at Pesach **Rabbi Bernard Hooker** Council of Christian and Jews 1999 LONDON

Proclaiming the Resurrection **P M Head, Ed.** Paternoster Press 1998 CARLISLE

Psalms Vol. 1 New Century Bible **A A Anderson** Oliphants 1972 LONDON

Remember Jesus **Steve Motyer** Christian Focus 1995 FEARN, ROSSHIRE

Romans, Introduction and Commentary **F F Bruce** Inter-Varsity Press 1963 LEICESTER

Roots and Branches **John Fieldsend, Managing Ed.** PWM Trust 1998 BEDFORD

Spiritualism (Revised Ed.) **K N Ross** SPCK 1965 LONDON

Systematic Theology **Louis Berkhof** Banner of Truth 1958 EDINBURGH

The Acts of the Apostles **William Neil** New Century Bible Oliphants 1973 LONDON

The Book of Jeremiah **J A Thompson** *The New International Commentary on the Old Testament* Wm B Eerdmans Publishing 1980 GRAND RAPIDS

The Epistle to the Galatians **Herman N Ridderbos** *New London Commentaries* Marshall, Morgan & Scott 1961 LONDON

The Gospel According to Luke **G H P Thompson** *New Clarendon Bible* Oxford University Press 1972 OXFORD

The International Standard Bible Encyclopaedia **Geoffrey W Bromiley** Wm B Eerdmans Publishing 1979 GRAND RAPIDS

The Interpreters Dictionary of the Bible **G A Buttrick, Ed.** Abingdon Press 1962 NASHVILLE

The Lamb Wins **Richard Bewes** Christian Focus 2000 FEARN

440

The Lion Handbook to the Bible **David & Pat Alexander** Lion Publishing 1973 BERKHAMSTEAD

The Lord is King **Ronald S Wallace** *The Message of Daniel* Inter-Varsity Press 1979 LEICESTER

The Man Born to be King **Dorothy L Sayers** Victor Gollancz 1943 LONDON

The Man They Crucified **R T France** Inter-Varsity Press 1975 LEICESTER

The New Bible Dictionary **J D Douglas, Ed.** Inter-Varsity Fellowship 1962 LONDON

The Passion **Geza Vermes** Penguin Books 2005 LONDON

The Religion of Jesus the Jew **Geza Vermes** SCM Press Ltd. 1993 LONDON

The Second Epistle to the Corinthians New Testament Commentaries **C K Barrett** A & C Black 1972 LONDON

The Seder **Jane Clements & Rachel Montague** The Council of Christians and Jews 2001 LONDON

The Trial and Death of Jesus **Haim Cohn** Weidenfeld & Nicholson 1967 LONDON

Who Moved the Stone? **Frank Morison** Faber & Faber 1930 LONDON

Lightning Source UK Ltd.
Milton Keynes UK
03 November 2009

145750UK00001B/2/P